YEARFUL OF CIRCLE TIMES

YEARFUL OF CIRCLE TIMES

By:
Liz & Dick Wilmes

Art:
Nel Webster

A **BUILDING BLOCKS** Publication
38W567 Brindlewood, Elgin, Illinois 60123

Resource Consultant: Vohny Moehling

About the Artist: Nel Webster is a free lance artist currently sharing her talents with Building Blocks, as a regular contributor to the Newspaper, illustrator of *Everyday Bulletin Boards* and now *Yearful of Circle Times*. In addition Nel is the staff artist for Gail Borden Library in Elgin, Illinois, specializing in the children's departments. She earned her Master's Degree in Fine Arts from the University of Tennessee.

Book List Compiled by:
Jill Braddish, Children's Librarian
Gail Borden Library
Elgin, Illinois 60120

Published by:
BUILDING BLOCKS
38W567 Brindlewood
Elgin, Illinois 60123

Distributed by:
GRYHPON HOUSE, INC.
P.O. Box 275
Mt. Rainier, Maryland 20712

ISBN 0-943452-10-4

DEDICATED TO

. . . young children who are learning to play and work together

CONTENTS

Page

INTRODUCTION 8

TIME FOR AUTUMN

"Hello" New Friends 12
Signs of Fall 16
Be Squirrely 20
Dress For Fall 24
In the Pumpkin Patch 28
Magic Carpet 32
Scarecrows 36
Autumn Harvest 40
Birds 44
The First Thanksgiving 48
Preparing For Winter 52
Gingerbread Family 56
Gifts 60

TIME FOR WINTER

'Twas the Night Before Christmas 66
Gift Boxes 70
Bells 74
I Can Do It 78
Snowman Fun 82
Boots and Mittens 86
Tracks and Trails 90
Hibernation 94
Hearts 98
Birthdays 102
Teddy Bear and His Friends 106
Nursery Rhymes 110
Up, Up and Away 114

TIME FOR SPRING

Think Green .120
Turtles and Frogs 124
Backwards Day 128
In Your Easter Basket 132
Animal Homes 136
Ducks 140
Puddlin' Around 144
Rainbows 148
"Good-bye" Old Friends 152
Marching Bands 156
Vegetable Garden 160
Wheels and Tires 164
Safety First .168

TIME FOR SUMMER

Summer Colors 174
Bouncing Balls 178
Summer Breezes 182
Fireworks 186
Picnics 190
Blast-Off 194
On the Road 198
Me and My Shadow 202
Shoes 206
Holes 210
It's In the Bag 214
In Your Neighborhood 218
Community Helpers 222

INTRODUCTION

Circle Time is that segment of the day when the group children gather together to enjoy participating in a variety of activities.

Each of the topic areas in YEARFUL OF CIRCLE TIMES is divided into eight sections.

For Openers—These opening activities offer a wide variety of ideas, stories, rhymes, and games to immediately involve the children in the topic.

Fingerplays—Children enjoy active rhymes. Whenever possible add actions to the fingerplays, rhymes, and poems suggested for each topic. Extend the rhymes with various activities.

Recipes—A snack each day is a time for nourishment as well as friendship. Enjoy making foods with the children at the beginning of the day. Later in the day enjoy eating the foods with the entire group.

Classroom Visitor—People have many talents, do a variety of jobs, and have available resources. Invite these people to visit your class to share their special knowledge and abilities with the children.

Field Trips—Many of the field trips suggested in YEARFUL OF CIRCLE TIMES are within walking distance of most Centers. Often they are special types of 'walks.' The trips help children learn how important the neighborhood is to their world.

Active Games—The active games allow the children to become physically involved with the topic and concept. At the same time, these games strengthen the child's wide range of physical skills such as balance, coordination, movement, and rhythm.

Language Games—The language games expand each child's knowledge of the topics and enhance his wide range of language, cognitive, small muscle, and social skills. Some of the activities have EXTENSIONS. These are coordinated activities to give your children more experience with a specific concept. Other activities have VARIATIONS. These activities are simply different ways to enjoy the same game. To take full advantage of the language games, the authors suggest that:

- The children should be exposed to as many 'real' objects and examples as possible, such as real food, toys, clothes, flowers, and so on. Models and pictures are necessary, but the more experience children have with the 'real,' the better understanding they will have of the abstract.

- When making teaching aids, such as felt board pieces, puppets, and learning games, enlarge the illustrations in this book to the appropriate size.

- Make the teaching aids and real objects that you used during Circle Time available to the children for further exploration and manipulation during their free choice times.

- Each child has a defined space in which to sit. A small carpet square or other designation is appropriate.

- You consider the developmental age of the children, whenever an activity suggests making a 'list.' If the children are not ready for letters, then draw the list using simple pictures or add pictures to the written list.

Books—The suggested books offer only a beginning. Visit your library and choose books you like and will enjoy reading to your group of children.

HELLO NEW FRIENDS

FOR OPENERS

ASK THE CHILDREN TO COVER THEIR EYES AND THINK OF WHAT THEY SAY AND DO WHEN THEY MEET A FRIEND. AFTER THE CHILDREN HAVE HAD THE OPPORTUNITY TO THINK, HAVE THEM SHARE THEIR IDEAS. AS EACH CHILD SHARES HIS IDEA, HAVE HIM WALK OVER TO ANOTHER CHILD AND SHOW EVERYONE HOW HE SAYS, "HELLO." CONTINUE SHARING AND SHOWING EVERYONE'S IDEAS.

FINGERPLAYS

FRIENDS

I say "Hello" to friends at school,
I'm happy as can be.
They are my special school friends,
I like them all, you see.

TWO LITTLE FRIENDS

Two little friends are better than one,
And three are better than two,
And four are much better still,
Just think!
What four little friends can do.

FRIENDSHIP TREE

We have a special thing at school,
It's called a "Friendship Tree."
It's filled with children's pictures,
And one of them is me.

If you could come and visit,
I'm sure that you would see
A bunch of happy faces
On our "Friendship Tree."
 Dick Wilmes

"GOOD MORNING"

Say "Good Morning" to your neighbor
Say "Good Morning" across the way.
Say "Good Morning" to _____. (teacher's name)
And wish them all a "Happy Day."
 Dick Wilmes

HOW DO YOU DO

Turn toward your neighbor
And say "How do you do?
My name is _____. (One child says name)
What can I call you?" (Other child says name)

SCHOOL FRIENDS

Today was the day
For school to begin.
We met our new teacher,
Who talks with a grin.

There are Amy and Sue,
Keith, Kevin, and Paul.
As hard as I try
I can't remember them all.

It's really exciting
To have some new friends.
I'll know all their names
Before the year ends.
    Dick Wilmes

WAVE A GREETING

Wave a greeting to another,
Wave a greeting to a friend,
Turn around and face your neighbor,
Wave and turn again.

Bow a greeting to another,
Bow a greeting to a friend,
Turn around and face your neighbor,
Bow and turn again.

Shake hands with another,
Shake hands with a friend,
Turn around and face your neighbor,
Say "Hi" to your new friend.
    Dick Wilmes
(Add more stanzas the children think of)

RECIPES

FRIENDSHIP MIX

YOU'LL NEED

Variety of bite-size crackers
 such as oyster crackers
Pretzel circles
Chow mein noodles

TO MAKE: Have each child put a handful of crackers or pretzels into a big friendship bowl (mixing bowl). Stir the ingredients several times until mixed. Serve with glasses of juice.

CLASSROOM VISITORS

• Have different adults whom the children will meet while at school visit the class during circle time. These visitors should introduce themselves and tell the children where in the school they work, what they do, and how they can help the children each day. If possible have the visitor lead the children down to his/her workroom or office and show them around.

LANGUAGE GAMES

WHO WILL IT BE?	Have the children cover their eyes with their hands. Everyone says, "*1, 2, 3, who will it be?*" and then uncovers his eyes. You begin describing one of the children. When someone thinks he knows, he should stand and tell the others who he thinks you're describing. Respond either, "*You guessed it!*" or "*Keep listening for more clues.*" Continue.
SAYING "HELLO"	Have the children sit in a group. Say, "*Good morning/afternoon Nel.*" Have Nel say "*Good morning*" back to you and then turn to a child near her and say, "*Good morning*" to that child using the child's name. (Help with names when necessary.) The game continues until everyone has said "*Good morning*" to each other.
WAVING	One way to greet friends is to wave to them. Have a child show the others how he waves and then let all of the children wave that way. Encourage others to show how they wave.
TELL US ABOUT YOURSELF	Write each child's name on a strip of paper. Put all of the names in a basket. Have a child come up, pull a name out of the basket, and give it to you. Read the name on the strip. That child should stand up and tell the class something about himself, do an exercise and then have the others repeat it, or whisper something to you that you can tell the class. Give the child his name strip to put in his pocket. Repeat this with several children each day until the basket is empty. EXTENSION: Throughout the year, take photos of the children enjoying different activities. Include these in a scrapbook. You can enjoy the scrapbook all year and use it again in the spring when you do the activities in "*Good-Bye, Old Friends.*"

ACTIVE GAMES

PARACHUTE HELLO
Have everyone sit around a bedsheet or a parachute. Have the children hold the chute with two hands and slowly lift it up as they count "*1, 2, 3.*" When they get it over their heads, they should duck their heads under the chute and say "*Hi*" to friends on the other side. Count "*1, 2, 3*" as they lower the chute. Repeat, this time whispering "*Hello*" to friends. Do it again and wave with one hand. Continue with other greetings.

FRIENDLY CARDS
Duplicate each card enough times so that the children each have one card and you have a complete set.
Have the children sit in a circle. Pass out one card to each child. Have the children look at their cards. Hold up one of your cards. The children who have matching cards should hop to the middle of the circle and do what is indicated on the card, such as wave, smile, shake hands, wink, hug, and so on. Then they should hop back to their places. Hold up another card and continue. Remember, you can repeat cards that you have already held up or hold up several at one time.

HELLO, NEW FRIEND
Help the children get to know each other through the song 'Hello, New Friend'.

Hello, New Friend
(tune: Happy Birthday To You)

Hello, new friend, hello, new friend,
Hello, new friend, and how do you do?

After the children have learned the song, have them sing it and turn to one of the children next to them and shake hands.

BOOKS

TOMI DePAOLA – ***BILL AND PETE***
ROBERT KRAUS – ***THREE FRIENDS***
ARNOLD LOBEL – ***FROG AND TOAD ARE FRIENDS***

ARNOLD LOBEL – ***FROG AND TOAD ALL YEAR***
JAMES MARSHALL – ***GEORGE AND MARTHA***
COLLECTION OF POEMS – ***BEST FRIENDS***

SIGNS OF FALL

FOR OPENERS

COLLECT DIFFERENT SIGNS OF FALL FOUND IN YOUR NEIGHBORHOOD AND PUT THEM IN A SACK.

PASS THE SACK AROUND, LETTING EACH CHILD CAREFULLY TAKE ONE OBJECT OUT. AFTER EACH CHILD HAS HIS OBJECT, HAVE EVERYONE NAME HIS. NOW ENCOURAGE EACH CHILD TO LOOK AT HIS OBJECT CAREFULLY AND DISCOVER ONE THING ABOUT IT. GIVE EACH CHILD THE OPPORTUNITY TO TELL THE GROUP ABOUT HIS DISCOVERY. AFTER EVERYONE HAS HAD AN OPPORTUNITY TO TALK, LET THE CHILDREN PUT THEIR OBJECTS BACK IN THE SACK.

EXTENSION: PUT THE SACK ON THE DISCOVERY TABLE FOR THE CHILDREN TO EXPLORE LATER. YOU MIGHT ADD MAGNIFYING GLASSES FOR EVEN CLOSER EXAMINATION.

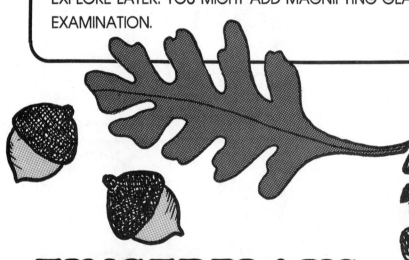

FINGERPLAYS

AUTUMN

Leaves are floating softly down,
They make a carpet on the ground.
Then swish, the wind comes whistling by,
And sends them dancing to the sky.

GENTLY FALLING LEAVES

Little leaves fall gently down,
Red and yellow, orange and brown,
Whirling, whirling 'round and 'round,
Quietly, without a sound,
Falling softly to the ground,
Down - and down - and down - and down.

RECIPES

LEAF ROLL-UPS

YOU'LL NEED

Spinach and/or lettuce leaves
Soft cheese

TO MAKE: Spread the cheese on the
spinach and/or lettuce leaves. Roll up
each one and put on a serving plate.
Enjoy with a wheat cracker and drink.

BIRD TREATS

YOU'LL NEED

Pinecones
Peanut butter
Birdseed

TO MAKE: Spread the pinecones with
peanut butter and then roll them in
birdseed. Put the bird treats in nearby trees
for the birds to enjoy.

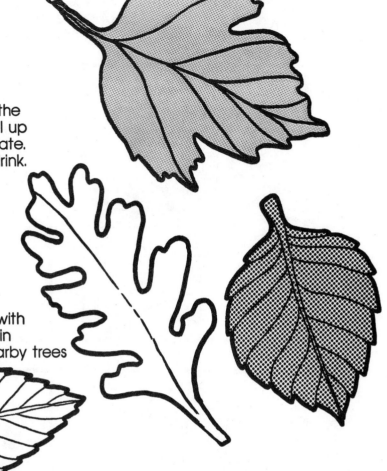

FIELD TRIPS

• On a nice fall day, take a walk to a nearby park. Have the children
collect different signs of fall and put them in a box. In addition, encourage
each child to look for a special leaf and put it in the box too. Bring the box
back to class. Have the children glue the fall objects from the box onto a
long piece of butcher paper. Use the special leaves as a border. Title it and
display for all to enjoy.

LANGUAGE GAMES

EXPLORING
FALL NATURE

Place several examples of fall nature on a tray (leaves,
acorns, different nuts, pinecones, evergreen sprigs, twigs,
and so on). Holding the tray, walk over to a child and
have him choose one thing off of it. Have the child look
at his object and tell the others one thing about it and
then give the object to another child to explore. After
he has explored the object, have him tell one more
thing about it and then pass the object to a third child.
Continue until the children have noted many of the
characteristics.

17

GROWTH SEQUENCE

Duplicate the pictures provided, color them, and back them with felt. Bring the pieces and felt board to circle time. Place the pictures in order on the felt board and talk about leaves from spring through winter. Mix up the pictures and have the children put them back in order.

LEAF COUNT

Before circle time, make a leaf chart similar to the one pictured. Find fifteen real leaves and bring them along with the chart to circle time. Put the chart in the middle of the circle time area. Point to the first row. It has one leaf in it. Have a child pick up one leaf and put it on top of the pictured leaf. Have everyone count aloud "One." Look at the second row. Count the leaves in that row. Now have a child pick up two leaves and match them. Continue adding and counting real leaves until the chart is full of leaves.

FALL LEAVES — Cut out red, green, brown, and gold leaves from construction paper. Pass them out to the children. As you say the rhyme, have the children listen for the color of their leaves. When each hears the color, have him hold his leaf up high and then toss it into the air to float to the ground.

FALL LEAVES

Leaf of red, leaf of green,
Prettiest leaf I've ever seen.
Leaf of brown, leaf of gold,
Sometimes flat, sometimes rolled.

Falling from the trees so high,
Blowing in the autumn sky.
Soon the snow will begin to blow,
Then in spring new leaves will grow.
Dick Wilmes

ACTIVE GAMES

LEAF HUNT — Collect all colors of leaves found in your area. Using construction paper, cut leaves of the same colors so that each child will have at least one paper leaf.

Hide all of the real leaves around the room. Have a basket in the middle of the circle time area. Give each child a paper leaf. When you say, "*Look for the leaves,*" the children should look for leaves that are the same color as their paper leaves. As the children find leaves, they should put them in the basket. After all of the leaves have been found, pass the basket around so that the children can look at the leaves. Let each child put his paper leaf in the basket with the real leaves. Put the basket on a window ledge, table, or counter.

ACORN TOSS — Buy or find a bagful of acorns or nuts in the shell. Have several baskets with large openings.

Divide the children into small groups depending on the number of baskets you have. Taking turns, have the children pretend that the baskets are squirrel nests and that they are squirrels tossing acorns into the nests for winter food.

FALL DANCING — Have at least one fall-colored streamer for each child. Let each child choose one or more. Find appropriate music to move to such as 'Autumn Leaves' by Roger Williams. Start the music and encourage the children to pretend that they are fall leaves waving and floating in the breeze.

BOOKS

CINDY WHEELER – *MARMALADE'S YELLOW LEAF*   JACK KENT – *ROUND ROBIN*
JIM ARNOSKY – *RACCOONS AND RIPE CORN*

BE SQUIRRELY

FOR OPENERS

SQUIRRELS DO LOTS OF CLIMBING, SCAMPERING, HUNTING, RUNNING, CHEWING, AND DARTING, SO THEY NEED TO BE IN GOOD SHAPE. HAVE THE CHILDREN PRETEND TO BE SQUIRRELS WARMING UP FOR A DAY OF HURRY-SCURRY.

"Exercise your legs by running in place."

"Stand in place and quickly open and close your mouth." Do 5-6 times.

"Puff out your cheeks. Hold the air. Let it go." Do several times to get your cheeks ready for storing nuts.

"Get down on all fours, crawl as fast as you can without bumping into other squirrels. Practice turning."

"Swish your bushy tail back and forth."

FINGERPLAYS

FIVE LITTLE SQUIRRELS

Five little squirrels sitting by the door,
One ran away and then there were four.
Four little squirrels climbing up a tree,
One ran away and then there were three.
Three little squirrels with coats so new,
One ran away and then there were two.
Two little squirrels warming in the sun,
One ran away leaving only one.
One little squirrel wasn't having any fun,
He ran away and then there were none.

GRAY SQUIRREL

Gray squirrel, gray squirrel,
Swish your bushy tail.
Gray squirrel, gray squirrel,
Swish your bushy tail.
Wrinkle up your little nose.
Hold a nut between your toes.
Gray squirrel, gray squirrel,
Swish your bushy tail.

SQUIRREL'S BREAKFAST

A squirrel from his tree-house
Poked out his head.
"It's high time for my breakfast!"
He gaily said.

So he ran down the tree trunk
And pattered around.
His bushy tail a-trailing,
Nose to the ground.

He looked here, then he looked there.
Through the white snow
Till he found a nut,
Hidden deep down below.

And into his cheek he popped
The nut with glee.
Then Mr. Squirrel scampered
Back up the tree.

If you look very sharply
Perhaps you will spy,
Mr. Squirrel at his door
Ever so high.

Have the children close their eyes as you read this rhyme to them. Talk about how a squirrel finds his breakfast.

THE SQUIRREL

Whisky, frisky, hippity hop,
Up he goes to the tree top!
Whirling, twirling, 'round and 'round,
Down he scampers to the ground.

Furly, curly, what a tail!
Tall as a feather, broad as a sail!
Where's his supper? In the shell,
Snappity, crackity, out it fell.

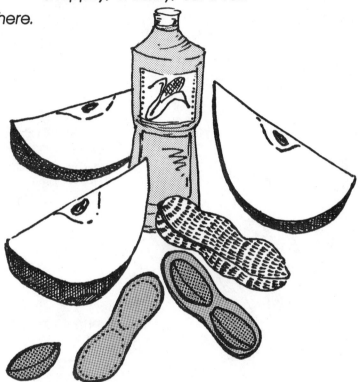

RECIPES

SQUIRREL TREATS

YOU'LL NEED

Peanuts (roasted in shells)
Corn oil
Apples
Wheat germ

TO MAKE: First make peanut butter. Have the children remove the peanuts from the shells. Remove the brown skins. Put one tablespoon of oil in a blender. Gradually add about one cup of peanuts and blend until it is crushed and blended into a smooth texture.

Wash and quarter the apples. Spread the peanut butter on the apple sections and sprinkle with a little wheat germ.

CLASSROOM VISITORS

• Invite a forest preserve ranger or naturalist to visit your children and tell them about squirrels and other animals. Encourage him/her to talk about the habits squirrels have, how and what they eat, where they live, what they do all day long, what colors they are, etc. Let the children say one of their squirrel fingerplays for the visitor. Maybe you can all take a walk and look for squirrels near your school. (If you have a camera take it with you and snap a few photos of your walk.)

21

LANGUAGE GAMES

**CRUNCHY
FOOD FOR
WINTER**

Remind the squirrels to hide acorns for winter by singing this song.

CRUNCHY FOOD FOR WINTER
(tune: Where is Thumbkin?)

*Where is gray squirrel? (Fists behind
    back)
Where is gray squirrel?
Here I am. (Fist in front, wiggle thumb)
Here I am. (Repeat with other fist)
How are you today squirrel?
How are you today squirrel?
Busy, busy, busy. (Roll fists around)
Busy, busy, busy. (Roll fists faster)*

*Where are your acorns?
Where are your acorns?
Here they are! (Wiggle 4 fingers)
Here they are! (Wiggle other 4 fingers)
Crunchy food for winter,
Crunchy food for winter,
Hide them quickly! (Hide hand behind
    back)
Hide them quickly! (Hide other hand)*
            Liz Wilmes

EXTENSION: On your Discovery Table, have a display of different nuts in shells along with magnifying glasses.

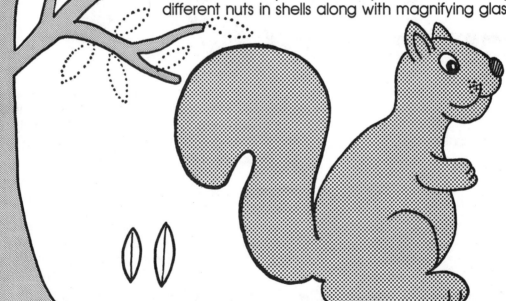

**WHERE IS THE
SQUIRREL?**

Using the examples provided, cut a felt tree and a squirrel. Bring the felt board and shapes to circle time. Put the tree on the board. Talk about its branches, trunk, and leaves. Place the squirrel on the board. Ask the children where the squirrel is in relation to the tree. For example, it might be on, near, in back of, under, next to, or on top of it. Have a child come up to the felt board and move the squirrel to another place. Now where is the squirrel?

22

SAY AND DO — Have the children imitate squirrel activities such as climbing trees, eating acorns, and swishing their tails. Once they have practiced being squirrels, enjoy this game. Say a squirrel movement and then act it out in this following 4-step sequence.

Everyone says: *"Swish your tail."*

Everyone says and does: *"Swish your tail."* (Say the action while waving your squirrel tail.)

Everyone whispers and does: *"Swish your tail."* (Quietly say the action while doing it.)

Everyone thinks and does: (Think the words while doing the action.)

MAKE A LIST — Have a piece of shelf paper and a marker. Have the children think of all of the things they have seen squirrels doing. Write down the children's observations. Hang the list near the window and add to it as children see squirrels doing more things.

ACTIVE GAMES

SQUIRREL SCAMPER — Have the children sit in a circle. One child is the squirrel. He walks around the circle and says *"Nut"* as he taps each child on the head. When he gets to the child he wants to chase him, he taps that child on the head and says *"Squirrel."* The two squirrels chase each other around the outside of the circle with the first one trying to get back to the hole before the other one catches him. During the chase all of the children encourage the squirrels by clapping and shouting *"Scamper, scamper, scamper . . ."* The second squirrel continues the game.

PEANUT HUNT — Trim or fold a large brown grocery bag to about six inches high. Put it in the center of the circle time area for the squirrel's hole. Hide peanuts in the shell around the room.

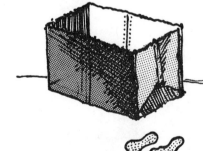

When you say *"Hunt,"* the children should get down on all fours and move like squirrels looking for nuts. When they find one, they should crawl over to the hole and drop it in. Then go back and look for more. When all of the peanuts have been found, gather the squirrels around the hole. Together count how many peanuts were found. Then shell the peanuts and have them for a snack.

EXTENSION: Use the shells for collage material in the art area.

BOOKS

JANE BELK MONCURE – ***WHAT WILL IT RAIN?***
GENE ZION – ***MEANEST SQUIRREL I EVER MET***
ANNE CARTER – ***SCURRY'S TREASURE***
BRIAN WILDSMITH – ***SQUIRRELS***

DRESS FOR FALL

FOR OPENERS

HAVE THE CHILDREN BRING THEIR JACKETS OR SWEATERS TO CIRCLE TIME. SHOW THEM AN EASY WAY TO PUT THEIR GARMENTS ON. FIRST, HAVE THEM LAY THEIR GARMENTS ON THE FLOOR WITH THE COLLARS POINTING AT THEIR FEET. NEXT, THEY SHOULD STICK BOTH OF THEIR ARMS THROUGH THE ARMHOLES, AND THEN FLIP THE GARMENTS OVER THEIR HEADS. IF IT IS COOL OUTSIDE, HELP THOSE WHO NEED ASSISTANCE FASTEN THEIR JACKETS/SWEATERS. TAKE A FALL WALK AROUND THE NEIGHBORHOOD.

FINGERPLAYS

LITTLE LEAVES

*The little leaves are falling down,
'Round and 'round, 'round and 'round.
The little leaves are falling down,
Falling to the ground.*

RECIPES

WARM APPLE SAUCE

YOU'LL NEED

Apples
Cinnamon
Honey (to taste)

TO MAKE: Wash and quarter the apples. Remove the stems, seeds, and cores. Add a little water to the pan. Put the apples in the pan and cook over a medium heat until very soft. Remove the apples and mash them. Choose whether you want to eat or remove the apple skins. Add a little honey if you want. Top with cinnamon and serve warm on a cool fall day.

FIELD TRIPS

● On a cool fall day, have the children put on their fall outer-wear and take a walk around your school neighborhood. Before you go outside, have the children look at each other and discuss what everyone is wearing. How many different types of clothes can they discover?

Go outside and begin your walk. As you're walking, have the children look for other people who are wearing fall clothes. What are they wearing? Why?

25

LANGUAGE GAMES

YOUR FALL DRAWER

Collect a variety of types of clothes, some of which are more appropriate for fall (sweats, sweater, jacket, hat) and some more appropriate for other seasons, (mittens, snowboots, swimsuits, tanktop). Fold all of the clothes. Get a grocery bag and a small dresser drawer or a large, fairly shallow empty box.

Bring the clothes, bag, and drawer/box to circle time. Tell the children that you got all of your clothes mixed up and you're trying to figure out which ones should go in your drawer for fall. Talk about the fall weather and the types of activities people do. Then hold up the first piece of clothing. Have the children name it. Discuss if it is usually worn in the fall. If so, put it in the fall drawer. If not, put it in the bag for storage. Continue with the other clothes. When finished name all of the fall clothing.

EXPLORING FALL CLOTHES

Bring the drawer of fall clothes to circle time. *(See 'Your Fall Drawer.')* Divide the children into small groups of two or three each. Pass the drawer to each group and have the children choose one garment from the drawer. Encourage them to explore the piece of clothing by feeling the cuffs, buttons, hems, pockets, collars, openings, etc. Have them rub the clothing on their cheeks and decide if each is rough, scratchy, smooth or soft. Let the children in each group tell the others about the clothing they examined.

WHO IS WEARING FALL CLOTHES?

Have the children look at the clothes they are wearing. Whoever thinks he is wearing something for fall should stand up. Give each child an opportunity to tell the others what fall clothes he is wearing.

FALL SPINNER

Before circle time, cut out a large circle from white posterboard or use a large pizza board. Divide the circle into six to eight equal sections. Find pictures of fall clothing in magazines or catalogues. Glue one picture in each segment. Attach a spinner to the middle of the circle.

Bring the fall spinner to circle time. Point to each picture and have the children call out the name of the clothing. Put the spinner in the middle of your group. Have a child flick the spinner. When it stops he should look at the picture the spinner stopped on and call out the name of the clothing being pictured. Then have all of the children who have this type of clothing pretend to put it on. Talk about when you would wear it.

26

ACTIVE GAMES

SIMON SAYS

Play this variation of Simon Says. You be Simon. Tell the children to put on different articles of fall clothing, such as sweatpants, sweatshirts, sweaters, jeans, hats, gloves, jackets, scarves, etc. In between telling the children to put on fall clothes, tell them to put on clothes which are more appropriate for other seasons. When you give them these commands, they should call out, "*Not in the fall.*" You could begin with this sequence and then continue:

Simon says, "*Put on your red sweater.*"

Simon says, "*Slip on your sweatpants.*"

Simon says, "*Pull your sweatshirt over your head.*"

Simon says, "*Put on your swimsuit.*" (To this the children would respond, "*Not in the fall.*")

Simon says, "*Put your sweatshirt on and zip it up.*"

FALL
FASHION
SHOW

Hang a clothesline across the circle time area. Hang different types of fall clothes on the line. Call on a child and tell him which article of clothing to take off of the line and carry back to his place. When all of the clothes are off of the line, have the children holding clothes put them on.

After each child has put the article of clothing on, have him stand up. When all of the children are standing, have a fashion show. The children wearing the clothes should parade around the area so everyone can see the different clothes. As each child passes you, have him stop. Then have everyone look, and call out the name of fall clothing the child is wearing. Continue with each child in the show.

BOOKS

LINDA STRAUSS EDWARDS – ***DOWNTOWN DAY***

IN THE PUMPKIN PATCH

FOR OPENERS

GET SEVERAL REAL PUMPKINS DIFFERING IN SIZE, SHAPE, AND COLOR. PUT THEM IN A ROW SO THAT THE CHILDREN CAN EASILY SEE THEM. ENCOURAGE THE CHILDREN TO TALK ABOUT WHAT THEY SEE. NOW SPREAD THE PUMPKINS OUT AND LET SEVERAL CHILDREN AT A TIME COME UP AND TOUCH THE PUMPKINS. HOW DOES EACH ONE FEEL? DOES IT HAVE SMOOTH SKIN? BUMPY? HOW DOES THE STEM FEEL? ANY LEAVES?

CAREFULLY CUT THE TOP OFF OF EACH PUMPKIN. PASS THE PUMPKINS AND LET THE CHILDREN TAKE A SECOND LOOK. WHAT DO THEY SEE THIS TIME? NOW LET THEM FEEL THE INSIDE. HOW DOES IT FEEL? DOES THE PUMPKIN SMELL?

PUT ONE PUMPKIN ON A CUTTING BOARD. CAREFULLY CUT THE PUMPKIN IN HALF AND THEN INTO ENOUGH PIECES SO THAT EACH CHILD CAN HAVE ONE. PUT THE PIECES INTO PLASTIC BOWLS AND PASS THEM TO THE CHILDREN. GIVE EACH CHILD OR PAIR OF CHILDREN A MAGNIFYING GLASS. HAVE THE CHILDREN EXAMINE THEIR PIECES CAREFULLY AND SHARE THEIR OBSERVATIONS.

HAVE PLASTIC BAGS AVAILABLE. LET EACH CHILD PUT HIS PUMPKIN PIECE INTO A BAG. ATTACH HIS NAME TO THE BAG. (REFRIGERATE IF NECESSARY.) HAVE THE CHILDREN TAKE THE PUMPKIN PIECES HOME AND TELL THEIR PARENTS ABOUT THEM.

FINGERPLAYS

THREE LITTLE PUMPKINS

Three little pumpkins laying very still
In a pumpkin patch on a little hill.
This one said, "I'm very green,
But I'll be orange by Halloween."
This one said, "I'm on my way
To be a jack-o-lantern some day."
This one said, "Oh my, oh my,
Today, I'll be a pumpkin pie."

PUMPKIN PIE

My father bought a pumpkin
And much to my surprise,
We didn't carve a funny face
We made two pumpkin pies.
Dick Wilmes

WHAT AM I?

A face so round,
And eyes so bright,
A nose that glows
My, what a sight!

MY PUMPKIN GROWS

I dig, dig, dig,
I plant some seeds.
I rake, rake, rake,
I pull some weeds.
I wait and watch
And soon I know,
My pumpkin sprouts
And starts to grow!

RECIPES

PUMPKIN CAKES

YOU'LL NEED

1/2 cup margarine
3/4 cup honey
2 eggs
1 t. molasses
2 cups pumpkin
2 cups whole wheat flour
2 t. baking soda
1 t. cloves
1 t. salt

TO MAKE: Cream the shortening and honey together. Beat the eggs well. Mash the pumpkin. Mix all of the ingredients together. Pour the batter into cupcake molds. Bake at 325 degrees for about 20 minutes. Test with a toothpick. Serve with apple juice.

FIELD TRIPS

• Visit a nearby pumpkin farm, vegetable stand, or grocery store. Look at all of the different pumpkins and gourds. Can you find the smallest one? Largest? Tallest? Fattest? Talk about the different characteristics. Buy several pumpkins for the classroom. If you are walking, you may want to bring a wagon to put the pumpkins in on your way back.

LANGUAGE GAMES

**IN THE
PUMPKIN**

Fill a plastic pumpkin with different orange objects. Have a child come up, and without looking, put his hand into the pumpkin. Have him pull out an object and hold it up for everyone to see. The children should call out what it is. Continue with the other objects.

**PUMPKIN
PATCH
MATCH**

Cut different colored pumpkins and matching stems out of felt.

Put the pumpkins on the felt board. Pass out the stems to the children. Point to one child holding a stem. He should walk up to the felt board as the children say the following rhyme using the child's name and the color of the stem he will put on the pumpkin.

PUMPKIN, PUMPKIN

*Pumpkin, pumpkin, without a stem,
Laying in the pumpkin patch,
Here comes* (child's name) *to look for you
With a stem of* (color) *to match.*

MR. PUMPKIN

Say this rhyme with the children. After you say it, talk with the children about what Mr. Pumpkin is thinking about as he sits on the post.

MR. PUMPKIN

*Pumpkin red, pumpkin yellow,
He's a funny, funny fellow.
He's a jolly, funny sight,
Sitting on the post at night.*

**ALL AROUND
THE PUMPKIN**

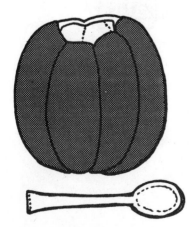

Get a plastic pumpkin or a real pumpkin which has been cleaned out. Get pairs of four or five objects which can easily fit inside the pumpkin, such as a spoon, a block, a crayon, etc.

Put the pumpkin on the floor so that the children can easily see it. Choose one pair of objects such as the spoons. Put one of the spoons *'inside the pumpkin.'* Ask the children where you put the first spoon. (Answer.) Then ask them where they would like you to put the other spoon. Put it where they tell you. Then repeat where the two spoons are located in relation to the pumpkin. For example, *"The first spoon is 'inside' the pumpkin and the second spoon is 'under' the pumpkin."* Continue with other objects.

30

ACTIVE GAMES

PUMPKIN,
PUMPKIN

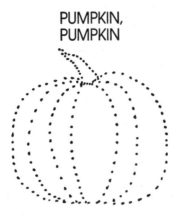

Have a small plastic pumpkin and one of the children's favorite records.

Have the children sit in a circle and put their hands behind their backs. Choose one child to sit in the middle and cover his eyes with his hands. Give one child the pumpkin and start playing the music. The children should pass the pumpkin behind their backs until the music stops. When it does the child who has the pumpkin should hold it. The child in the middle should look at all of the children and guess who has the pumpkin. When he guesses correctly the children trade places and the game continues.

PUMPKIN
PATCH

Play *'Pumpkin Patch'* to the tune of *'Here We Go 'Round the Mulberry Bush.'* Begin by walking in a circle and singing the first verse. Add more verses and continue.

PUMPKIN PATCH

This is the way we walk to the patch,
Walk to the patch, walk to the patch.
This is the way we walk to the patch,
On a sunny day in the fall.

This is the way we pick a pumpkin.

This is the way we wash a pumpkin.

This is the way we carve a pumpkin.

This is the way we bake a pumpkin cake.

This is the way we stir pumpkin soup.

This is the way we rinse pumpkin seeds.

BOOKS

*LENART HELLSING - **THE WONDERFUL PUMPKIN***
*RICHARD SHAW - **THE KITTEN IN THE PUMPKIN PATCH***
*ALVIN TRESSELT - **AUTUMN HARVEST***

MAGIC CARPET

FOR OPENERS

HAVE A FAIRLY LARGE RUG, BEDSPREAD, OR SHEET THAT AS MANY AS FOUR TO SIX CHILDREN CAN SIT ON. BRING IT TO CIRCLE TIME AND INTRODUCE IT TO THE CHILDREN AS THEIR 'MAGIC CARPET,' A CARPET THAT WILL ALLOW THEM TO TAKE IMAGINARY TRIPS, CREATE STORIES, PRETEND THAT THEY ARE OTHER PEOPLE, AND SO ON.

LET THE CHILDREN TRY OUT THEIR NEW CARPET. HAVE THEM ALL CLOSE THEIR EYES AND THINK OF AN ANIMAL THEY WOULD LIKE TO BE. GO AROUND THE GROUP AND TAP SEVERAL CHILDREN ON THE HEAD AND HAVE THEM SIT ON THE CARPET. AS THEY ARE MOVING TO THE CARPET, HAVE EVERYONE SAY THE FIRST VERSE OF THE RHYME BELOW.

THE CHILDREN ON THE CARPET SHOULD MAKE THE SOUNDS OF THEIR ANIMALS. THE CHILDREN IN THE CIRCLE SHOULD GUESS WHAT ANIMALS ARE ON THE MAGIC CARPET. AFTER ALL OF THE ANIMALS HAVE BEEN IDENTIFIED, EVERYONE SAY THE SECOND VERSE OF THE FOLLOWING RHYME AND THE CHILDREN ON THE CARPET SHOULD MOVE BACK TO THE CIRCLE.

MAGIC CARPET

MAGIC CARPET, MAGIC CARPET
TAKE US ALL AWAY.
BRING US TO FANTASYLAND
TO TALK AND DANCE AND PLAY.

MAGIC CARPET, MAGIC CARPET
TAKE US BACK WE SAY.
RETURN US TO OUR CLASSROOM
THERE'S NO MORE TIME TO PLAY.
LIZ WILMES

LET ANOTHER GROUP OF CHILDREN TRY OUT THE MAGIC CARPET. HAVE ALL OF THE CHILDREN CLOSE THEIR EYES AND THINK ABOUT BEING TOYS IN TOYLAND. WHEN THEY OPEN THEIR EYES, TAP SEVERAL CHILDREN ON THE HEAD, AND LET THEM MOVE TO THE MAGIC CARPET. EVERYONE ELSE SAY THE FIRST VERSE OF THE RHYME. WHEN THE CHILDREN REACH THE CARPET, LET THEM PRETEND TO BE TOYS IN TOYLAND. TALK ABOUT THE DIFFERENT TOYS AND THEN HAVE THE CHILDREN MOVE BACK AS THE OTHERS SAY THE SECOND VERSE. CONTINUE, ENCOURAGING CHILDREN TO BE SINGERS ON STAGE, ADULTS AT WORK, CHILDREN PLAYING IN THE SNOW, ETC.

FINGERPLAYS

HOLD ON TIGHT

Hold on tight, we're flying through the stars,
There goes Jupiter, here comes Mars.
Fly so high, floating in the sky.
Our magic carpet is flying high.

RING AROUND THE MAGIC CARPET

Ring around the magic carpet
Try to grab a star,
Stardust, stardust,
Fall where you are.

RECIPES

MAGIC PIE

YOU'LL NEED

4 eggs
2 cups milk
1/2 cup flour
1/3 cup butter
1 cup coconut
1 t. vanilla
1/2 t. nutmeg
Pinch of salt

TO MAKE: Measure everything into a blender, turn on high speed and count to ten. Grease a pie pan and fill it with magic mixture. It will settle into three layers: crust, custard filling, and coconut topping. Bake at 350 degrees for 40 minutes.
from COME AND GET IT
by Kathleen Baxter

FIELD TRIPS

• Call your local children's librarian and make an appointment for the children to visit the library. Ask the librarian to show your children different books in which the children in the stories use their imaginations, enjoy dressing up in costumes, or take adventurous trips such as *'Peter Pan'*, *'Where the Wild Things Are'* or *'Dream Child.'* If possible, have the librarian show a short filmstrip or read one of the books to your children.

CLASSROOM VISITORS

- Invite a local actor to visit your class. (You could contact the high school or college drama club.) Encourage him/her to act out or pantomime very short stories or ideas with the children. See if s/he could bring make-up or parts of costumes for the children to try on.

LANGUAGE GAMES

MAGIC CARPET RIDE

Have a large sheet of paper and a wide marker. Put the magic carpet in the middle of the circle time area. Have the children form a circle around it. Give each child a piece of yarn about five or six feet long. Have several children at a time put one end of their pieces of yarn on the carpet and hold the other ends in their laps. When all of the 'extenders' have been attached to the carpet, everyone can go on the sky ride.

Say the first verse of the Magic Carpet rhyme and take off. As the children are flying around, have them call out different things that they see up in the sky or down on the ground. Make a list of all of their sightings. Continue the ride looking for objects, people, flowers, clouds, etc.

When the ride is over, say the second verse of the rhyme, land the magic carpet, and detach the *extenders*. Talk about all of the things that the children saw on their magic carpet ride. Continue this idea, taking rides to places that the children have chosen. EXTENSION: Have the children keep their 'extenders' in their pockets so they can take rides whenever they would like.

WHAT COULD IT BE?

Put several semi-large objects which could easily be hidden under the magic carpet in a box so that the children cannot see them. Put the magic carpet in the middle of the circle time area with the children sitting around it. Have the children cover their eyes. Go over to the box, select one object, and put it under the carpet.

Have the children uncover their eyes and look at the carpet. Tell the children several things about the object such as *"It is a toy and it rolls."* Let a child go over and look at it more closely. Maybe he could put his hand on the carpet and feel around the object. Let him tell the others something else about the hidden object. Let another child look at it and see if he can add something different. Maybe he could gently tap the magic carpet to see if the object makes a noise. Give the children several more clues. Let other children explore it closely. Guess. Uncover the object. *"Did you guess it? How did you know or why were you fooled?"* Play again with another object.

MAGIC CARPET CHARADES

Before circle time, have the children make headbands for themselves depicting a character, animal, or object they would like to pretend to be. Have them wear their headbands to circle time.

Say to the children, "*Today we're going to pretend to be lots of different things when we board our magic carpet. Who would like to go first?*" (Child boards the magic carpet.) "*OK, Gene, you're on the magic carpet and you're wearing your headband. Do something to let us know who or what you are.*" (The child does something and everyone guesses. After they have guessed, another child boards the magic carpet and the pantomimes continue.)

HEADBAND RIDDLES

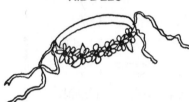

Have the children wear their headbands. Go around the group and have each child whisper who he is in your ear. Begin describing one of the characters. The children should try to guess who you are describing. When the child is guessed he boards the magic carpet. Continue until the magic carpet is full of children waiting to take a ride. "*Where will you go today? Have fun!*"

ACTIVE GAMES

ACTING SILLY

Put a clown hat in the middle of the magic carpet. Have one child board the magic carpet, place the clown hat on his head, and do something silly like bounce side to side, bow up and down, change into an animal, stand very quietly, or turn in circles. Then let everyone be silly by following the action of the child on the magic carpet. Let other children board the magic carpet, put on the clown hat, and lead the others in an action.

MAGIC CARPET

Let the children each take individual magic carpet rides. Give each child a piece of construction paper. Have him sit on it, close his eyes, and pick a place he'd like to go. Begin to play quiet music such as 'Puff the Magic Dragon' or 'Somewhere Over the Rainbow.' Have the children take off to their magic lands. When the music stops, they should all come back to the circle time area, sit on their magic carpets, and tell the others where they've been.

BOOKS

EZRA JACK KEATS – *THE TRIP*
ANN JONAS – *THE TREK*
JILL MURPHY – *WHAT NEXT, BABY BEAR?*

DAYAL KAUR KHALSA – *I WANT A DOG*
PHYLLIS ROOT – *MOON TIGER*

SCARECROWS

FOR OPENERS

MAKE A VERY SIMPLE SCARECROW WITH THE CHILDREN. YOU'LL NEED A PAIR OF OLD PANTS, AN OLD SHIRT, A PLASTIC MILK BOTTLE, COLLAGE MATERIALS INCLUDING YARN, STRAW OR PAPER TO STUFF YOUR SCARECROW, AND A BROOM.

HAVE THE MATERIALS READY IN SEVERAL DIFFERENT AREAS OF THE CLASSROOM. FOR EXAMPLE, HAVE THE PANTS AND STUFFING MATERIALS IN ONE AREA, THE SHIRT AND MORE STUFFING MATERIALS IN A SECOND AREA, AND THE MILK BOTTLE WITH THE COLLAGE MATERIALS ON THE ART TABLE. DIVIDE THE CHILDREN INTO SMALL GROUPS WITH AN ADULT FOR EACH GROUP. HAVE THE CHILDREN WORK TOGETHER, EITHER TEARING, WADDING, AND STUFFING THE CLOTHES OR CREATING A FACE. REMEMBER TO TIE THE OPENINGS OF THE PANTS AND SHIRT CLOSED IF THE STUFFING IS COMING OUT.

WHEN THE PARTS OF THE SCARECROW ARE FINISHED, BRING THEM TO THE CIRCLE TIME AREA. HAVE A CHAIR READY. CAREFULLY SIT THE STUFFED PANTS ON THE CHAIR. STICK THE STRAW END OF THE BROOM INTO THE BACK OF THE PANTS. NOW STICK THE SHIRT ON THE PANTS BY SLIDING THE HANDLE UP THROUGH THE BACK OF THE SHIRT. ATTACH THE OPENING OF THE MILK BOTTLE TO THE TOP OF THE BROOM HANDLE AS IT SITS ON THE NECK OF THE SHIRT. TIE THE SCARECROW SECURELY TO THE CHAIR.

LET THE CHILDREN NAME THE SCARECROW AND DECIDE WHERE TO PLACE HIM SO THAT HE CAN WATCH THE CHILDREN PLAY AND VISIT WITH THEM EACH DAY.

FINGERPLAYS

THE FLOPPY SCARECROW

I flop my arms,
I flop my feet.
I let my hands go free.
I am the floppiest scarecrow
That you ever did see.

THE SCARECROW

The scarecrow stands,
With hanging hands,
Beside the farmer's barn.
He scares the jay and crow away,
With a smile made of yarn.

LET'S BUILD A SCARECROW

First the body
And then the head.
A big straw hat
And a scarf of red.
Buttons for eyes,
And a carrot nose,
And a mouth made of stitches
In two smiling rows.

RECIPES

SCARECROW FACES

YOU'LL NEED

Hamburger buns
Peanut butter
White and/or orange spreadable cheese
Vegetable bits
Olive circles
Raisins

TO MAKE: Spread the cheese or peanut butter on hamburger halves. Using the vegetables, olives, and raisins, have fun creating different scarecrow faces.

FIELD TRIPS

• Ask your parents if any of them make scarecrows for their gardens or fields. If so, arrange to visit the family. Let the person/s who constructed the scarecrow tell the children how s/he did it.

CLASSROOM VISITORS

• Invite a parent/s to come into the classroom to do scarecrow make-up. During the time the parent/s is there, children who want can have their faces changed into scarecrow faces. Have a full length mirror near the make-up area for the children to see themselves.

LANGUAGE GAMES

**SCARECROW
SECRETS**

Bring the scarecrow to circle time and use him as a big puppet. (See *For Openers.*) Have the children each think of a secret to tell the scarecrow. Have him call on children and ask each to come up and whisper something in his ear. For example, *"Maria, I get so lonely just sitting in this chair. Please tell me a secret."* (Let Maria come up and talk to the scarecrow.) Continue with other children in a similar way. When four or five children have had a chance to tell the scarecrow a secret, say *"I just cannot remember any more secrets. Would the rest of you please wait until tomorrow to tell me your secrets? Thank you. I'm really tired. I'm going to take a nap."* Repeat for several days.

**SCARECROW
PUZZLE**

Make your puzzle by having an adult lie down on a piece of butcher paper and have someone trace around his whole body. Have the children paint the body tracing. Let it dry and cut it out. Now cut the scarecrow shape into as many pieces as you have children. (To make the puzzle more sturdy, use spray glue and glue each piece to posterboard and recut.)

Bring all of the pieces to circle time. Pass them out to the children. Start with the feet. Have the children who have the feet pieces lay them on the floor. Talk about who might have the leg pieces. Put them in place. Continue until you have the entire puzzle put together.
EXTENSION: Place the pieces in a brownie pan and put it with the other puzzles. Encourage the children to do the puzzle during their free choice time.

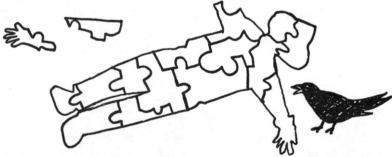

**SCARING
CROWS**

Have the children sit in a circle to make a farmer's field. Choose one child to pretend to be the scarecrow in the middle of the field. Have him wear a straw hat or a flannel shirt. Point to another child. Have him pretend to be a crow flying around the farmer's field towards the scarecrow. As the crow gets closer to the scarecrow, have the scarecrow scare the crow away by saying something, giving the crow a scary look, or waving his arms at the crow. The crow should fly back to his place.

Once the children understand how to play you might have several *'crows'* teasing the scarecrow at one time, or you might have a pair of scarecrows in the field.

SCARECROW WEATHER CHART

Have a chart (plain or calendar) and several copies of the different types of weather. Have a child look out of the window to check the weather and then choose one (or more) of the weather pictures to describe it. Have him paste the picture on the chart.

Talk about how they think scarecrows like this weather. *"How would a scarecrow feel in this weather?"* (warm, just right, shivery, freezing, wet, cold, etc.) *"What should scarecrows wear today?"* (sunglasses, raincoats, boots, etc.)

ACTIVE GAMES

SCARECROW DANCE

Have the children close their eyes and imagine they are scarecrows dancing down the sidewalk. *"How do their legs look all stuffed with straw? What are their arms doing? How does it feel to have a broom sticking up through their backs?"* Now turn on some dancing music such as 'Follow the Yellow Brick Road' from The Wizard of Oz, and let the children dance as if they were scarecrows.

SCARECROW-CHILD

Have the children talk about and show each other how to make different scary faces. Then play 'Scarecrow-Child.' Have the children stand up. You say, *"Scarecrow."* The children should look at each other and pretend to be scarecrows with scary faces. Then say, *"Child."* They should change back to how a child would stand and look. Say *"Scarecrow"* again. They should look at each other with different types of scary poses.

Continue by alternating *"Scarecrow-Child,"* or you might want to repeat *"Scarecrow"* or *"Child"* several times in a row to add more of a listening challenge.

BOOKS

SID FLEISCHMAN – ***SCAREBIRD***
KAY DANA – ***ROBBIE AND THE RAGGEDY SCARECROW***

AUTUMN HARVEST

FOR OPENERS

SEND A NOTE HOME AND ENCOURAGE EACH OF THE CHILDREN TO BRING EITHER A FRUIT OR VEGETABLE TO SCHOOL. (HAVE SEVERAL EXTRA FRUITS AND VEGETABLES FOR THOSE CHILDREN WHO FORGET THEIRS.)

HAVE TWO CORNUCOPIA BASKETS: ONE FOR FRUITS AND ONE FOR VEGETABLES. LET EACH CHILD HOLD UP HIS PIECE OF PRODUCE AND TELL THE OTHERS WHAT HE BROUGHT. IF HE WANTS, HE CAN TELL SOMETHING ELSE ABOUT IT SUCH AS ITS COLOR, SHAPE, TASTE, OR WHERE HE GOT IT. AFTER HE'S FINISHED TALKING, HE SHOULD PUT IT IN THE FRUIT OR VEGETABLE BASKET.

WHEN BOTH BASKETS ARE FULL, PICK UP THE FRUIT BASKET. HOLD UP EACH PIECE OF FRUIT AND HAVE THE CHILDREN CALL OUT ITS NAME. REPEAT WITH THE VEGETABLES IN THE VEGETABLE BASKET. DURING FREE CHOICE, USE THE FRUIT TO MAKE A FRUIT SALAD FOR SNACK OR LUNCH. SAVE THE VEGETABLES UNTIL THE NEXT DAY WHEN THE CHILDREN CAN CLEAN AND CUT UP THE VEGETABLES AND THEN ENJOY THEM WITH A DIP FOR SNACK OR LUNCH.

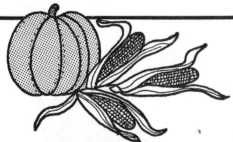

FINGERPLAYS

PICKING APPLES

Here's a little apple tree,
I look up and I can see,
Big red apples, ripe and sweet,
Big red apples, good to eat!
Shake the little apple tree,
See the apples fall on me.

Here's a basket, big and round,
Pick the apples from the ground,
Here's an apple I can see,
Waiting there just for me.
It's ripe and sweet.
That's the apple I will eat!

JACK FROST

Who comes creeping in the night
When the moon is clear and bright?
Who paints tree leaves red and gold
When the autumn days turn cold?
Up the hill and down he goes
In and out the brown corn rows,
Making music crackling sweet,
With his little frosty feet?
Jack Frost!

FARMER PLANTS HIS WHEAT
(tune: "Farmer In the Dell")

The farmer plants the wheat,
The farmer plants the wheat,
Hi, ho, the dairy-o,
The farmer plants the wheat.

The sun comes out to shine, etc.

The rain begins to fall, etc.

The seeds begin to grow, etc.

The farmer cuts the wheat, etc.

The farmer grinds the wheat, etc.

And now we'll bake some bread.

RECIPES

VEGETABLE DIP

YOU'LL NEED

1/2 cup cottage cheese
1/2 cup sour cream
Pinch of dill weed to taste
1 T. onion to taste
1/4 t. celery seed

TO MAKE: Lightly mix all of the ingredients. Serve with favorite vegetables.
from COME AND GET IT
by Kathleen Baxter

FRUIT DIP

YOU'LL NEED

Plain yogurt
Honey
Vanilla

TO MAKE: Put the yogurt in a bowl. Add the honey and vanilla to taste. Mix well and serve with pieces of fresh fruit.
from COME AND GET IT
by Kathleen Baxter

FIELD TRIPS

• Take a walk to a nearby grocery store or fruit/vegetable market. Have one of the employees show the children where the produce is delivered, how it is delivered, cared for, and then displayed.

• Go to an apple orchard and enjoy picking apples from the trees. Bring them back for juicy snacks during the next week or so.

LANGUAGE GAMES

FRUITS
VEGETABLES,
PRODUCE

Collect a variety of fruit and vegetables. Put them all in a basket. Have a tray. Put three or four pieces on the tray. Say *"fruit," "vegetables,"* or *"produce."* If you say *"fruit"* the children should begin naming the fruit on the tray. If you say, *"vegetables"* they should name the vegetables. If you say *"produce"* they should name all of the things on the tray.

As you take the first assortment of produce off of the tray, let the children name each piece. Put another assortment on the tray. Point to each piece and have the children name those pieces. Then you say *"fruit,"* *"vegetables"* or *"produce"* as above. The children call out the names of those specific items.

Continue with different assortments of fruit and vegetables.

CRUNCH TEST

Clean and cut a variety of fruits and vegetables into fairly small pieces. Put them on a tray. Pass the tray around and let each child pick a piece of produce. As each child picks his piece, either have him name what it is or tell him what he chose.

After everyone has a piece, have the children eat, listening very carefully to hear if his piece makes a crunching noise as he chews it. After everyone has given his piece the *'crunch test,'* let each child tell the others what he ate and if it crunched or not.

  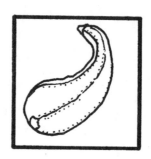 

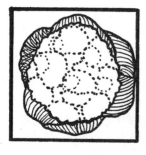   

VEGETABLE MATCH

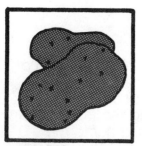

Using the examples provided, make picture cards for a variety of vegetables. Duplicate as many as necessary so that each of the children will have several cards. Get real vegetables to match the pictures.

Bring the cards and vegetables to circle time. Pass several cards to each child. Put one vegetable on the floor in front of you. Have the children call out its name and then look at their pictures. Those who have a matching picture should bring it up and place it near the real vegetable. Lay the next real vegetable on the floor. Continue as above.

EXTENSION: Put the game on a table so the children can play it during their free choice time.

FEEL AND GUESS

Fill a mesh bag with different types of produce. Pull each one out and have the children identify it. Put them all back in the bag. Have an empty basket.

Begin walking around the group holding the bag. Stop in front of a child. Have him close his eyes, put one hand in the bag, and feel a piece of produce. After he has felt it, have him guess what it is, pull it out, open his eyes, and see if he guessed correctly. Then he should put his piece of produce in the basket. Continue walking around the group, stopping at other children, and proceeding with the game.

ACTIVE GAMES

FRUIT SALAD

Get enough pictures of different fruits so that each child will have at least one. (Duplicates are OK.) Punch a hole in each fruit picture and tie a piece of yarn through it to make a necklace.

Teach the children this song which they will use for the fruit salad game.

FRUIT SALAD
(tune: Head, Shoulders, Knees, and Toes)

Apples, cherries, bananas, and pineapple
Apples, cherries, bananas, and pineapple
Apples, cherries, bananas, and pineapple
All mixed up in a fruit salad.
Liz Wilmes

TO PLAY: Using a long rope make a circle in the middle of the circle time area to represent the fruit bowl. Give each child a fruit necklace. Decide which four fruits will go into the fruit salad. Using those four fruit names, sing the song. While everyone is singing, the children wearing those necklaces go into the fruit bowl, hold hands, and jump up and down and all around mixing up the fruit. An adult or child can be standing near the fruit bowl pretending to stir and mix up the fruit.

When the song is over, the *'fruits'* walk out of the circle as everyone pretends to eat the fruit salad. The teacher says, *"I'm still hungry. Let's make another salad."* Choose four more fruits and repeat changing the names of the fruits being used.

Continue until all of the children have had at least one opportunity to be in the fruit bowl. At the end someone says, *"I'm really full, no more fruit salad for me."*

BOOKS

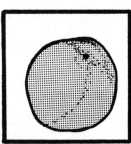

DARLOV IPCAR – **_HARD SCRABBLE HARVEST_**
ALVIN TRESSELT – **_AUTUMN HARVEST_**

BIRDS

FOR OPENERS

CUT OUT A BARE TREE TO HANG ON ONE OF YOUR SMALLER BULLETIN BOARDS. FIND PICTURES OF A VARIETY OF DIFFERENT BIRDS SUCH AS A CARDINAL, OWL, TURKEY, ROBIN, EAGLE, STORK, ETC. (BE SURE THERE ARE ENOUGH FOR ALL OF THE CHILDREN. DUPLICATES ARE FINE.) HIDE THEM AROUND THE ROOM.

HAVE THE CHILDREN GATHER. TELL THEM THAT THEY ARE GOING TO PRETEND TO BE BIRDS AND GO ON A BIRD HUNT TO FIND PICTURES OF THEIR FRIENDS. TELL THEM THAT WHEN THEY FIND A PICTURE, THEY SHOULD BRING IT OVER TO YOU AND YOU WILL TACK IT ON THE GROUND OR IN THE TREE ON THE BULLETIN BOARD WHERE ALL OF THE BIRDS ARE GATHERING. HAVE THE CHILDREN FLAP THEIR BIRD WINGS AS THEY LOOK FOR PICTURES OF THEIR BIRD FRIENDS.

AFTER ALL OF THE BIRDS ARE ON THE BULLETIN BOARD, HAVE THE CHILDREN HELP YOU IDENTIFY EACH OF THEM.

FINGERPLAYS

BIRD STORY

A father and mother bird
Lived in a tree,
In their nest were babies,
One, two, three.

The parent birds fed them
All day long.
And soon the babies
Grew big and strong.

They fluttered down
From the nest one day,
And hid in some bushes
Not far away,

The father bird saw
A cat creep by,
He cried: "My children,
You'll have to fly!

"You needn't be fearful,
Just follow me!"
And off they flew
To their nest in the tree.

BIRDS

If I were a bird
I would learn to fly
Twisting and turning
All over the sky.

Up to the cloud
Down to the ground
Stretching my wings
As I turned all around.

Come pretend and fly
With me
Up to our home
In the top of a tree.
Dick Wilmes

44

ONCE I SAW A LITTLE BIRD

Once I saw a little bird
Go hop, hop, hop.
And I cried, "Little Bird,
Will you stop, stop, stop?"

I was going to the window
To say "How-do-you-do,"
But he shook his little tail
And far away he flew.

IF I WERE A BIRD

If I were a bird, I'd sing a song,
And fly about the whole day long,
And when the night came I'd go to rest,
Up in my cozy little nest.

RECIPES

BIRD GARLANDS

YOU'LL NEED

Blunt needle and heavy-duty thread
Raisins
Stale bread
Stale donuts
Cheese bits

TO MAKE: String any of the above ingredients onto the thread. Hang the bird treats in a nearby tree.

BIRD MIX

YOU'LL NEED

Clean sand
Cracked corn
Crushed dog biscuits
Sunflower seeds
Thistle seeds

TO MAKE: Mix all of the above ingredients. Pour into your bird feeder. Replace as it gets low.

FIELD TRIPS

• On a nice day, take a *'Bird-Walk'* with the children. Before the walk talk with the children about where they might see birds and what the birds might be doing. Remind the children that they are bigger than most birds and that they need to walk very quietly so they do not scare the birds.

Walk quietly looking for birds. When you see several in a tree or sitting on the grass, stop and sit down, trying to make as little movement as possible. Have the children cup their hands to make binoculars and carefully watch what the birds do. After the birds fly away, get up and continue your walk. Stop again when you see more birds and look at them through your binoculars. Continue and then return to the classroom.

Discuss what you all saw on your walk. Write down on a large piece of paper what the children say. Hang the list in the language area.

45

LANGUAGE GAMES

BIRD
WATCHING

Hang a bird feeder near one of the windows in your room. Encourage the children to quietly stand near the window and watch the birds fly to the feeder, land, eat, and then fly away.

After the children have had several days to watch the birds, talk about how the birds hang onto the feeder. *"How do they get the food out? Do they eat from the ground or the feeder? What colors of birds come to the feeder? What color bird is the biggest bird? The smallest? Do any of the birds make noises? What do you think they are saying?"*

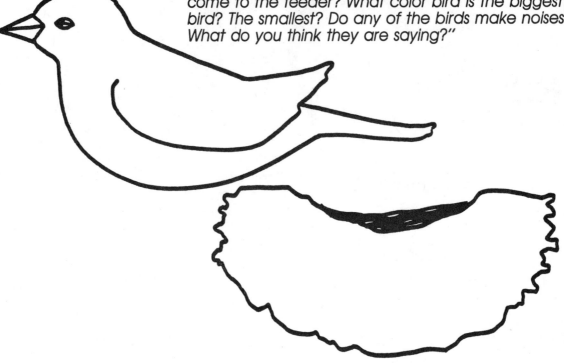

BIRD MATCH

Using the bird and nest illustrations and different colors of felt, cut matching bird and nest shapes. Put the birds in one container and the nests in another container. Have the felt board nearby.

First hold up each bird and have the children call out its color. Now have a child come up and choose a nest and put it on the felt board. That child should call on a friend to come up and find the bird that sits in that nest. The friend should put the bird in the matching nest and call on another child to come up and find another nest. Continue in this manner until all of the birds and nests have been matched.

TALK ABOUT
THE BIRDS

Fold down the edges of a paper grocery bag to make a nest. Get four to six of the birds which you made for the opening activity. Put the birds in the nest and bring it to circle time.

Have a child come up, take one of the birds out of the nest, and slowly fly it around showing it to all of the children. Identify what kind of bird it is and then talk about its different characteristics. When finished, have the child who is holding the bird fly it back to the bulletin board to rehang later. Repeat with the other birds.

BIRDS IN THE NEST

Using construction paper and popsicle sticks, make as many bird stick puppets as you have children. If your children can read numerals, number the birds one through the number of children you have. Paint a piece of styrofoam brown. This will be the nest. Stick all of the birds in the nest. Bring it to circle time.

Pass the nest around and have each child take a bird. Now sing the following song and have the children hold up their birds. If the birds have numerals on them, the children should hold them up when their number is sung. If there are no numerals, point to children when they should hold them up.

BIRDS IN THE NEST

1 little, 2 little, 3 little birds
4 little, 5 little, 6 little birds
7 little, 8 little, 9 little birds
10 birds in the nest.

11 little, 12 little, 13 little birds
14 little, 15 little, 16 little birds
17 little, 18 little, 19 little birds
20 birds in the nest.

Repeat the song to return the birds to the nest. If the birds have numerals on them, the children can fly their birds back when their number is sung. If there are no numerals, point to children to fly their birds back to the nest.

ACTIVE GAMES

BIRD MOVEMENT

Give all of the children feathers and have them pretend that they are birds. Chant this bird rhyme as they move around the room:

Fly like a bird, fly like a bird
Fly, fly, fly!

Swoop like a bird, swoop like a bird
Swoop, swoop, swoop!

Peck, tweet, dig, flutter, rest, etc.

IN AND OUT THE WINDOW

Have the children stand in a circle and join hands. Choose one child to stand in the middle. Have that child name one of the birds or colors of birds that you've talked about.

The child in the middle is the bird and begins to fly around. The children sing 'In and Out the Window' as they raise and lower their arms for the bird.

IN AND OUT THE WINDOW

Fly in and out the window,
Fly in and out the window,
Fly in and out the window,
Small, red bird. (Substitute the
color or name of the bird which
the child chose to be.)

BOOKS

EDITH THACHER HURD – **LOOK FOR A BIRD**
BRIAN WILDSMITH – **BRIAN WILDSMITH'S BIRDS**
LEONARD BASKIN – **HOSIE'S AVIARY**
ASHLEY WOLFF – **YEAR OF BIRDS**
MARTHA STILES   – **DOUGAL LOOKS FOR BIRDS**

FIRST THANKSGIVING

FOR OPENERS

GO TO YOUR LOCAL LIBRARY AND CHECK OUT A CHILDREN'S BOOK WHICH TELLS ABOUT THE FIRST THANKSGIVING, SUCH AS *SQUANTO AND THE FIRST THANKSGIVING* BY JOYCE K. KESSEL. BRING IT TO CIRCLE TIME ALONG WITH A FEATHER. READ THE BOOK TO THE CHILDREN OR TELL THEM THE STORY WHILE SHOWING THEM THE PICTURES.

AFTER THE STORY, GIVE THE FEATHER TO A CHILD. LET HIM TELL SOMETHING ABOUT THE STORY OR ASK A QUESTION. THEN HAVE HIM PASS THE FEATHER TO ANOTHER CHILD AND LET THAT CHILD TELL THE OTHERS HIS FAVORITE PART ABOUT THE FIRST THANKSGIVING. CONTINUE, GIVING ALL OF THE CHILDREN THE OPPORTUNITY TO SHARE THEIR THOUGHTS.

FINGERPLAYS

TURKEY GOBBLER

*I met a turkey gobbler
When I went out to play.
Mr. Turkey Gobbler, "How are you today?"
"Gobble, gobble, gobble, that I cannot say,
Don't ask me such a question on
Thanksgiving Day."*

IN THE FOREST

*This is the forest of long ago,
These are the trees standing all in a row.
Look very closely, what do you see?
Indians peering out—one, two, three.*

*Now they are hiding; the forest is still.
Now they are hurrying over the hill.
Ever so quickly, now they are nearing
The teepees at the edge of the clearing.*

MR. DUCK AND MR. TURKEY

Mr. Duck went out to walk,
One day in pleasant weather.
He met Mr. Turkey on the way
And there they walked together.
"Gobble, gobble, gobble."
"Quack, quack, quack."
"Good-bye, good-bye, good-bye."
And then they both walked back.

...TTLE PILGRIM

...lgrim
Went ... a bear.
He looked in the woods.
He looked everywhere.

The brave little pilgrim
Found a big bear.
He ran like a rabbit.
Oh, what a scare!

RECIPES

CORN BREAD

YOU'LL NEED

2 eggs
4 T. honey
1 cup wheat flour
2 cups yellow corn meal
1 t. salt
1 rounded t. baking soda
2 cups buttermilk (or sour milk)
2 T. vegetable oil

TO MAKE: Beat the eggs and honey together. Measure the dry ingredients and mix them alternately with milk. After everything is well mixed, add the oil. Grease a 9" × 13" pan, pour in the batter, and bake at 425 degrees for 30 minutes.

FIELD TRIPS

• Schedule your class to visit your local library. Have the librarian tell the children about Thanksgiving and then read them a Thanksgiving story. Share one of your Thanksgiving rhymes with the librarian.

• Visit a turkey farm or game preserve in your vicinity.

49

LANGUAGE GAMES

NATIVE
AMERICAN
STORIES

Before circle time, get a long sheet of mailing paper and draw several simple, easily recognizable pictures or symbols on it. Bring the sheet to circle time. Have the children sit around the mailing paper and look at the first picture/symbol. Pretending they are Native Americans, have them create a story which relates to the illustration. Continue with other illustrations.

Once they have told their stories, have several children carry the paper over to the art area. After circle time encourage the children to add more designs, symbols, or pictures. Write the children's names near their drawings. After several days, bring the paper back to circle time and allow each child to tell a story about the drawing he made.

TURKEY DASH

Make simple turkey finger puppets for each of the children. Have them put the puppets on their fingers and move the turkeys as they say the rhyme, *'Run Fast Little Turkey.'*

RUN FAST LITTLE TURKEY

The brave little Pilgrim (Hide turkey puppet)
Went out in the wood (Other hand over eyes)
Looking for a meal
That would taste really good. (Rub tummy)

First she picked cranberries (Pick)
Out in the bog.
Then she saw a turkey (Slowly show turkey)
Hiding in a log.

Run fast little turkey. (Wiggle turkey away)
Run fast as you may.
Or you'll come to dinner
On Thanksgiving Day.
Dick Wilmes

WHAT'S FOR DINNER?	Talk about all of the different foods and drinks that the children would like to have for Thanksgiving dinner. Then say a series of three or four words, two or three of which are food words and one which is not. After listening to the series, have the children tell you which were the food words you said. For example, you might say, *"milk, pudding, cheese, bed."* The children would repeat *"milk, pudding, cheese."* Continue in this manner with other series of words.
OVER THE RIVER	Teach the children the words to the song *'Over the River and Through the Woods.'* Encourage them to help you think of hand gestures to go with the lyrics. Now enjoy it even more using the movements you have made up.

ACTIVE GAMES

PILGRIM'S PROGRESS	Talk about the Pilgrims sailing across the ocean to a new country. (For example: Loading the ship, waving good-bye, looking for land, rejoicing when they found it, looking for a place to build their new homes, building their homes, planting crops, preparing for the first Thanksgiving celebration.) You be the leader and play a follow-the-leader type game and act out the Pilgrims' journey to the first Thanksgiving.
THANKSGIVING GAMES	Play some of the games the Pilgrims and Native Americans may have played on the first Thanksgiving such as running, jumping, and relay races. Pretend to shoot bows and arrows at targets by tossing bean bags at a certain spot. Weather permitting, go outside and play hide and seek.
TURKEY TROT	Get an instrumental version of the *'Bunny Hop.'* Teach the children the dance. Now let them pretend they are turkeys doing the *'Turkey Trot.'*

BOOKS

MARC BROWN – **ARTHUR'S THANKSGIVING**
LYDIA MARIA CHILD – **OVER THE RIVER AND THROUGH THE WOOD**
CRESCENT DRAGONWAGON – **ALLIGATOR ARRIVED WITH APPLES**
GAIL GIBBONS – **THANKSGIVING DAY**
JOYCE KESSEL – **SQUANTO AND THE FIRST THANKSGIVING**

PREPARING FOR WINTER

FOR OPENERS

SEND A NOTE HOME WITH THE CHILDREN ASKING THE PARENTS TO TALK WITH THEIR CHILDREN ABOUT GETTING READY FOR WINTER. NEAR THE BOTTOM OF THE NOTE, LEAVE SPACE FOR AN ADULT TO WRITE ONE THING THAT HIS CHILD HAS PICKED AS A FAVORITE THING THAT THE FAMILY DOES TO PREPARE FOR WINTER. THE CHILDREN SHOULD BRING THE NOTES BACK.

BRING A LARGE SHEET OF NEWSPRINT OR BUTCHER PAPER TO CIRCLE TIME ALONG WITH A WIDE-TIPPED MARKER. TALK WITH THE CHILDREN ABOUT HOW THEIR FAMILIES ARE PREPARING FOR WINTER. AS EACH CHILD SAYS WHAT HIS FAMILY IS DOING, WRITE IT ON THE PAPER. FOR EXAMPLE, *"DAN'S FAMILY IS STACKING WOOD FOR THE FIREPLACE."* OR YOU COULD SIMPLY WRITE, *"STACKING WOOD."* CONTINUE WITH ALL OF THE CHILDREN. AFTER CIRCLE TIME, DRAW A VERY SIMPLE PICTURE NEXT TO EACH CHILD'S IDEA. THIS WILL REMIND EVERYONE WHAT WAS SAID. HANG THE EXPERIENCE CHART LOW ON THE DOOR OR WALL SO THE CHILDREN CAN *'READ'* IT.

IN THE NEXT PARENT NEWSLETTER, SHARE THE CHILDREN'S IDEAS WITH ALL OF THE FAMILIES.

FINGERPLAYS

WINTER WEATHER

Let's put on our mittens
And button up our coat.
Wrap a scarf snugly
Around our throat,

Pull on our boots,
Fasten the straps,
And tie on tightly
Our warm winter caps.

Then open the door
And out we go
Into the soft
And feathery snow.

MY HOUSE

I'm going to build a little house,
With windows big and bright,
With chimney tall and curling smoke,
Drifting out of sight.

In winter when the snowflakes fall,
Or when I hear a storm,
I'll go sit in my little house,
Where I'll be snug and warm.

WHEN THE COLD WINDS BLOW

When cold winds blow,
And bring us snow,
At night what I like most
Is to climb in bed
And hide my head
And sleep as warm as toast.

"Shhhhhhhh - good night!"

RECIPES

VEGETABLE SOUP

YOU'LL NEED

6 cups water
1 qt. tomatoes
1 medium onion
1-2 carrots
1-2 stalks of celery
Other favorite vegetables
2 bay leaves
Salt and pepper to taste
Noodles (Optional)

TO MAKE: Simmer the tomatoes, water, and seasonings. Peel and chop the onion. Clean and chop the other vegetables. Add to the broth. Simmer for 1/2 hour. Add noodles if you would like. Cook until noodles are soft. Serve with peanut butter crackers.
from COME AND GET IT
by Kathleen Baxter

CLASSROOM VISITORS

• Invite a park ranger or naturalist to talk with your children about how the forest animals prepare for winter– what they eat, how their bodies adapt, and where they live. If possible, compare the animal habits to things the children are doing.

LANGUAGE GAMES

GETTING DRESSED

Collect snowpants, a coat, boots, mittens, a scarf, and a hat that will fit most of your children. Talk about each of the items. Discuss the order in which the clothes are put on.

Have the children sit in a circle. Pass out the different articles of clothing. (You might give the boots and mittens to four separate children.) Pick one child who is going to get dressed. Have him stand in the middle. The child who has the snowpants says, *"I'm first. Come put on the snowpants."* The child goes over to the child holding the snowpants and puts them on. The child holding a boot says, *"I'm next, I have a boot."* The child who is dressing goes over to him and puts on the first boot. The game continues until the child has all of the winter clothes on.

Then he stands in the middle and takes off the outerwear. As he takes each piece of winter clothing off, have everyone call out what it is.

MITTEN MATCH

Hang a clothesline in the circle time area between two chairs. Collect all of the children's mittens. Using a clothespin, clip one from each pair on the clothesline. Put the mates in a box or basket.

At circle time pass all of the mates out. Have a child hold up the mitten he has. Let the others name all of the colors/designs on it. Then have him go to the clothesline, find the mate, and clip the two mittens together to make a mitten match. Everyone claps.

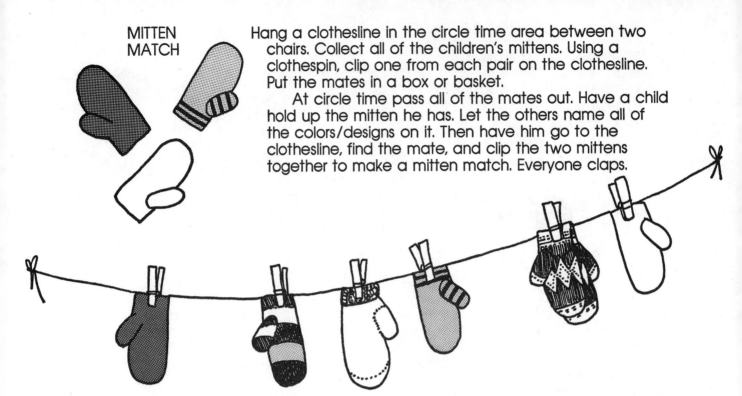

THE BIG SNOW

Read the book *'The Big Snow'* by Hader and Hader to the children. Read it several more times each time presenting it in a slightly different way:

- Begin with the first page. As you encounter each animal or person in the story, have the children talk about how that character prepares for winter.

- Write down all of the animals and people named in the story. Bring the list to circle time. Read the first name on the list. Ask if any of the children have ever really seen that animal/person. *"What was he doing when the child saw him? Who can remember how that animal/person got ready for winter?"*

- Have the children pretend that they are the different animals getting ready for the big snow. For example, ask, *"Who would like to be a bird?"* Choose several children and let them fly around getting ready. Then say, *"The snow is beginning to fall."* The birds should fly to their shelter. Pick another animal, such as the squirrels, and continue in the same manner.

When all of the children are protected in their winter habitats, pretend you are *'the big snow'* and come rushing through the classroom. As you sprinkle snow on each group of animals, say things like, *"The squirrels are protected in their holes. The birds are sheltered by the tree branches."* Since everyone has prepared for the big snow, everyone will be safe.

THINK WINTER

Have the children think of words which relate in any way to winter. Tack the list on the door. Add to it whenever a child thinks of another word. You might draw a simple picture next to each word.

ACTIVE GAMES

BEAR HUNT — Bears hibernate for the winter. Have the children go on a bear hunt and look for bears that are preparing for the winter chill.

GOING ON A BEAR HUNT

Let's go on a bear hunt.
All right. (Slap hands on thighs)
Let's go!

Oh look,
I see a wheat field!
Can't go around it,
Can't go under it,
Let's go through it.
Swish, swish, swish.

Oh look,
I see a tree!
Can't go through it,
Can't go under it,
Let's climb it.
Up, up, up, up.

Continue the walk as above.

I see a swamp! (Swim, swim, swim)
I see a bridge! (March, march, march)

Oh look,
I see a cave!
Can't go around it,
Can't go under it,
Let's go in it.
Walk, walk, walk.

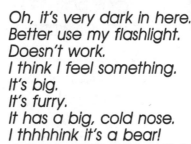

Oh, it's very dark in here.
Better use my flashlight.
Doesn't work.
I think I feel something.
It's big.
It's furry.
It has a big, cold nose.
I thhhhink it's a bear!
A BEAR, LET'S GET OUT OF HERE!

Reverse the walk and run back home.

Oh look
I see our house!
Quick open the door.
Lock the door.
Whew, we made it back safely.

BOOKS

LYDIA DABCOVICH – *SLEEPY BEAR*
DICK BRUNA – *I CAN DRESS MYSELF*
EMILY ARNOLD McCULLY – *FIRST SNOW*

DOUGLAS FLORIAN – *WINTER DAY*
ALVIN TRESSELT – *THE MITTEN*

GINGERBREAD FAMILY

FOR OPENERS

USING THE SHAPES PROVIDED, MAKE A STICK PUPPET GINGERBREAD FAMILY. VARY THE SHAPES TO MAKE AS MANY MEMBERS AS YOU THINK ARE APPROPRIATE FOR YOUR GROUP OF CHILDREN.

BRING THE GINGERBREAD FAMILY TO CIRCLE TIME AND INTRODUCE EACH MEMBER TO YOUR CHILDREN. YOU MIGHT WANT TO INCLUDE EACH PERSON'S AGE AND A LITTLE BIT ABOUT HIM/HER. LET THE CHILDREN GIVE EACH MEMBER OF THE GINGERGREAD FAMILY A FIRST NAME. AS YOU INTRODUCE THE FAMILY, TALK WITH THE CHILDREN ABOUT THE PEOPLE IN THEIR FAMILIES. TELL THE CHILDREN THAT THE GINGERBREAD FAMILY IS GETTING READY TO CELEBRATE A HOLIDAY. ASK THE CHILDREN IF THEIR FAMILIES ARE ALSO PREPARING FOR A HOLIDAY. TALK ABOUT THE HOLIDAY/S.

TELL THE CHILDREN THAT THE MEMBERS OF THE GINGERBREAD FAMILY WILL NEED THE CHILDREN'S HELP TO GET READY FOR THEIR HOLIDAY. THE CHILDREN SHOULD PUT ON THEIR THINKING CAPS SO THEY ARE READY TO HELP THE GINGERBREAD FAMILY THINK OF GIFTS THAT THEY CAN GIVE EACH OTHER, SPECIAL THINGS THEY CAN DO FOR EACH OTHER, A DELICIOUS HOLIDAY MENU, AND FESTIVE HOLIDAY DECORATIONS.

RECIPES

GINGERBREAD CHILDREN

YOU'LL NEED

1 box butterscotch pudding mix
1/2 cup shortening
1/2 cup brown sugar
1 egg
1-1/2 cups flour
1-1/2 t. ginger
1/2 t. cinnamon
1/2 t. baking soda

TO MAKE: Cream the shortening and brown sugar. Add the egg and mix well. Add the pudding mix, flour and spices. Mix.

Roll the dough 1/8 to 1/4 inch thick and cut into one large gingerbread character or small ones. Bake on a greased cookie sheet at 350° for ten (10) minutes.
from THE EVERYTHING BOOK
by Valerie Indenbaum & Maria Shapiro

56

CLASSROOM VISITORS

• Have a simple holiday party including the children and their families. You might want to have an inexpensive *'gift grab.'* For example you could make batches of brown playdough and give some to each child along with a gingerbread cookie cutter.

To make the playdough: Mix 4-5 cups of flour, 1 cup of salt, 4 tablespoons of alum, and 2 tablespoons liquid cooking oil in a large bowl. Boil 3 cups of water. Add a little blue and red food coloring to the water and then enough yellow food coloring to make a brown color. Add the colored water to the other ingredients. Stir until the mixture has cooled a little. Put on a table and knead until the dough is thoroughly mixed. (Add more flour if the dough is too moist and feels sticky.)

LANGUAGE GAMES

THE GINGERBREAD HOUSE

Bring a large piece of styrofoam about two to three inches thick, a permanent wide-tipped marker, and the members of the Gingerbread family to circle time.

Hold up each family member and have the children whisper each gingerbread character's name. Hold up the piece of styrofoam and tell the children that this is going to be the Gingerbread family's home. Talk with the children about which rooms the family will need to have in their home. After the children have decided, use the marker to divide the styrofoam into rooms.

Pass out the family members to the children. Ask, *"Which room of the house is the mom in? What is she doing to get ready for the holiday?"* (The child holding the mom chooses the room he wants her in, sticks the puppet into the styrofoam, and tells what the mom is doing there to get ready for the holiday the family is celebrating.) Continue until all of the members of the Gingerbread family are in the home.

EXTENSION: Put the house in the art area for the children to further decorate.

HOLIDAY MENU

Using brown strips of construction paper, make a headband for each child. Have the children wear their headbands to circle time. Bring a sheet of white shelf paper, posterboard, and a marker.

Have the children pretend they are members of the Gingerbread family and they are planning the holiday menu. Have the children name foods they would like to eat. Print all of their ideas on the shelf paper.

After all of the ideas have been written down, bring out a piece of posterboard. On the top left side of the posterboard print *"Drinks,"* in the middle print *"Meal,"* and near the right side print *"Desserts."* Have the list of foods which you wrote on the shelf paper nearby. Read the first food on the list. Have the children decide if it is a drink, part of the meal, or a dessert. Print it in the proper column. Continue with all of the foods. Ask the children if they would like to add anything else to the menu.

EXTENSION: Have the children decorate the border of the holiday menu and then hang it up for all to enjoy.

GINGERBREAD FAMILY GIFTS	Bring the members of the Gingerbread family to circle time. Pass them out to different children. Name one family member, for example the baby brother. Whoever is holding the baby brother crawls to the middle of the group and tells everybody one thing he would like to receive for a gift. Then say, "*What else could we buy for* (name)." After the children have named several gifts for the baby brother, have him crawl back to the edge of the circle.

Name another member of the family and have the child holding that person move to the center. The child mentions one gift and you all think of several more. Continue with other family members.

THOUGHTFUL DEEDS	Hold up two Gingerbread family puppets. Ask the children to think of nice things each of those family members could do for each other. After talking about those two members, hold up two others and discuss nice things they could do for each other.

ACTIVE GAMES

CAN'T CATCH ME	Have the children sit in a circle. Bring one of the gingerbread headbands. (See '*Holiday Menu.*') Give the headband to a child to wear. He's the gingerbread child. He walks around the circle and taps each child on the head. When he comes to the child he wants to chase him, he says, "*Catch me if you can*" as he taps the child's head. The chase begins. As the two children are chasing each other, the others chant:

> "*Run, run, as fast as you can.*
> *You'll never catch him,*
> *He's the gingerbread man.*"

A new child wears the gingerbread headband and the game continues.

FAMILY SING-ALONG	Bring the Gingerbread family puppets to circle time. Have the children teach the family the words and actions to their favorite holiday rhymes, fingerplays, and songs.

BOOKS

GINGERBREAD BOY
SEABURY PRESS, 1975 – *PAUL GALDONE*
KNOPF, 1987 – *SCOTT COOK*

GIFTS

FOR OPENERS

BRING A LARGE PIECE OF BUTCHER PAPER TO CIRCLE TIME. THE CHILDREN SHOULD COVER THEIR EYES AND THINK OF TWO GIFTS THEY WOULD EACH LIKE TO RECEIVE. THEN THEY OPEN THEIR EYES AND EACH SHARE ONE IDEA. WRITE DOWN EACH CHILD'S NAME AND WHAT HE SAYS. AFTER EVERYONE HAS MADE ONE WISH, GO AROUND AGAIN AND HAVE EACH CHILD TELL THE OTHERS HIS SECOND WISH, WRITING EACH ONE OF THEM DOWN ALSO. DRAW A VERY SIMPLE PICTURE NEXT TO EACH WISH AND THEN HANG THE *"WISH LIST"* ON A DOOR OR WALL WHERE THE CHILDREN AND THEIR PARENTS CAN EASILY READ IT.

EXTENSION: WHEN YOU TAKE THE LIST DOWN, CUT IT INTO SECTIONS SENDING EACH CHILD'S WISHES HOME WITH HIM.

RECIPES

TREATS IN ICE

YOU'LL NEED

Grapes   Your favorite fruit juice
Cherries
Raisins

TO MAKE: Fill your ice cube trays about 3/4 full of your favorite juice. Add a treat to each section. Freeze the juice. Use the special cubes with a holiday punch.

HOLIDAY PUNCH

YOU'LL NEED

Club soda or seltzer water
Your favorite fruit juice

TO MAKE: Mix the two ingredients half and half in a large bowl. Add the special ice cubes. Float fresh orange slices on top.

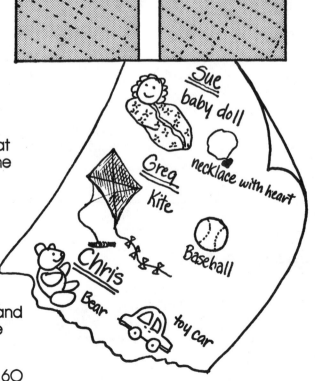

Sue
baby doll

necklace with heart

Greg
Kite

Baseball

Chris
Bear

toy car

FIELD TRIPS

• Visit a nearby shopping center. Note the holiday gifts, decorations, and music. Make arrangements to have the children tour a toy store or toy department. Have one of the employees show the children different toys which are appropriate for their age and within the price range of the families you serve. Call ahead of time to discuss this with the employee who will be leading your children.

LANGUAGE GAMES

MATCHING
GIFTS

Wrap several different sizes and shapes of boxes in a variety of holiday wrapping papers, so that you can lift off the top or open one side. Gather ten to fifteen types of gifts and put them in a sack.

Put the boxes out so all of the children can easily see them. Talk about the different sizes and shapes. The children could even imagine what gifts might be wrapped in the different boxes. Then take one of the gifts from the sack. Name it and talk about it.

Tell the children that you need help wrapping the gifts that you're giving for the holiday. Give the gift to a child and ask him to help you find the best box for it. Have the child hold it next to the first wrapped box. If the children think that the box is just the right size, they should say, *"Just right."* If it is too small, they should say, *"Too small."* If it is too large, they can say, *"Too big."*

Once the children have decided which box is best for the gift, have a child open the box and see if it fits. If it does, lay the gift near the box. If not, continue looking. Follow the same procedure with the rest of the gifts.

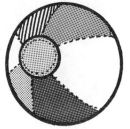

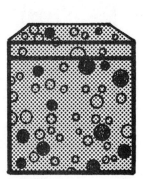

GIFT GUESS

Get five or six different boxes. Put a different toy in each one. Wrap them in holiday paper. Cut a hole in each box just large enough for the children to slip one of their hands through.

At circle time, ask the children to help you figure out what's in the boxes. Give a gift box to a child. Have him slip his hand into it, feel the gift, and think of what it could be. When he slips his hand out, have him whisper what he thinks the gift is to you. Give the gift to another child. Have him repeat the activity. Then say *"Albert thinks the gift is a ball. Albert, why did you guess a ball?"* (Albert can give his reasons.) *"Marion thinks that it is a ball also. Marion, why do you think it is a ball?"* (Let Marion give her reasons.) Now give the box to another child. Have him shake it. *"Does he think it is a ball?"* Take the top off of the box and discover what is really in the package. Continue with the remaining gifts.

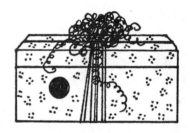

GIFT SHAPES

Using magazines and catalogues, cut out pictures of different gifts which have fairly distinguishable shapes, such as a beach ball for a circle, a party hat for a triangle, a music box for a square, and a package of gum for a rectangle. Put each picture of a gift in an envelope. Be sure to have at least one for each child. Cut out a large circle, square, triangle, and rectangle from posterboard.

Lay the posterboard shapes on the floor in the middle of the circle time area. Have a child be the letter carrier and pass out the envelopes to the other children. Point to a child. Have him open his letter, look at the picture, and tell the others what it is. He should walk over to another child, show him the picture and let him decide what shape the gift looks like. Then the second child can put the picture of the gift on the matching large shape in the middle of the area. He should return to his place and open his envelope. Continue until all of the envelopes are open.

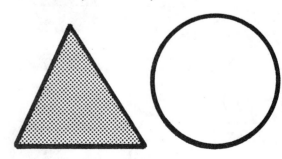

TALK ABOUT
GIFTS

Bring one or two gifts to circle time to show the children. Name each gift and talk with the children about who would like to receive that gift, how the person would use it, and who the person might share the gift with. On other days, bring several more gifts and discuss them in the same way.

ACTIVE GAMES

GIFT IN THE
BOX

Have each child think of a gift he would like to pretend to be. Ask who would like to go first. Have that child go into the middle and curl up like a gift in the box. Say the *Jack in the Box'* rhyme changing the first two lines to "*Gift in the box.*"

> *Gift in the box,*
> *Gift in the box,*
> *Will you come out?*
>
> *Yes, I will!* (Child pops out.)

After the child pops out, he begins to act like his pretend gift. The other children try to guess what he is. When someone guesses correctly, pick another child to go into the middle. Continue in this manner.

BOW
BONANZA

Wrap a fairly large box in white newsprint or butcher paper. Put it in the art area and have the children decorate it with washable markers.

Put the gift box in the middle of the circle time area. Give each child a bow with adhesive or a loop of tape on the back. Have the children stick the bows to the back of their hands.

Point to a child, have him crawl to the box, close his eyes, crawl around in a circle, and then stick the bow to the box. Point to another child (or several at one time) and continue until the gift box is filled with bows. EXTENSION: Use the box to store the small gifts you may be giving the children at the holidays.

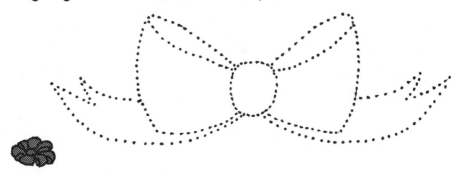

BOOKS

LEONARD EVERETT FISHER – ***BOXES, BOXES***
RUTH RADLAUER – ***WHAT CAN YOU DO WITH A BOX?***

'TWAS THE NIGHT BEFORE CHRISTMAS

FOR OPENERS

READ THE CHILDREN THE POEM "'TWAS THE NIGHT BEFORE CHRISTMAS" BY CLEMENT C. MOORE. AS YOU READ IT, SHOW THE CHILDREN THE PICTURES AND RELATE THE PICTURES TO WORDS WITH WHICH THEY MAY NOT BE FAMILIAR. FOR EXAMPLE, POINT TO THE REINDEER WHEN THE POEM MENTIONS "COURSERS."

LANGUAGE GAMES

BEDTIME STORIES

Before reading the poem the second time, make stick puppets of the different characters for each of your children. (Make duplicates if you have more children than characters.) Spread a large blanket on the floor in the middle of the circle time area. Have the children sit around the blanket and tuck their legs under it as if they were snuggling into bed. Pass the stick puppets out to the children. Read the poem and have the children listen carefully. When they hear their characters mentioned, they should hold up their puppets.

When you have finished reading, talk about what the different characters did in the story.

ACTIVE GAMES

ACTING OUT

Pass out the stick puppets to the children. Have one child hold his up and point to a child who is not holding a puppet. That child names the character and then goes to an open area and does something that the character did in the story, such as a reindeer prancing on the rooftop or a child sleeping.

Happy Christmas to all. And to all a good night.

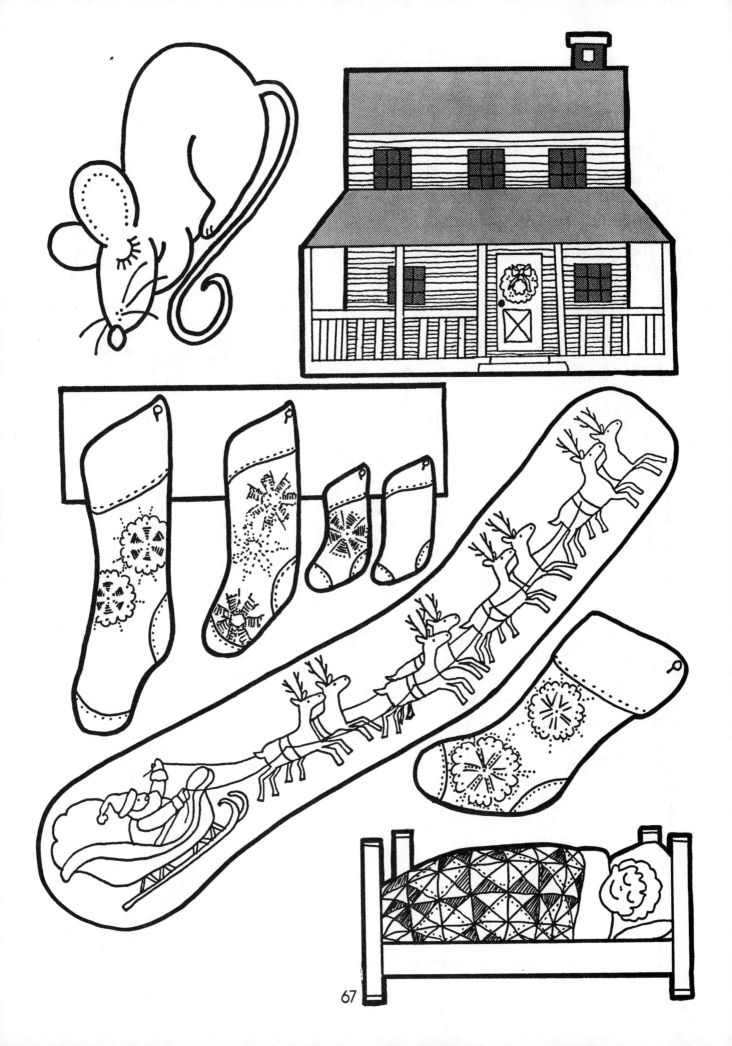

BOOKS

CLEMENT C. MOORE – *NIGHT BEFORE CHRISTMAS*
DODD, 1986 — ROBIN SPOWART
SCHOLASTIC, 1985 — JAMES MARSHALL
KNOPF, 1984 — ANITA LOBEL
HOLIDAY — 1980 — TOMI DePAOLA
LIPPINCOTT, 1976 — ARTHUR RACKHAM

GIFT BOXES

FOR OPENERS

PUT A LARGE PIECE OF CARDBOARD ON THE FLOOR IN THE MIDDLE OF THE CIRCLE TIME AREA. COLLECT ENOUGH GIFT BOXES SO EACH CHILD CAN HAVE AT LEAST ONE. PASS THEM OUT. TELL THE CHILDREN THAT YOU WANT THEM TO USE THEIR BOXES TO BUILD A TOWER, BUILDING, OR AN IMAGINARY STRUCTURE. YOU'LL START BY PUTTING THE FIRST BOX ON THE PIECE OF CARDBOARD. (LAY YOUR BOX ON THE CARDBOARD.) *"WHO WANTS TO GO NEXT?"* (LET A CHILD PUT THE NEXT BOX DOWN.) EACH CHILD CAN ADD A BOX UNTIL ALL OF THE BOXES ARE ON THE PIECE OF CARDBOARD. TALK ABOUT THE STRUCTURE.

NOW CALL ON A CHILD TO COME AND REMOVE ONE BOX FROM THE STRUCTURE TRYING NOT TO LET ANY OF THE OTHER BOXES MOVE. CONTINUE, LETTING THE CHILDREN CAREFULLY TAKE OFF ONE BOX AT A TIME. ONCE ALL OF THE BOXES HAVE BEEN REMOVED, CALL ON A CHILD TO BEGIN THE BUILDING PROCESS AGAIN. WHEN FINISHED, TALK ABOUT THE NEW STRUCTURE AND COMPARE IT TO WHAT THE CHILDREN REMEMBER ABOUT THE FIRST ONE.

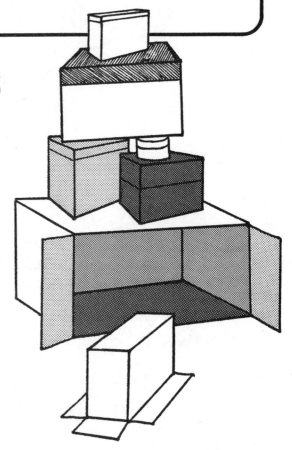

FINGERPLAYS

GIFT BOXES

Gift boxes, gift boxes, everywhere.
Empty now, they're lighter than air.
Some tiny as bugs, one big as a bear.
Round, rectangular, even square.
Vohny Moehling

RECIPES

Each day prepare a simple snack. Put it in a gift box and cover it. Before passing it, give the children clues about what the snack is. When they have guessed, take the top off of the box, pass the snack, talk about what it is, and then enjoy it with a drink.

You could prepare: Crackers and cheese, peanut butter balls, oatmeal cookies, finger gelatin, bread squares and cream cheese, etc.

70

CLASSROOM VISITORS

• Ask a person who does gift wrapping for one of the stores to visit your classroom. Ask him/her to bring a sample of the different size boxes s/he uses for gifts. Encourage the children to think of gifts that would fit in each of the boxes.

LANGUAGE GAMES

BOX PUZZLE

Before circle time cut a large piece of butcher paper. Collect all of the boxes. Using one side from each box, trace around it with a black marker on the butcher paper. (Depending on your group, you may want to mark a large "X" on the side of the box which you traced around.)

Lay the butcher paper on the floor in the circle time area. Have the children sit around it. Pass out a box to each child. Have the children look at all sides of their boxes. Then have them look at the shapes on the butcher paper. See if each child can find a shape which matches one side of his box. Lay the boxes so they fit on the shapes. Any boxes left? Any shapes on the paper empty? Why?

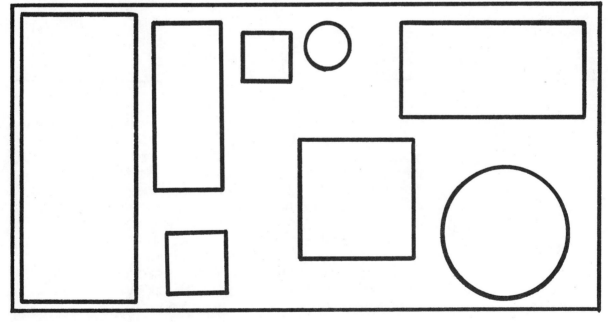

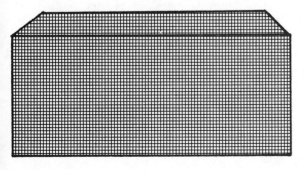

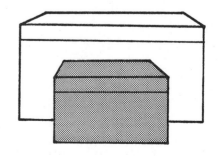

WHAT'S IN THE BOX?

Collect duplicates of a variety of objects (ball, rubber band, brick, safety pin, bell). Put one of each object on a tray for the children to see. Put the duplicate objects in a bag. Have a box with a lid.

Turn your back. Put one object from the bag into the box. Turn around. Shake the box. Pass it to several children. Do they think the object is heavy? Looking at the objects on the tray, which one do they think is in the box? Open the box. Did they guess the match? Have a child take the object from the box and lay it next to the matching one on the tray. Repeat with the other objects.

STACK AND NEST

Choose four to seven boxes of different sizes. Lay them in a line going from largest to smallest. Talk about the sizes. Then stack the boxes with the children, putting the largest one on the bottom. Have a child take the next one and put it on top of the largest one. Continue until all of the boxes are stacked. You might want to try the reverse, with the smallest one on the bottom and see what happens. Maybe the children could predict and then see if their prediction comes true.

Once the children have had experience stacking the boxes, try nesting them. Did it work? Why or why not? Would different boxes work better?

TALLER OR SHORTER

Have several children help you build a box tower in the middle of the circle time area. It should be about as tall as the height of your average child. Have a child stand next to the tower. All of the children look at the child and the tower. If the child is taller than the tower have the group call out *"Taller."* If shorter than the tower, call out *"Shorter."* If the same, call out *"Same."*

ACTIVE GAMES

BALANCING ACT

Pass out a box to each child. Have one child stand where everyone can see him. Have him balance his box on a part of his body, such as on his shoulder, knee, hand, or wherever. Then encourage everyone to try to do the same with his box. Can everyone balance his box in the same place? Why or why not? Maybe some boxes are too big to balance in that place. Have another child balance his box, maybe on his head. Everyone copy him. Continue balancing until everyone who wants has led the balancing act.

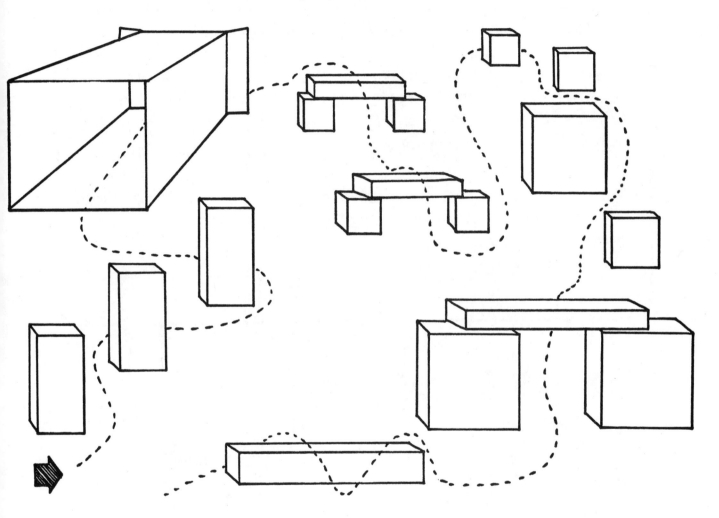

OBSTACLE COURSE

Collect all of the boxes and use them to make an obstacle course around your room. Adapt the illustration for a possible path.

BOOKS

LEONARD EVERETT FISHER – *BOXES, BOXES*
RUTH RADLAUER – *WHAT CAN YOU DO WITH A BOX?*

BELLS

FOR OPENERS

COLLECT A VARIETY OF DIFFERENT BELLS. (USE DUPLICATES SO YOU HAVE ENOUGH FOR EACH CHILD TO HAVE ONE.) PUT THEM IN A BOX WITH A LID. WALK INTO CIRCLE TIME SHAKING THE BOX SO THE CHILDREN WILL REALLY HEAR ALL OF THEM JINGLING. ASK THE CHILDREN WHAT THEY THINK IS IN THE BOX. *"WHY DO THEY THINK IT IS BELLS?"* LIFT OFF THE LID AND SHOW THE BELLS TO THE CHILDREN.

PASS THE BOX AROUND AND LET EACH CHILD CHOOSE A BELL FROM THE BOX. THEN SAY, *"WHOEVER HAS A LARGE BELL STAND UP. SHAKE YOUR BELLS FOR US."* (DO IT.) *"EVERYBODY WHO HAS A VERY TINY BELL, STAND UP. SHAKE THEM FOR US."* TALK ABOUT THE DIFFERENCES BETWEEN THE TWO SOUNDS. (YOU MIGHT WANT TO HAVE THE CHILDREN WITH THE LARGER BELLS RING THEM AGAIN.) NOW HAVE THE CHILDREN WITH MEDIUM SIZE BELLS RING THEIRS. *"DOES THE SOUND OF THE MEDIUM SIZE BELLS SOUND MORE LIKE THE LARGE BELLS OR THE VERY TINY ONES?"*

HAVE THE CHILDREN GENTLY RING THEIR BELLS WHILE SINGING *"JINGLE BELLS."*

FINGERPLAYS

HERE'S A BELL

Here's a bell,
And here's a bell,
And a great big bell I see.
Shall we ring them?
Yes we will.
One (ting-a-ling),
Two (ting-a-ling, ting-a-ling)
Three (dong, dong, dong)

HOLIDAY TIME
(tune: Row, Row, Row Your Boat)

Ring, ring, ring, the bells.
Ring them loud and clear
To tell the children everywhere
That Holiday Time is here.

FIVE LITTLE BELLS

Five little bells, hanging in a row,
The first one said, "Ring me slow."
The second one said, "Ring me fast."
The third one said, "Ring me last."
The fourth one said, "I'm like a chime."
The fifth one said, "Ring me at Holiday Time."

RECIPES

DING-DONG BELLS

YOU'LL NEED

3 T. unflavored gelatin
12 oz. frozen juice concentrate
12 oz. water

TO MAKE: Mix 1/2 cup of juice with the gelatin. Boil another 1/2 cup of juice and add it to the gelatin. Mix until the gelatin is thoroughly dissolved. Add the remaining juice. Pour into a flat dish and refrigerate until set. Remove and cut the gelatin into bell shapes with cookie cutters.

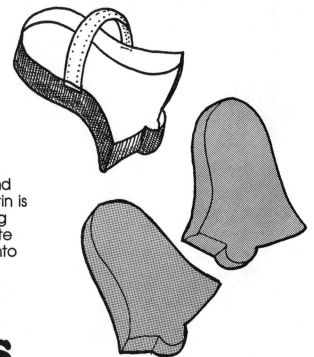

FIELD TRIPS

- Visit a facility which uses bells for signals on a regular and frequent basis. For example, a fire station or a hospital. Have an employee show the children the different types of bells and how they are used. If possible, let the children have opportunities to ring them.

CLASSROOM VISITORS

- Have an adult who collects bells for a hobby bring in his/her collection for the children to see. While there, have him/her talk about the different types of bells and ring several of them for the children to hear. Depending on the types of bells in the collection, let the children have opportunities to ring the bells. Encourage the visitor to stay in the classroom for a little while after circle time and talk with the children in small groups and individually.

LANGUAGE GAMES

BELL MATCH   Collect five to seven pairs of bells. Tie a short ribbon to each bell so that you can easily ring each of them. Put them in a box. Pick two matching bells and one that is different.

Have the children cover their eyes. Tell the children to listen while you ring three bells and see if they can figure out which two sound the same. Ring the first bell. Wait a second. Ring the second one. *"Does it sound like the first?"* (Answer.) Ring the third one. *"Does it sound like the first or second bell?"* (Answer.) Ring the two bells which the children thought sounded the same. Do they still think that the sounds match? Have the children cover their eyes again. Pick three new bells and play again.

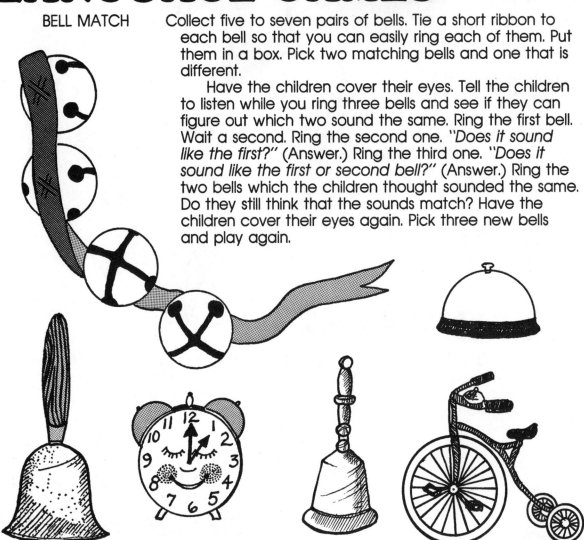

BELL TALK   Talk with the children about the different ways that bells are used. For example, ask the children, *"How many children have doorbells at their homes? When they hear the doorbell, what does it mean? What other bells can they think of and what do they mean?"* (fire bell, school bell, church bell, sleigh bells, bells on a hat, bells on baby shoes, etc.)

BELL SOUNDS   Put one bell in a box and cover it. Give the box to one child. Have him move the box so the bell rings. The children should listen carefully to the sound. Have him slowly and carefully pass the box to another child, trying to keep the bell silent. Have the child move the box in a different way and see if the bell sounds differently. Once again pass the box quietly and have a third child move the box in yet another way to give the bell another sound. Continue trying to get the bell to sound as many different ways as possible. Repeat with another bell.

GIVE A JINGLE

Pass out bells to the children. Read or tell them a story which frequently repeats a word or short phrase such as in *'The Three Little Pigs,' 'The Three Bears,' 'Brown Bear, Brown Bear, What Do You See?'*, and so on.

Begin reading the story. Whenever you say the repetitious word or phrase the children should *'Give a Jingle.'*

WHO'S AT THE DOOR?

The children sit in a circle. Pick one child to sit in the middle and cover his eyes. Very quietly give a bell to a child. The child should ring the bell. The child in the middle uncovers his eyes and the children say *"Who's at the door?"* The child in the middle tries to guess who rang the bell. If he can't, have him close his eyes again and let the child with the bell ring it again. When he guesses, the child with the bell comes into the middle to guess *"Who's at the door?"*

ACTIVE GAMES

PARACHUTE JINGLE

Put twenty to thirty small bells on the parachute. Have the children sit around the chute and lift it several inches off of the ground. Sing *'Jingle Bells'* as you gently move the parachute side to side.

JINGLE BELL

Hang five or six different size bells from the ceiling at varying heights so that the children could reach them if they jumped and swung at them with their hands.

Call on a child and give him directions on how to move and which bell to swing at. For example:

"Troy, run to the largest bell and try to hit it."

"Paula, hop to the smallest bell, jump up and tap it gently."

"Heather, skip to any bell you want and tap it with your pointer finger."

BOOKS

ASHLEY WOLFF – *BELLS OF LONDON*
MARYANN KOVALSKI – *JINGLE BELLS*
PAT HUTCHINS – *DOORBELL RANG*

I CAN DO IT

FOR OPENERS

GET A COFFEE CAN WITH A PLASTIC LID. COVER THE CAN WITH PAPER. WRITE "I CAN" ON IT. CUT AN OPENING IN THE TOP. CUT 2"×6" STRIPS OF PAPER. BRING THE CAN, STRIPS, AND A MARKER TO CIRCLE TIME. SHOW THE CHILDREN THE CAN. TELL THEM THAT IT IS A VERY SPECIAL CAN. DURING THE NEXT SEVERAL DAYS THEY WILL BE FILLING IT WITH STRIPS OF PAPER TELLING MANY OF THE THINGS THAT THEY ARE ABLE TO DO.

NOW TELL THE CHILDREN TO CLOSE THEIR EYES AND THINK OF ALL OF THE THINGS WHICH THEY CAN DO BY THEMSELVES, SUCH AS PUT ON THEIR SHOES, BUTTON THEIR SHIRTS, CLEAR THE DISHES, RUN FAST, PAINT AT THE EASEL, AND SO ON. THEN THEY SHOULD CHOOSE THEIR FAVORITE THING. WHEN A CHILD HAS THOUGHT OF ONE, HAVE HIM OPEN HIS EYES. GO OVER AND HAVE HIM TELL YOU WHAT IT IS. YOU WRITE HIS NAME AND SKILL ON A STRIP OF PAPER. GIVE THE STRIP TO THE CHILD AND HAVE HIM DROP IT INTO THE 'I CAN.' DO THIS WITH SEVERAL MORE CHILDREN. TELL THE OTHERS THAT YOU ARE GOING TO PUT THE 'I CAN' IN THE LANGUAGE CENTER AND THAT DURING FREE CHOICE TIME YOU WILL WRITE THE REST OF THE STRIPS AND HAVE THE CHILDREN PUT THEM IN THE 'I CAN.'

WHEN EVERYONE HAS A STRIP IN THE 'I CAN' BRING IT BACK TO CIRCLE TIME AND SHARE EVERYONE'S TALENTS WITH THE GROUP. ENCOURAGE THE CHILDREN TO ADD MORE AND MORE STRIPS. PERIODICALLY READ THEM TO THE GROUP.

EXTENSION: HAVE AN 'I CAN' FOR EACH CHILD. CONTINUE TO FILL IT OVER THE COURSE OF THE YEAR.

FINGERPLAYS

ALL BY MYSELF

There are many things that I can do
All by myself;
I can comb my hair and lace my shoe,
All by myself;
I can wash my hands and wash my face,
All by myself;
I can put my toys and blocks in place,
All by myself.

TEN LITTLE FINGERS

I have ten little fingers,
And they all belong to me.
I can make them do things,
Would you like to see?

I can close them up tight,
I can open them wide.
I can put them together,
I can make them all hide.

I can hold them up high,
I can hold them down low.
I can fold them up quietly,
And hold them just so.

HELPING'S FUN

When I come in from outdoor play
I take my boots off right away.
I set them by the door just so,
Then off my cap and mittens go,
Zip down my coat and snowpants too,
And hang them up when I am through,
I'm a helper, don't you see?
Helping's fun, as fun can be.
(Talk with the children about what
they do with their outerwear when they
are finished playing.)

THINGS I CAN DO

Hat on head, chin strap here,
Snap just so, you see;
I can put my cap on
All by myself—just me!

One arm in, two arms in,
Buttons one, two, three;
I can put my coat on
All by myself—just me!

Toes in first, heels push down,
Pull, pull, pull and "Whee!"
I can put my boots on
All by myself—just me!

Fingers here, thumbs right here,
Hands are warm as can be;
I can put by mittens on
All by myself—just me!

RECIPES

Plan snacks which the children can easily help you prepare.

ANTS ON A LOG

YOU'LL NEED

Celery
Peanut butter
Raisins

TO MAKE: Wash the celery. Cut it into short pieces. Fill each piece with peanut butter. Add several raisins to each one.

APPLE GOODIE

YOU'LL NEED

Apples
Cream cheese
Banana

TO MAKE: Wash and core the apples. Cut them into quarters. Spread cream cheese onto each one. Top each one with a banana slice.

FIELD TRIPS

• Take a *'Shadow Walk'* on a sunny day. Stop along the way and have the children find their shadows. Once the children have found them, encourage the children to discover what their shadows can do. Encourage the children to do *'tricks,'* such as wave their arms, stand on one foot, etc. What are the shadows doing?

LANGUAGE GAMES

PEEK-A-BOO
PICTURES

In the middle of a piece of construction paper cut an opening about two to three inches in diameter. Collect pictures of children doing different activities: self-help skills, playing outside on different equipment, playing inside with a variety of things, helping with chores, etc.

Bring the pictures and the peek-a-boo construction paper to circle time. Hold up each picture and have the children talk about what the child in the picture is doing. Now mix up the pictures. Do not let the children see them.

Take the first picture and put it behind the peek-a-boo paper so that only a portion of the picture is showing. Have the children look at the clue and then guess what is happening in the rest of the picture. After guessing show them the entire picture. Did they guess what was happening? Then talk with the children about times when they might have been doing the same thing that the child in the picture is doing. Do they like doing that particular activity? Are they good at it or could they get better? Is the child doing it the same way that they do it?

tie shoes
set table
empty trash
dry dishes

BUSY HANDS

Before circle time put a piece of posterboard on the art table. Have several bowls of paint for hand prints. Have the children make hand prints along the bottom half of the board.

Bring the posterboard to circle time. Ask the children to name all of the things that they do with their hands. Write them down as the children say them. As you are writing, have the children clap for the person who thought of the idea. Hang the posterboard low on a wall or door.

CALL FOR
HELP

Talk with the children about times when they might need to use the phone or run to a neighbor's home to call for help. If your community has an emergency number such as '911,' teach it to the children.

Now have one child stand up and tell about a time when he might need to call for help. When he is finished relaying the story, have all of the children chant, "And what did you do?" The child says "I phoned (ran to a neighbor) for help and this is what I said." (Child pretends to phone and talk to an operator or run and talk to a neighbor.) Repeat with several other children.

BABY-CHILD

Talk with the children about all of the things that they did when they were babies and what they can do now that they are older. You might want to record their thoughts in two columns on a piece of posterboard. EXTENSION: Name one of the skills the children mentioned. If it is something that they did when they were a 'baby' they should call out "Baby." If it is a skill they can do now, they should call out "Child."

ACTIVE GAMES

IN MOTION

Have children take turns leading the other children in their favorite exercises. After doing the exercise, talk about which parts of their bodies they seemed to use the most, such as their arms, legs, feet, stomach, and/or head.

HOKEY-POKEY

Put on a record of the 'Hokey-Pokey' and have the children dance to the directions. When finished, talk about which body parts they used in the song. Discuss other things they do with those same body parts, such as run with their legs and throw with their arms.

BOOKS

PEGGY PARISH – *I CAN, CAN YOU?*
SHIGEO WATANABE – *HOW DO I PUT IT ON?*
DICK BRUNO – *I CAN DRESS MYSELF*
JEAN HOLZENTHALER – *MY HANDS CAN*

SNOWMAN FUN

FOR OPENERS

CUT OUT A LARGE POSTERBOARD SNOWMAN AND ALL OF HIS CLOTHES AND FEATURES. LAY THE SNOWMAN IN THE MIDDLE OF THE CIRCLE TIME AREA. PASS OUT ALL OF THE PIECES. DESCRIBE ONE OF THE PIECES, SUCH AS, *"I SIT ON TOP OF THE SNOWMAN'S HEAD. I AM BLACK. WHAT AM I?"* (THE CHILD WITH THE HAT BRINGS IT UP AND PUTS IT ON THE SNOWMAN.) CONTINUE UNTIL THE SNOWMAN IS COMPLETE.

EXTENSION: PUT THE SNOWMAN PUZZLE ON A TABLE FOR THE CHILDREN TO PUT TOGETHER ON THEIR OWN.

FINGERPLAYS

ROLLING A SNOWMAN

Roll the snow over and over,
Roll the snow over the ground,
Pat it and shape it,
Making a snowball round.

Two balls we make for a body,
One for the snowman's head,
Top with a hat worn and shabby,
Tie on a scarf, winter red.

Roll the snow over and over,
Roll the snow over the ground,
Making a smiling, old snowman
Is the jolliest fun we have found.

BUILDING A SNOWMAN

I will build a snowman,
Make him big and tall.
See if you can hit him,
With a big snowball.

RECIPES

SNOWBALLS

YOU'LL NEED

Cream cheese
Round crackers

TO MAKE: Give each child a small piece of cream cheese. Have him roll it into a ball. Put the balls on a plate and refrigerate. Serve on round crackers with a glass of milk.

WHITE FRUIT

YOU'LL NEED

Bananas
Apples
Pineapple
White grapefruit
Fresh coconut
Coconut flakes

TO MAKE: Choose two or more fruits plus coconut flakes. Clean and cut the fruit. Sprinkle it with snow (coconut flakes).

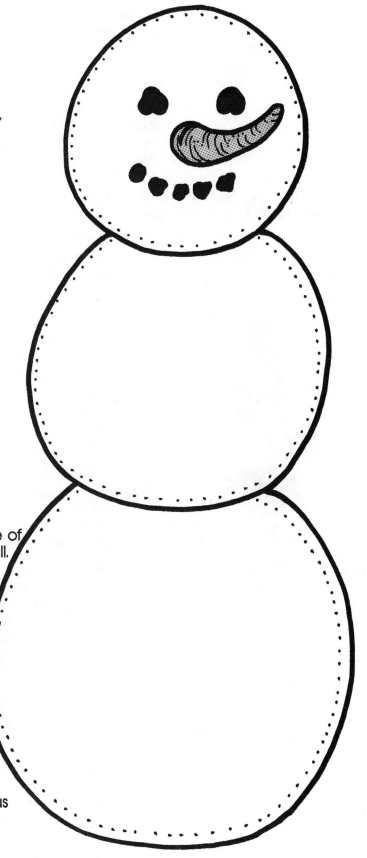

FIELD TRIPS

• Go outside with the children to collect snow for the water table. Just before you leave, give each child a small plastic container. Print names on them. When you get to the snow piles encourage each child to scoop as much snow into his container as possible. Put the containers in one area and enjoy playing in the snow for a while. When you go in, take your containers of snow. Dump the snow in the water table. Enjoy building indoor snowmen. (Remember to wear mittens.)

• If you do not have snow, put styrofoam pieces in your water table along with rounded toothpicks. Pretend the styrofoam pieces are snowflakes. Build a big snow sculpture by linking the styrofoam pieces together with the toothpicks.

LANGUAGE GAMES

BUILDING A
SNOWMAN

Talk with the children about the steps in building a snowman. What do they do first? (Pretend to form a little snowball and then roll and roll it into a giant snowball.) What next? (Make another big snowball.) Then ask, "How do you get it on top of the first one? Do you need another snowball for your snowman? Now that your snowman is made, what else does he need?" Talk about his features and how the children will put them on.

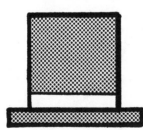

headband with flat tophat

MAGIC HATS

Before circle time, make simple magic hats for all of the children. Have them wear their hats to circle time. Tell the children that when they wear the hats they can pretend to be anyplace they would like, such as swimming at the beach, building a snow fort in the park, etc. Have all of the children touch their hats and think of a place they would like to be. Share their ideas. Did any of the children pick the same place?

WHAT'S
MISSING?

Bring the snowman and his accessories, which you made for the opening activity, to circle time. Put all of the accessories on a tray. Name each of them. Have the children cover their eyes. Take one or more pieces off of the tray. The children should uncover their eyes, look at the tray, and decide what is missing. After everyone has looked, have them quietly call out what they think is missing. Bring it back. Were they right? Put the piece/s back on the tray or add it to the snowman. Play again and again.

DRESS YOUR SNOWMAN	Before circle time cut a snowman from white felt and several hat and mitten sets from different colors of felt.

Put the snowman on the felt board. Lay the mittens and hats randomly on a tray. Have two children come up and find the mittens and hat that match and dress the snowman. Have all of the children call out what color the snowman is wearing. Do any of the children have hats or mittens that color? Remove the mittens and hat and have two different children dress the snowman.

ACTIVE GAMES

DANCING THROUGH TOWN

Bring the magic hats (second language activity) and a whisk broom to circle time. Have the children sit in a circle. Pass out the magic hats and have the children put their hats behind them. Give one child the whisk broom.

Play the song *'Frosty the Snowman.'* Pass the whisk broom around the circle. Stop the music. Whoever is holding the broom puts on his magic hat, pretends to be *'Frosty,'* saunters into the middle, and does a dance. When the music starts again he waltzes back to his place, sits down, takes his magic hat off, and starts passing the whisk broom again. Continue as above so other children can be *'Frosty.'*

VARIATION: Use several whisk brooms at a time.

SNOWBALL TOSS

Get a large white plastic waste basket. Using wide permanent markers draw a big snowman on one side. Using a sharp knife (remember safety) cut out two or three large buttons in your snowman. Get white yarn balls (or tennis balls, ping-pong balls, etc.) and put them in a bucket. Have the children toss the balls through the snowman's buttons.

BOOKS

EZRA JACK KEATS – *A SNOWY DAY*
RAYMOND BRIGGS – *SNOWMAN*
M.B. GOFFSTEIN – *OUR SNOWMAN*

BOOTS AND MITTENS

FOR OPENERS

DURING FREE CHOICE TIME HAVE THE CHILDREN MAKE A BOOT PRINT MATCHING GAME. YOU'LL NEED:

- A LONG SHEET OF BUTCHER PAPER DIVIDED INTO 12"×6" SECTIONS ALONG THE EDGES OF THE PAPER. (SEE ILLUSTRATION.)
- POSTERBOARD CUT INTO 12"×6" PIECES (ONE PER CHILD).
- TEMPERA PAINT POURED INTO SHALLOW BROWNIE PANS.
- ONE BOOT FROM EACH CHILD.
- BUCKET OF WATER AND A SCRUB BRUSH OR USE YOUR WATER TABLE WITH ONE TO TWO INCHES OF WATER IN IT.

TO MAKE: LAY THE PIECE OF BUTCHER PAPER ON THE FLOOR IN A SECLUDED AREA OF THE ROOM WITH THE BROWNIE PANS AROUND THE EDGES OF IT. BRING THE POSTERBOARD PIECES. WHEN EACH CHILD COMES OVER TO MAKE HIS PART OF THE GAME, HAVE HIM BRING ONE OF HIS BOOTS ALONG.

HAVE THE CHILD SLIP ONE HAND INTO HIS BOOT, PICK ONE SECTION OF THE BUTCHER PAPER, PLACE HIS BOOT IN THE PAINT, THEN MAKE ONE BOOT PRINT ON THE SECTION HE CHOSE AND THEN A MATCHING PRINT ON ONE OF THE POSTERBOARD SECTIONS. WRITE HIS NAME ON EACH PRINT. AFTER HE HAS MADE HIS TWO PRINTS, HAVE HIM WASH OFF HIS BOOT. REPEAT WITH EACH CHILD. LET THE GAMEBOARD AND POSTERBOARD PRINTS DRY.

WHEN DRY, BRING THE GAMEBOARD TO CIRCLE TIME. HAVE THE CHILDREN SIT AROUND IT. PASS OUT ALL OF THE POSTERBOARD SECTIONS. HAVE THE CHILDREN LOOK AROUND THE GAMEBOARD FOR THE PRINT WHICH MATCHES THE PRINT ON THE POSTERBOARD PIECE EACH IS HOLDING. AS EACH CHILD FINDS HIS MATCHING PRINT, HAVE HIM LAY THE POSTERBOARD SECTION ON THE GAMEBOARD SECTION. CONTINUE UNTIL ALL OF THE PAIRS HAVE BEEN MATCHED.

THEN GO AROUND THE BOARD TO EACH PRINT AND READ THE NAMES, PICKING UP SECTIONS WHICH DO NOT MATCH. DOUBLE CHECK ALL OF THE PRINTS AND RE-MATCH THE PRINTS BY HOLDING UP ONE POSTERBOARD PRINT AND HAVING ALL OF THE CHILDREN LOOK AROUND AND FIND THE MATCHING PRINT. LAY THE POSTERBOARD PRINT ON ITS MATE. CONTINUE UNTIL ALL OF THE PRINTS HAVE BEEN MATCHED.

EXTENSION: PUT THE GAME IN THE CLASSROOM FOR CHILDREN TO PLAY AGAIN AND AGAIN.

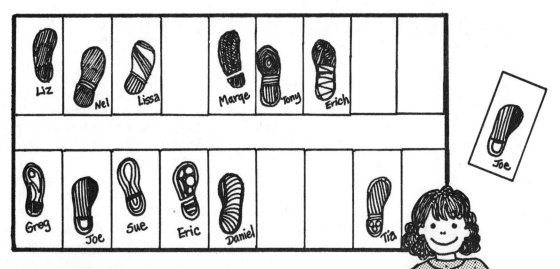

RECIPES

SNOWBALL COOKIES

YOU'LL NEED

2 cups of flour
1 t salt
2/3 cup of oil
4-5 T water
Powdered sugar (optional)

TO MAKE: Put all of the ingredients into a bowl. Mix with your hands or a fork. Roll the dough into small balls. Bake on a greased cookie sheet at 325 degrees for ten minutes. Let cool, sprinkle with a little powdered sugar, and enjoy with a glass of milk.

FIELD TRIPS

• Take a 'Snow Walk' after a new snowfall. Before the walk, give each child a small plastic bag. Just before you return to the classroom, have the children scoop some snow into their bags and close them. Bring the bags inside and set them on a large tray or brownie pan. After everyone has taken off his coat, explore several bags of snow. Watch the snow for the rest of the day. Periodically stop and describe what is happening inside the bags.

CLASSROOM VISITOR

• Invite a parent or grandparent who knits to your classroom. Ask him/her to stay for several hours and work on knitting a pair of mittens. Encourage the children and volunteer to talk about knitting, snow, mittens, etc.

LANGUAGE GAMES

MITTEN MATES

Use pairs of real mittens or cut pairs of construction or wallpaper mittens. Have a clothesline and spring loaded clothespins. String the clothesline between two chairs in the circle time area. Clip one mitten from each pair onto the clothesline. Several children might like to help you. Put the mitten mates in a bag.

Hold up the bag. Have a child come up and pull one mitten out of the bag. He should look at the mittens hanging on the clothesline and find the mitten that matches the one that he is holding. Have him clip it next to the matching one. Continue until all of the mittens have been matched.

MITTEN CLAP

Have the children wear their mittens to circle time. Say a series of three words, one which is associated with cold weather and snow and two which are not. When the children hear the cold weather word they should clap. For example, "*necklace, swimmer, boots.*" When they hear "*boots*" they should clap.
EXTENSION: Enjoy a cold weather rhyme or two.

WINTER WEATHER

*Let's put on our mittens
And button up our coats,
Wrap a scarf snugly
Around our throats,
Pull on our boots,
Fasten the straps,
And tie on tightly
Our warm winter caps.*

*Then open the door . . .
. . . and out we go
Into the soft and feathery snow.*

MITTEN WEATHER

*Thumbs in the thumb place,
Fingers all together,
This is the song we sing
In mitten weather.*

*Doesn't matter whether
They're made of wool or leather.*

*Thumbs in the thumb place,
Fingers all together.
This is the song we sing
In mitten weather.*

WILL THE BOOTS FIT?

Have several sizes of boots. Put them in the circle time area so that all of the children can easily see them. Now say the name of a person, such as "*Dad.*" As you're saying the word, point to a pair of boots. If they would fit a dad, the children should say "*Yes.*" If not, they should say "*No.*" Point to another pair. "*Would that pair fit a dad?*" "*Yes*" or "*No?*" Continue until you get to the pair that would fit a dad. Continue, naming other people such as a big brother, firefighter, baby sister, babysitter, etc.
EXTENSION: Put the boots in the Dramatic Play area for the children to explore later.

MITTEN SORT   Lay about ten single mittens of different sizes, colors, and patterns on the floor. Tell the children that together you and they are going to sort the mittens into two groups. Ask them how they would like to sort the mittens. If a child has an idea let him explain it and then group the mittens the way he suggested. If not, suggest that the children group them by size, those which are big and those which are small.

Hold up one mitten. Ask the children, "*Big or Small?*" If the children say "*Big*," put the mitten in the big pile; if they say "*Small*," put it in the small pile. Continue until all of the mittens are sorted by size. Put all of the mittens back together, sort another way, maybe those which have a '*snowflake design*' on them and those which do not or those which have '*red*' in them and those which do not.

ACTIVE GAMES

BOOT HUNT   Have all of the children bring their boots to circle time. Put the boots in the middle of the area. Mix them up. (Have the children take off their shoes to make the game easier.) Point to two children. They should run to the middle, find their pair of boots, put them on and run back to their places. Continue until all of the children have their boots on.

SNOW   Teach your children the '*Snow*' rhyme. When they know the words, challenge them to say the words and do the actions a little faster-faster-faster!

SNOW

Snow on my forehead (touch forehead)
Snow on my knee (touch knee)
Snow on my glasses (touch eyes)
Getting hard to see.

Snow on my boots (touch shoes)
Snow in my hair (touch hair)
Snow on my mittens (touch hands)
Snow everywhere (touch head to toe)
　　　　Dick Wilmes

BOOKS

ANN SCHWEININGER – ***HUNT FOR RABBIT'S GALOSH***
RON ROY – ***WHOSE SHOES ARE THESE?***
EVE RICE – ***OH, LEWIS***
JEAN ROGERS – ***RUNAWAY MITTENS***
ALVIN TRESSELT – ***THE MITTEN***

TRACKS AND TRAILS

FOR OPENERS

ENJOY GOING ON A BEAR HUNT WITH YOUR CHILDREN

LET'S GO ON A BEAR HUNT

Let's go on a bear hunt,
All right,
Let's go.
Open the door. (Slap thighs as if walking)

Oh look,
I see a wheat field! (Point)
Can't go around it, (Shake head "No")
Can't go under it, (Shake head "No")
Let's go through it. (Spread wheat away with hands)
All right,
Let's go.
Swish, swish, swish.

Oh look,
I see a tree! (Point)
Can't go over it, (Shake head "No")
Can't go under it, (Shake head "No")
Let's go up it. (Climb up hand over fist)
All right,
Let's go.
Climb, climb, climb.

Oh look!
I see a swamp! (Point)
Can't go around it, (Shake head "No")
Can't go under it, (Shake head "No")
Let's swim through it. (Swim)
All right,
Let's go.
Swim, swim, swim.

Oh look!
I see a bridge! (Point)
Can't go around it, (Shake head "No")
Can't go under it, (Shake head "No")
Let's cross over it. (Stomp feet)
All right,
Let's go.
March, march, march.

Oh look!
I see a cave! (Point)
Can't go over it, (Shake head "No")
Can't go under it, (Shake head "No")
Let's go in it.
All right,
Let's go.

Golly—it's dark in here.
Better use my flashlight. (Get out of pocket)
Doesn't work.
I think—I feel something. (Reach out)
It's big!
It's furry!
It's got a big nose!
I think—it's a bear!
IT IS A BEAR!
LET'S GO!
Reverse the order and actions to get away from that bear. Hurry back home!

RECIPES

TRAIL MIX

YOU'LL NEED

Choose from the ingredients listed below and add others you know your children like to eat:

Sunflower seeds
Almonds
Walnuts
Peanuts
Raisins
Dates
Cereals which are not sugar-coated

TO MAKE: Mix some of the above ingredients in a large bowl. Scoop a little into individual muffin cups and serve with glasses of milk.

FIELD TRIPS

• Take a walk right after a new snowfall. Look at the tracks your boots make. Be careful not to walk over your tracks or those of your friends.
   Look carefully at the snow. Do you see tracks that animals or other people might have made?

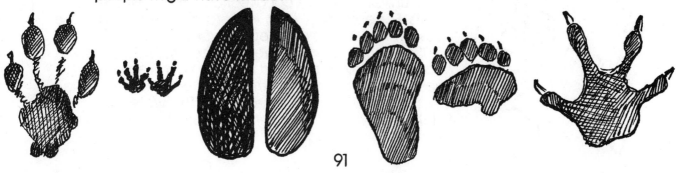

LANGUAGE GAMES

BIG OR LITTLE TRACKS?
Say the name of an animal. If the children think the animal would make big tracks, they should say in a big voice, *"BIG TRACKS!"* If the children think the animal would make small tracks, they should say in a little whisper voice, *"little tracks."* Continue naming other animals and having the children decide what size tracks each makes. After a while, let the children name animals they think of.
EXTENSION: Bring snow inside and put it in your water table. Add plastic animals and encourage the children to make animal tracks in the snow.

MYSTERY TRAILS
Have the children pretend that they are going to make a trail in the snow for their friends to follow. They don't want to make the trail by just walking on their feet because that would be too easy. What ways could they make their trail? For example, they could tiptoe or hop to make the trail. Maybe they could crawl. Encourage them to keep thinking of as many ways as they can to make their trail.
EXTENSION: Have the children pretend that they are in the snow and playing *'Follow the Leader'* using the different ways they had thought of to make trails.

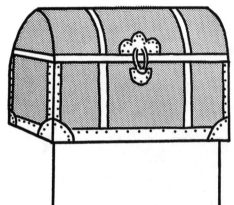

Insert into slit

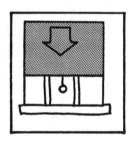  

JOB TRAIL
Before circle time, make a helper chart by cutting a 6" slit for every child in a piece of posterboard. Write each child's name next to a slit. (See the illustration.) Decide how many jobs you want the children to do. Find a picture for each job. Cut one treasure chest for each job. Glue one of the job pictures to each of the treasure chests.

Hide the chests around the room. Have a child stand up. Give him verbal directions to one of the chests. For example, *"Dan, walk to the round table. (He does.) Take three giant steps toward the window. We'll all count for you. (Everyone count, '1,2,3.') Now hop to the flower pot and look for your treasure chest."* When he finds it, he brings it back and tells the others what his job is for the week. (The watering can tells him to water the flowers.) He puts the chest in the slit next to his name.

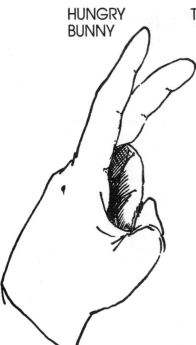

HUNGRY BUNNY

Teach your children this rhyme about a bunny looking for food.

HUNGRY BUNNY

Hop little bunny
Twitching your feet,
Sniffing the snowbanks
For something to eat.
Dick Wilmes

After the children know the rhyme, have them put up their index and middle fingers, pretending their hands are bunnies on the trail of good food. Have the children say the first two lines of the rhyme, then stop and pretend to sniff the snowbanks while you say the last two lines. Then call on several *'bunnies'* and ask them what foods they are looking for. Repeat the rhyme and see what foods other *'bunnies'* are hunting for. You might want to make a list of all of the *'bunny foods.'*

ACTIVE GAMES

FOLLOW THE TRAIL

Trace around the children's feet on pieces of construction paper. Cut out each child's pair of feet several times. While the children are out of the room, use their paper feet to make a trail. Have the trail wind around, go in and out of the room, maybe up and down some stairs. (Tape the feet down for safety.) At the end of the trail have bags of trail mix in a basket for the children's snack.

When the children return, point to the trail and talk about it. Ask the children, *"Who might have made it?"* Then gather together and follow it. Say something like *"I wonder where the trail will lead us? Is it exciting to follow the trail?"* When you get to the basket at the end of the trail, talk about it. Guess what might be in it Then open it up and enjoy the snack.

BIRD TRAILS

Give each child a small bag of bird seed. Take a walk to your outdoor bird feeder. As you are walking, sprinkle a trail of birdseed. When you get to the feeder, check to see if it is full. Add more seed if necessary.

If you are going to play outside for a little while, be careful not to disturb your birdseed trail. When you come to school the next day, check your trail. Is it still there? Who do you think ate some of the seeds?

BOOKS

FRANKLYN BRANLEY – ***BIG TRACKS, LITTLE TRACKS***
MARK TAYLOR – ***HENRY THE EXPLORER***
MASAYUKI YABUUCHI – ***WHOSE FOOTPRINTS?***

HIBERNATION

FOR OPENERS

ANIMALS WHO HIBERNATE ARE DIVIDED INTO TWO CATEGORIES, HIBERNATORS AND SLEEPERS. SLEEPERS ARE ANIMALS WHOSE BODY TEMPERATURES DROP SLIGHTLY, BREATHING DOESN'T SLOW DOWN, AND THEY WAKE UP TO EAT NOW AND THEN. HIBERNATORS ARE ANIMALS WHOSE BODY TEMPERATURES DROP VERY LOW, THEIR HEART RATE ALMOST STOPS, AND THEY SLEEP FOR SEVERAL MONTHS.

SLEEPERS

ANIMALS	WINTER QUARTERS
BEAR	CAVE, HOLLOW TREE, ROCK PILE
CHIPMUNK	TWISTED UNDERGROUND TUNNEL
SKUNK	NEST OF DRY LEAVES AND GRASSES
RACCOON	HOLLOW TREE, CAVE

HIBERNATORS

GROUND HOG	UNDERGROUND BURROW
SALAMANDERS	UNDER LEAVES AT POND EDGE
EARTHWORM	UNDERGROUND
TOAD	MUD
FROG	MUDDY POND BOTTOM
WOODCHUCK	UNDERGROUND TUNNEL
TURTLE	MUDDY POND BOTTOM
SNAKE	UNDERGROUND
SNAIL	LOG, STONE
JUMPING MOUSE	TUNNEL

FINGERPLAYS

THE CHIPMUNK GATHERS NUTS

These are the brown leaves
Fluttering down,
And this is the tall tree
Bare and brown.

This is the chipmunk
With eyes so bright,
Hunting for nuts
With all his might.

This is the hole
Where day by day,
Nut after nut,
He stores away.

When winter comes
With its cold and storm,
He'll sleep curled up
All snug and warm.

GROUND HOG

Ground hog, ground hog, will you come out?
Yes sir, yes sir, if the sun is not about.
Groundhog, groundhog, the sun is shining bright.
I'll hop back in and curl up tight.
      Susan Spaete

RECIPES

HIDEOUTS

YOU'LL NEED

1 cup peanut butter
1/2 cup honey
3/4 to 1 cup powdered milk
Apple pieces
Raisins
Date bits

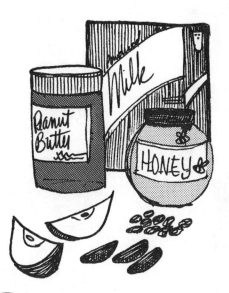

TO MAKE: Make the peanut butter hideouts by mixing the first three ingredients in a large bowl and then forming the mixture into small balls. When all of the *'hideouts'* have been formed, stick apple pieces, raisins, or dates in the middle and then smooth over the openings.

Before the children eat their snacks, talk about the *'hideouts'* and tell the children that a surprise is hibernating in the middle of each one.

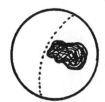 

FIELD TRIPS

• Visit your local forest preserve museum. Call ahead and arrange for a ranger to talk with your children about winter in the forest.

CLASSROOM VISITORS

• Invite a naturalist from your local forest preserve district to visit your classroom. Have him/her bring along slides or posters of animals who are hibernating.

LANGUAGE GAMES

LISTEN CAREFULLY

Have the children say the rhyme *'Winter Wind.'* Then have them curl up as if getting ready for their winter sleep. What sounds do they hear?

WINTER WIND

The winter wind is cold outside.
The snow is whirling 'round.
So under the covers my head I'll hide
And never make a sound.
Dick Wilmes

TO HIBERNATE OR NOT?

Read the story *'Beginning to Learn About Winter'* by Richard Allington and Kathleen Krull. Then have the children make a list of all of the things they like to do in winter. Talk about what the hibernating animals do in winter. Then let each child decide if in the winter season he would rather be a child or a hibernating animal. Why?

EXTENSION: Act out some of the winter fun the children said they enjoyed.

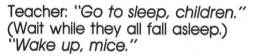

HIBERNATION HIDEOUT

Have the children sit in a circle on the floor. They should draw their knees up to their chests, wrap their arms around their legs, and put their heads on their knees as if they were sleeping. Now they're ready to play. The teacher begins by saying:

Teacher: *"Go to sleep, children."*
(Wait while they all fall asleep.)
"Wake up, mice."

Children: (They wake up pretending to be mice.) *"Squeek, squeek, squeek, etc."*

Teacher: *"Go to sleep, mice."* (Do it.)
"Wake up, chipmunks."

Children: (They wake up pretending to be chipmunks.) *"Chip, chip, chip. . . ."*

Continue, letting the children pretend to be other hibernating animals.

Teacher: (at the end) *"Wake up, children."*

WHO'S SLEEPING?

Have the children sit in a circle. Whisper to one of the children next to you, "*A bear is sleeping.*" That child should whisper the same message to the child sitting next to him and so on until you stop the progression by saying, "*Eric* (child's name), *tell us who's sleeping.*" The last child to receive the message should say the name of the animal that was passed on to him. Was that the animal in the original message? Walk over to the next child. Start a new message such as, "*A toad hibernates in mud.*" The children should pass it along until you stop them with a question such as, "*Lila* (child's name), *where do toads hibernate?*" Continue in this manner with different messages.

ACTIVE GAMES

PEANUT HUNT

Hide peanuts in the shells throughout the room. Put a basket in the middle of the circle time area. Have the children pretend that they are chipmunks gathering up peanuts to eat before their long winter's rest.

WAKE-UP SLEEPY HEADS

Have the children curl up in a ball as if they were at home hibernating. Then read the 'Hibernation' rhyme. Name a sign of spring. Have the children stretch their legs. Then name another sign of spring and have them stretch their arms. Say another one and have them stretch their necks and shoulders. Continue until they are wide awake and ready for spring adventures.

HIBERNATION

Deep underground I'll make my nest,
All curled up for a nice long rest.
Don't wake me for anything,
Until you see the first signs of spring.
Vohny Moehling

BOOKS

LYDIA DABCOVICH – ***SLEEPY BEAR***
LORNA BALIAN – ***A GARDEN FOR GROUNDHOG***
NADINE WESTCOTT – ***PEANUT BUTTER AND JELLY***
WENDY WATSON – ***HAS WINTER COME?***

HEARTS

FOR OPENERS

BEFORE CIRCLE TIME PRINT EACH CHILD'S NAME ON AN ENVELOPE. CUT PAIRS OF CONSTRUCTION PAPER HEARTS. PUT ONE HEART INTO EACH ENVELOPE.

BRING ALL OF THE ENVELOPES TO CIRCLE TIME. HOLD UP ONE ENVELOPE SO THAT ALL OF THE CHILDREN CAN READ THE NAME ON IT. HAVE THE CHILD WHOSE NAME IS ON THE ENVELOPE COME UP AND GET IT. CONTINUE UNTIL ALL OF THE ENVELOPES HAVE BEEN PASSED OUT. (IF CHILDREN DO NOT RECOGNIZE THEIR WRITTEN NAMES YET, READ THEIR NAMES AND HAVE THEM COME AND GET THEIR ENVELOPES.) AFTER ALL OF THE ENVELOPES HAVE BEEN PASSED OUT, LET THE CHILDREN OPEN THEIR ENVELOPES AND LOOK AT THE HEART INSIDE. HAVE THE CHILDREN WALK AROUND AND FIND THE MATES WHO HAVE THE SAME SIZE HEARTS AS THEIRS. THE *'HEART MATES'* WILL BE BUDDIES FOR THE DAY.

EXTENSION: HELP THE CHILDREN STRING THEIR HEARTS WITH YARN TO MAKE NECKLACES.

FINGERPLAYS

FIVE GAY VALENTINES

Five gay valentines from the ten-cent store.
I sent one to mother, now there are four.
Four gay valentines, pretty ones to see,
I gave one to brother, now there are three.
Three gay valentines, yellow, red and blue,
I gave one to sister, now there are two.
Two gay valentines, my we have fun,
I gave one to daddy, now there is one.
One gay valentine, the story is almost done,
I saved it for you, now there are none.

VALENTINE'S DAY

Flowers are sweet,
This is true.
But for my valentine,
I'll choose you.

VALENTINE'S DAY

Five little valentines were having a race,
The first little valentine was frilly with lace,
The second little valentine had a funny face.
The third little valentine said, "I love you."
The fourth little valentine said, "I do too."
The fifth little valentine was sly as a fox.
He ran the fastest to your valentine box.

VALENTINES

Valentines, valentines.
Red, white and blue.
I'll find a nice one
And give it to you.

RECIPES

HAVE A HEART

YOU'LL NEED

Refrigerator biscuits

TO MAKE: Give each child one biscuit. Have him roll the dough in a long strip and then form it into a heart shape. Following the directions on the package, bake the hearts.

FOLD →

FIELD TRIPS

• Visit a flower shop or nearby nursery and see how the florists are preparing the flowers for Valentine's Day. Plan for one of the florists to put a flower arrangement together while the children watch. When s/he's finished, buy it for your classroom.

CLASSROOM VISITORS

• Invite a nurse to talk with your children about their hearts – how a heart works, how to take care of it, and what it looks like.

LANGUAGE GAMES

CUPID
MAGIC

Bring a little confetti to circle time. Tell the children that Cupid is a make-believe character who comes around at Valentine's Day to help people show each other extra love. You are going to pretend to be Cupid and you've brought your 'cupid dust' with you. You're going to come and sprinkle one of them with 'dust' and tell him who to walk over to and how to show love. For example, you might walk over and sprinkle Dick, bend down, and tell him to walk over to Liz and give her a hug. Cupid continues to sprinkle 'dust,' helping all of the children share love with each other.

HEART PUZZLE

Before circle time, construct a giant heart puzzle. You'll need a piece of red, and pink or white posterboard. On one piece of posterboard draw as many hearts as you have children. Cut the hearts out. Cut each heart in two pieces using a different cut line for each one. Glue one piece from each heart onto the whole piece of posterboard. Put the loose halves in a valentine bag.

Bring the board and the valentine bag to circle time. Lay the board in the middle of the circle time area. Call on two or three children. Have them each take a heart piece out of the bag and look on the board for the heart which fits the piece they chose. Fit the heart pieces together. Call on several more children, have them each choose a piece and fit their hearts together. Continue until the puzzle is all put together.

EXTENSION: Put the heart puzzle with your other puzzles.

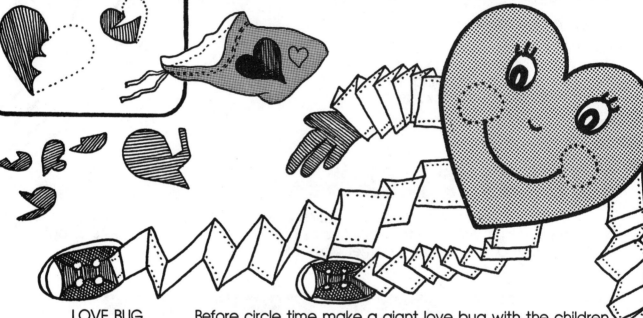

LOVE BUG

Before circle time make a giant love bug with the children and cut strips of paper. Get a large picture, maybe a poster, of people showing each other love. Bring the love bug, paper strips, picture, a marker, and a glue stick to circle time.

Hold up the picture for the children to see. Talk with them about the people in the picture. Now talk with them about how they show love to each other, their brothers, sisters, grammas, grandpas, and so on. Write down what they say on the strips of paper and glue the strips to the love bug. Hang the love bug in your language area.

On another day, talk with the children about how other people show love to them. Start with their moms. Ask the children, *"What do your moms do to let you know that they love you?"* Once again write the children's ideas down on strips of paper and glue them to the love bug.

EXTENSION: Share the two lists with all of your parents in the next parent newsletter.

100

FEELINGS   Using the illustrations provided, make a set of heart stick puppets portraying a variety of feelings. Bring them to circle time.

Hold up the first puppet. Ask the children, *"How do you think this heart feels? Why?"* (Discuss the children's different ideas.) Continue with the other puppets.

ACTIVE GAMES

HEALTHY
HEARTS
     Have the children stand up, put their hands over their hearts and feel how fast they are beating. Now have the children run in place starting slowly and going faster for ten to fifteen seconds. Slow down, stop, and have the children feel their hearts again. Now how fast are their hearts beating? Sit down, take several deep breaths, and rest. Have the children feel their hearts again. How fast are they beating now? Repeat with a different exercise, such as hopping or marching in place.

CUPID,
CUPID,
HEART
     Have the children sit in a circle. Give one child a construction paper heart. Have him walk around the outside of the circle tapping each child on the head saying *"Cupid"* to each one. When he comes to the child he wants to chase him, he drops the heart in that child's lap and says, *"Heart."* The child grabs the heart and chases the first child. The first child races to sit down before being caught. The child with the heart becomes *'it'* and walks around tapping children on the head saying *"Cupid"* each time.

BOOKS

PAUL SHOWERS – *HEAR YOUR HEART*
FELICIA BOND – *FOUR VALENTINES IN A RAINSTORM*
MARC BROWN – *ARTHUR'S VALENTINE*
GAIL GIBBONS – *VALENTINE'S DAY*

BIRTHDAYS

FOR OPENERS

PLAY 'HAPPY BIRTHDAY' WITH THE CHILDREN. FIRST MAKE THE 'TOP OF THE CAKE' BY USING A CLOTHESLINE TO FORM A FOUR TO FIVE FOOT CIRCLE IN THE CENTER OF YOUR CIRCLE TIME AREA. HAVE THE CHILDREN TAKE TURNS BEING 'CANDLES.' THE 'CANDLES' CAN PUT THE TIPS OF THEIR FINGERS TOGETHER OVER THEIR HEADS TO FORM 'FLAMES.'

NOW YOU ARE READY TO PLAY 'HAPPY BIRTHDAY.' PICK A CHILD TO BE THE BIRTHDAY CHILD. HE SHOULD TELL HOW OLD HE IS AND THEN POINT TO THAT MANY CHILDREN TO BE CANDLES ON HIS CAKE. THE 'CANDLES' SHOULD WALK ONTO THE CAKE. AN ADULT CAN WALK OVER TO THE CANDLES AND LIGHT THEM. AFTER THE FLAMES ARE LIT, EVERYONE SHOULD SING 'HAPPY BIRTHDAY' TO THE BIRTHDAY CHILD AND THEN HAVE THAT CHILD BLOW OUT HIS CANDLES. THE CANDLES CAN PRETEND TO GO OUT AND THEN MOVE OFF OF THE CAKE.

CONTINUE WITH SEVERAL OTHER BIRTHDAY CHILDREN. DO SEVERAL TIMES DURING THE WEEK SO ALL OF THE CHILDREN GET A CHANCE TO BE THE BIRTHDAY CHILD.

FINGERPLAYS

GROWING

When you were one, you were so small,
You could not speak a word at all.
When you were two, you learned to walk,
You learned to sing, you learned to talk.
When you were three, you grew and grew,
Today you're _____ , "Happy Birthday to you!"

POLLY'S BIRTHDAY
(substitute child's name)

Polly had a birthday;
Polly had a cake;
Polly's mother made it;
Polly watched it bake.

Frosting on the top,
Frosting in between;
Oh, it was the nicest cake
That you have ever seen!

Polly had some candles,
1, 2, 3, 4, 5.
Who can tell how many years
Polly's been alive?

TEN LITTLE CANDLES

Ten little candles on a chocolate cake;
"Wh! Wh!" Now there are eight.
Eight little candles on candlesticks;
"Wh! Wh!" Now there are six.
Six little candles and not one more
"Wh! Wh!" Now there are four.
Four little candles, red, white, and blue;
"Wh! Wh!" Now there are two.
Two little candles trying to run;
"Wh! Wh!" Now there are none.

RECIPES

PARTY PUNCH

YOU'LL NEED

1 quart cranapple juice
12 oz. can frozen lemonade concentrate
4 cups cold water

TO MAKE: Combine the ingredients and serve in party cups.

BIRTHDAY SUNDAES

YOU'LL NEED

Several types of yogurt
Variety of toppings such as:
  Berries
  Bananas
  Peaches
  Raisins
  Coconut
  Granola

TO MAKE: Have each child scoop some yogurt into a cup and sprinkle on his favorite toppings to make a birthday sundae.

CLASSROOM VISITORS

• Have a clown come into the classroom and entertain the children. While s/he is there, sing *'Happy Birthday,'* play several party games, and make your yogurt sundaes.

LANGUAGE GAMES

BIRTHDAY
SHARE

Choose a child to be the birthday child. Have everyone sing *'Happy Birthday'* to him. Then tell the birthday child something that you like about him or something that you wish for him. Go around the circle having the children share their thoughts and wishes for the birthday child. Choose another child and repeat the game. Play several times during the week so everyone has the opportunity to be the birthday child.

BABY-CHILD

Say different words associated with babies (rattles, diapers, teething rings, crawling) and with your children at their present age (painting, hopping, talking, tricycles). After you say each word, the children should respond *"Baby"* if the word is associated mainly with infants or *"Child"* if the word is associated with children their age.

GROWING

Talk with the children about what babies are able to do on the day they are born. Then about what most children can do on their first birthday, second birthday, third birthday, and what the children can do now.

After the discussion say, the 'Growing' fingerplay with the group.

104

HAPPY BIRTHDAY, ECHO

Say short sentences about birthdays for the children to repeat or echo. For example:

- *"Happy birthday to you."* (Children repeat.)
- *"Make a wish."* (Echo and then let the children make birthday wishes.)
- *"Happy unbirthday to the girls."*
- Continue.

EXTENSION: Use the game to echo facts about Lincoln and Washington on their birthdays. For example:

- *"Happy birthday to Abe Lincoln."*
- *"Lincoln grew up in a log cabin."*
- *"Lincoln's nickname was 'Honest Abe.'"* (Talk with the children about their nicknames.)
- *"Lincoln's birthday is February 12th."*
- *"George Washington was our first President."*
- *"George Washington rode a horse."*
- *"Washington's birthday is February 22nd."*
- *"Happy Birthday, George Washington."*

ACTIVE GAMES

CAKE AND CANDLES

Play a *'Pin the Tail On the Donkey'* type of game. Make a large cake and tape it to the wall. Cut candles and put a circle of tape on the back of each one.

As each child takes his turn, have him cover his eyes with one hand and hold the candle in the other. Lead him to the cake and let him put his candle on it. Clap for each child as he sticks his candle to the cake. After everyone has added a candle, count the candles.

BALLOON GOLF

Have a laundry basket, blown-up balloons, and a yardstick. Set the basket on its side. Have the children take turns hitting a balloon into the basket using the yardstick. (You may need to have several baskets, balloons, and yardsticks so that children are not waiting too long.)

BOOKS

PAT HUTCHINS – **HAPPY BIRTHDAY, SAM**
EVE RICE – **BENNY BAKES A CAKE**
ERIC CARLE – **SECRET BIRTHDAY MESSAGE**
MARJORIE FLACK – **ASK MR. BEAR**

TEDDY BEAR FRIENDS

FOR OPENERS

HAVE EACH OF THE CHILDREN BRING HIS FAVORITE STUFFED ANIMAL OR DOLL TO SCHOOL. (HAVE EXTRA FOR THOSE WHO FORGET.) LET EACH CHILD INTRODUCE HIS STUFFED FRIEND TO HIS SCHOOL MATES. THEN TAKE THE STUFFED FRIENDS OUT FOR A WALK. HAVE SEVERAL CHILDREN PULL THEIR FRIENDS IN WAGONS, LET SOME CHILDREN GIVE THE STUFFED FRIENDS RIDES ON TRICYCLES, STILL OTHERS CAN CARRY THEIR FRIENDS UNDER THEIR ARMS. WALK AROUND THE NEIGHBORHOOD AND ENCOURAGE THE CHILDREN TO TALK TO THEIR STUFFED FRIENDS AND TELL THEM ABOUT THE SCHOOL, NEIGHBORHOOD, PARK, ETC.

FINGERPLAYS

TEDDY BEAR

Teddy bear, teddy bear,
Turn around;
Teddy bear, teddy bear,
Touch the ground.

Teddy bear, teddy bear,
Show your shoe;
Teddy bear, teddy bear,
That will do.

Teddy bear, teddy bear,
Go upstairs;
Teddy bear, teddy bear,
Say your prayers.

Teddy bear, teddy bear,
Turn out the light;
Teddy bear, teddy bear,
Say, "Good-night!"

BEARS EVERYWHERE

Bears, bears, bears, everywhere!
Bears climbing stairs,
Bears sitting on chairs,
Bears collecting fares,
Bears giving stares,
Bears washing hairs,
Bears, bears, bears, everywhere!

HONEY BEARS

A little brown bear went searching for honey.
Isn't it funny, a bear wanting honey?
He sniffed in the breeze.
And he listened for bees.
And would you believe, he even climbed trees.

RECIPES

Prepare simple snacks and have the children bring their stuffed friends to the table with them.

SIMPLE SNACKS

- Yogurt with a piece of fruit on top
- Apple quarters topped with peanut butter
- Graham crackers spread with a little honey
- Raisin bread squares with cream cheese

FIELD TRIPS

- Visit your local zoo. Be sure to visit the real animals that your children's stuffed animals are named after.

LANGUAGE GAMES

GETTING
TOGETHER

Get a large box. Cut the top off and carefully sit or stand all of the stuffed friends in the box. Put the box in the middle of the circle time area.

Tell the children that all of the stuffed friends had gotten together for a party and now they are ready to come home. Look inside the box and then begin describing one of the stuffed friends. When a child recognizes his friend, he should come up, get it out of the box, and give it a big hug. Continue describing until all of the friends are back home.

GOOD-NIGHT,
FRIENDS

Spread a parachute or sheet out in the circle time area. Have the children sit around it with their stuffed friends in their arms. Have the children quietly tell their stuffed friends good-night stories and then gently lay them on the parachute towards the center. Still sitting, have the children lift the parachute up. Then very quietly move it side to side, while singing 'Rock-A-Bye Baby.' When they sing the words about the baby falling, gently lower the chute, cover the stuffed friends with the excess parachute fabric, and quietly tip-toe to another activity.

WHO
BELONGS TO
WHOM?

Have two or three children come up to the front of the circle time area with their stuffed friends. Each child should face the group and hold his stuffed friend so everyone can easily see the friend. Everyone in the group should look at each child and his friend. Now have the group cover its eyes while the children switch stuffed friends. Let the group uncover its eyes and take turns trying to pair the children back with their stuffed friends. Repeat until everyone has had a turn in front of the group.

TRICKY TEDDIES	Say the *'Teddy Bear'* rhyme below and then let a child tell the others a trick a teddy bear might do. Repeat.

TEDDY BEAR

Teddy bear, teddy bear turn around;
Teddy bear, teddy bear touch the ground;
Teddy bear, teddy bear show your shoe;
Teddy bear, teddy bear what can you do?

EXTENSION: Let the children pretend to be *'tricky teddies'* and do the suggested tricks.

ACTIVE GAMES

STUFFED FRIEND TAG	Have all of the children bring their stuffed friends to the game. Name one child to be *'it.'* When you say "Go," the child who is *'it'* tries to tag another child with his stuffed friend. When he does, then two children are *'it.'* Their stuffed friends each tag another child and then four children are *'it.'* The game continues until the stuffed friends have tagged all of the children.
HIDE 'N' SEEK	While the children are out of the room, hide all of the stuffed animals. When the children return, tell them that while they were gone all of their stuffed friends decided to hide. Have the children hunt for their friends. When each child finds his friend, he should bring the friend to the circle time area and read the friend a story. Continue until all of the friends have been found.

BOOKS

DON FREEMAN – **CORDUROY**
BARBARA DOUGLASS – **GOOD AS NEW**
KAY CHORAO – **MOLLY'S MOE**
DICK GACKENBACH – **POPPY THE PANDA**
SHIRLEY HUGHES – **DAVID AND DOG**

NURSERY RHYMES

FOR OPENERS

TEACH YOUR CHILDREN YOUR FAVORITE MOTHER GOOSE NURSERY RHYMES BY PLAYING 'NURSERY RHYME ECHO.' TO PLAY, READ OR SAY A RHYME, AND TALK ABOUT THE CHARACTER IN THE RHYME AND WHAT S/HE IS DOING. THEN GO BACK AND REPEAT THE FIRST LINE OR TWO AND HAVE THE CHILDREN ECHO IT BACK TO YOU. CONTINUE UNTIL YOU HAVE ECHOED THE ENTIRE RHYME. ENJOY SAYING THE ENTIRE RHYME TOGETHER.

FINGERPLAYS

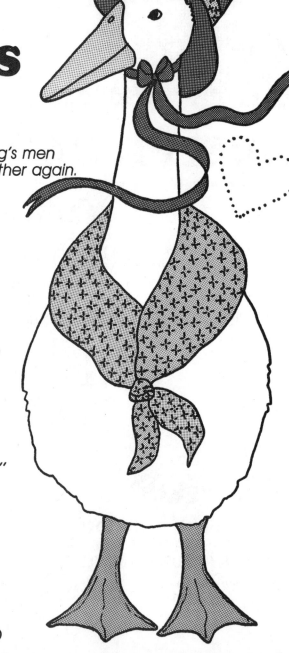

HUMPTY DUMPTY

Humpty Dumpty sat on a wall;
Humpty Dumpty had a great fall;
All the King's horses and all the King's men
Couldn't put Humpty Dumpty together again.

MISS MUFFET

Little Miss Muffet
Sat on a tuffet
Eating her curds and whey;
Along came a spider,
And sat down beside her,
And frightened Miss Muffet away.

LITTLE JACK HORNER

Little Jack Horner
Sat in a corner,
Eating his Christmas pie;
He put in his thumb,
And pulled out a plum,
And said, "What a good boy am I!"

JACK

Jack be nimble,
Jack be quick,
Jack jump over the candlestick.

RECIPES

HUMPTY DUMPTY EGGS

YOU'LL NEED

1 hard-boiled egg for each child
Mayonnaise
Mustard
Paprika (optional)

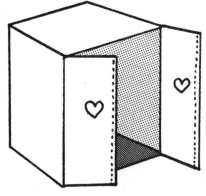

TO MAKE: Give the children hard-boiled eggs. Let them peel the eggs, cut them in half with a table knife, and carefully remove the yolks. Put the yolks, a little mayonnaise, and a little mustard in a bowl. Mash them with a fork. When the yolk mixture is finished, each child should spoon a little back into the egg halves and sprinkle with paprika.

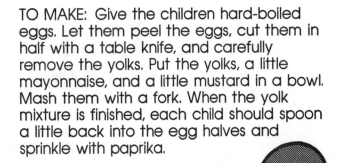

FIELD TRIPS

- Take 'Nursery Rhyme Walks' around your neighborhood.

    •• 'Jack Be Nimble Walk' – Pretend that all of the cracks in the sidewalk are candlesticks. Everytime you see one, jump over it and say, "Jack Be Nimble."

    •• 'Jack and Jill Walk' – Have the children walk in pairs to a nearby park. When they get there, find a hill or an open area. Run up the hill, fall, and roll down.

    •• 'Little Bo Peep Walk' – Before the walk hide small plastic sheep or pieces of styrofoam to represent sheep along the path you'll be walking.
    As you're beginning to walk, say the 'Little Bo Peep' rhyme. Have everyone look for sheep as he walks. When he finds one, have him put it in a shoe box.

LANGUAGE GAMES

OLD MOTHER HUBBARD'S CUPBOARD

Have a fairly large box representing Old Mother Hubbard's cupboard. Lay it on its side so the opening is facing the children.
    Say the 'Old Mother Hubbard' rhyme with the children. Then say something like, "Oh, no! There is nothing in Mother Hubbard's cupboard. Let's go to the grocery store and buy food for her."
    Sitting down, have the children use their hands to take a pretend walk to the store. When they arrive, have the children get a cart and pretend to put food in it that they think Mother Hubbard would like. Write down all of the items as the children say them.
    Walk back home. When the children get back home have them try to remember all of the foods that they bought. As the children name the foods, have them come up and pretend to put the foods in the cupboard. Check the foods off of the list as they are named. If there are any foods left on the list, read them, and have the children put them into the cupboard.

111

HUMPTY-DUMPTY PUZZLE

Using a piece of posterboard, draw a large Humpty Dumpty. Cut him into as many pieces as you have children or as many pieces as you think your children can comfortably put together.

Bring the pieces to circle time. Say the rhyme with the children. When you say, *"Humpty Dumpty had a great fall,"* dump the puzzle pieces on the floor. Call on children to each come and pick up one piece. Everyone looks at his piece. Have the children put the puzzle together in the middle of the circle time area.

EXTENSION: Put the Humpty Dumpty Puzzle on the shelf with the other puzzles.

WHERE IS LITTLE MISS MUFFET?

Say different Mother Goose rhymes with the children. After each one, you say the rhyme by yourself and let the children listen. When you get to a position word in the rhyme, stop and talk about where the character is. For example in 'Little Miss Muffet' she sat "*on*" a tuffet and the spider sat down "*beside*" her. In 'Hickory Dickory Doc,' the mouse ran "*up*" the clock and then ran "*down*" again.

LITTLE JACK HORNER

Before circle time, have the children use washable markers and draw plums on their thumbs.

During circle time, say the rhyme and have the children make a fist and pretend to be Jack sticking their thumbs in and out of the Christmas pie.

Now have the children think of their very favorite food. Point to a child. Have him stand up and tell the others his first and last name and his favorite food. Say the first line of the rhyme substituting the child's name for Jack Horner. Continue the rhyme and insert the child's favorite food for Christmas pie. As the children say the last three lines, have them put their thumbs in the new food and pull out plums from it. For example:

Little Greg Smith sat in a corner
Eating his macaroni and cheese.
He stuck in his thumb
And pulled out a plum,
And said, "What a good boy am I!"

ACTIVE GAMES

LITTLE BO PEEP LISTENS

Have a chair in the middle of the circle time area. Have one child be Little Bo Peep. That child sits there and covers his eyes. The rest of the children should be sheep and hide from Bo Peep. When all of the sheep have hidden, tap one of them on the head. Then signal for all of the sheep to begin wagging their tails as they sneak home. The one sheep that you tapped on the head should make loud "baaing" noises as he walks home. Little Bo Peep listens and tries to guess which one of her sheep is making the "baaing" noises before he tags her. Little Bo Peep trades places with one of the sheep and you're ready to play again.

JACK BE NIMBLE JUMP

Have a candle (real, paper towel or toilet paper roll) for each of the children. Have them hold their candles up and say the 'Jack Be Nimble' rhyme. Then have them put their candles on the floor. Repeat the rhyme. When they say the line, "Jack jump over the candlestick," have the children jump over their candles.

Keeping the candles on the floor, have the children pretend to be Jack doing other tricks with his candle.

- *Jack walk around your candlestick.*
- *Jack hop over your candlestick.*
- *Jack hold your candlestick way up high.*
- *Jack put your toes on your candlestick.*
- *Jack put your candlestick in this basket.*

BOOKS

RANDOM HOUSE BOOK OF MOTHER GOOSE
MOTHER GOOSE TREASURY
TOMI DePAOLA'S **MOTHER GOOSE**
JAMES MARSHALL'S **MOTHER GOOSE**

UP, UP, AND AWAY

FOR OPENERS

BRING A VARIETY OF THINGS TO CIRCLE TIME WHICH THE CHILDREN CAN FLY THROUGH THE AIR (KITE, BALLOON, FRISBEE, WOODEN MODEL AIRPLANE, PLASTIC LIDS FROM VARIOUS SIZE CONTAINERS, COMMERCIAL BUBBLE SOLUTION, ETC.). HOLD UP EACH ONE AND HAVE THE CHILDREN CALL OUT ITS NAME. TALK ABOUT TIMES WHEN THE CHILDREN MIGHT HAVE PLAYED WITH EACH OF THE OBJECTS.

OPEN THE BUBBLE SOLUTION. SHOW THE CHILDREN HOW TO DIP THE WAND INTO THE SOLUTION, SLOWLY BRING IT OUT, AND THEN BLOW INTO THE WAND. WHAT HAPPENS TO THE SOLUTION? NOW GIVE EACH CHILD A CHANCE TO BLOW. WALK TO EACH CHILD, HOLD THE BOTTLE FOR HIM, HELP HIM DIP IF NECESSARY, AND THEN LET HIM BLOW THE BUBBLE. HAVE THE CHILDREN WATCH THE BUBBLE, TRYING NOT TO TOUCH IT. TALK ABOUT THE SIZE, COLOR, AND/OR DESTINATION OF THE BUBBLE/S EACH CHILD BLOWS.

FINGERPLAYS

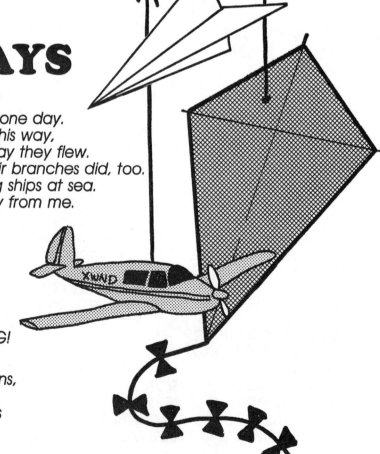

THE WIND

The wind came out to play one day.
He swept the clouds out of his way,
He blew the leaves and away they flew.
The trees bent low, and their branches did, too.
The wind blew the great big ships at sea.
The wind blew my kite away from me.

LITTLE BALLOON

I had a little balloon
That I hugged tight to me.
There was a great big BANG!
No more balloon, you see.

But if I had lots more balloons,
I wouldn't hug them tight!
I'd just hold on to the strings
And fly them like a kite.

114

CLOUDS

*What's fluffy-white
And floats up high
Like piles of ice cream
In the sky?*

*And when the wind blows hard and strong,
What very gently floats along?
What brings the rain?
What brings the snow, that showers down on us below?*

*What seems to have just lots of fun
Peek-a-booing with the sun?
When you look in the high, blue sky,
What are these things you see floating by?
(What do the children think they are?)*

THE AIRPLANE

*The airplane has great big wings;
Its propeller spins around and sings,
"Vvvvvvvv!"
The airplane goes up;
The airplane goes down;
The airplane flies high
Over our town!*

RECIPES

Let the children pretend to have their snack on an airplane. Get enough clear or styrofoam disposable containers for each child. Put pretzels and a little soft cheese in each one. Pretend that you are a flight attendant. Pass out the snacks. When the children are finished, collect all of the containers.

FIELD TRIPS

• Walk to a store which fills balloons with helium. Let each child buy a balloon and tie it around his wrist. Go to a nearby park and run around watching the balloons fly behind you.

• Visit your local airport. See how the pilots and mechanics take care of the airplanes. Note the variety of aircraft. Are there any helicopters at your airport?

LANGUAGE GAMES

YOUR
FRISBEE RIDE

Give each child a plastic cover from a margarine tub. Have him sit on it and get ready to take an imaginary frisbee ride. As the children take off, have the children look for different things that are happening on the ground. As the children mention the things they see, talk about each one. For example, you could begin by saying, *"Oh, I see my mother digging in the garden."* Continue with the children's observations. Does anyone see children playing outside at a park? What are they doing?

THE LOST
BUBBLE

Write a story with the children. Have a large piece of butcher paper and a wide-tipped marker. You begin the story.

> *"Once upon a time, two children were in the yard blowing bubbles. They were laughing and giggling and watching their bubbles float all around and then burst. But they noticed one bubble. It did not burst like the others. It floated by them and then started to drift away. It winked as it left as if to say......"*

Let the children continue from here. Write down what they say. Hang their story in the language area. Read it to them often. Add to it when they think of other things.

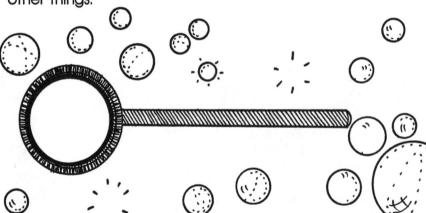

IN GREAT
DETAIL

Get a large, simple poster of a kite, hot air balloon, or other floating/flying objects. Have a tape recorder available. Talk with the children about the picture, recording their conversation. Play it back later, maybe while waiting for lunch or just before rest time.

WHAT FLIES?

Name three objects, one which flies/floats in the sky and two which do not. After the children hear all three words, have them whisper (shout) the one which flies/floats. For example, you might say, *"Horse, hammer, kite."* The children should whisper (shout) *"Kite."*
VARIATION: Talk about the things which do not fly/float in the sky.

ACTIVE GAMES

BALLOON FLOAT   Blow up a large balloon. Have the children stand around a parachute (bedsheet) holding it with both hands. Put the balloon on the chute. Count "*1,2,3*" and have the children lift the chute into the air letting the balloon rise to the ceiling. Let the chute slowly come back down. Watch the balloon. Where did it land? Enjoy several times. You might want to try several balloons at the same time.

KITE FLYING   On a nice day, bring several of the toys which you talked about in the opening activity outside. Let the children toss the frisbee around, fly the airplane, blow the bubbles, bat the balloons, and fly the kite.

BALLOONS AWAY   Blow up three or four balloons. Divide the children up into small groups. Give each group one balloon and all of the children wide-mouth straws. Encourage the children to blow the balloons around their areas. Do the balloons roll along the floor or float up off of it? How high?

PASS THE BALLOONS   Blow up different colored balloons. Put one of the children's favorite songs on the record player. Have the children sit in a circle. Give balloons to two or three children. When you begin the music, the children should start passing the balloons around the circle. Stop the music. The children holding the balloons should stand up, tell the others what color balloons they are holding, and then give them to you. Give other children different colors of balloons to pass. Start the music again and play in the same manner.

BOOKS

KATHERINE MARKO – *HOW THE WIND BLOWS*
PAT HUTCHINS – *THE WIND BLEW*
EDWARD FENTON – *BIG YELLOW BALLOON*
ALBERT LAMORISSE – *RED BALLOON*
BYRON BARTON – *AIRPLANES*
DOUGLAS FLORIAN – *AIRPLANE RIDE*
DENNIS NOLAN – *MONSTER BUBBLES*
MARGARET REY – *CURIOUS GEORGE FLIES A KITE*

THINK GREEN
FOR OPENERS

GET SWATCHES OF DIFFERENT SHADES OF GREEN FROM AN ART SUPPLY
OR PAINT STORE. GIVE ONE SWATCH TO EACH CHILD. PAIR THE CHILDREN.
HAVE THE CHILDREN IN EACH PAIR HOLD THEIR SWATCHES CLOSE
TOGETHER. TALK ABOUT THE COLOR IN EACH PAIR OF SWATCHES. WHICH
ONE IS DARKER? LIGHTER? WHICH COLOR DO THEY LIKE BETTER?

AFTER THE DISCUSSION, HAVE THE CHILDREN STAND UP. STARTING WITH
THEIR SHOES, HAVE THEM PUT THEIR SWATCHES NEXT TO EACH ARTICLE OF
CLOTHING THAT THEY ARE WEARING, TO SEE IF THE SWATCHES MATCH ANY
OF THEIR CLOTHES. WHEN A CHILD FINDS A MATCH, HAVE HIM WAVE HIS
SWATCH IN THE AIR AND SHARE THE MATCH WITH THE OTHERS.

FINGERPLAYS

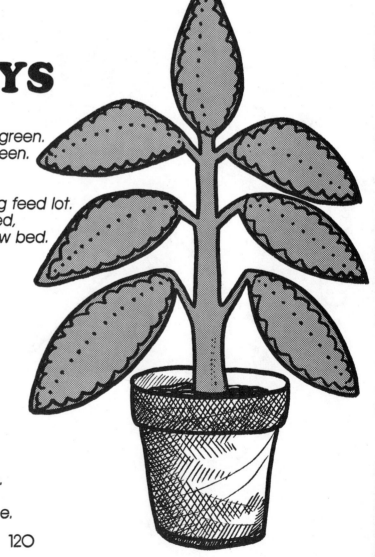

TEN LITTLE PONIES

Ten little ponies in a meadow green.
Ten little ponies, friskiest ever seen.
They go for a gallop.
They go for a trot.
They come for a halt in the big feed lot.
Ten little ponies fat and well fed,
Curl up together in a soft, straw bed.

THE FLOWER

Here's a green leaf,
And here's a green leaf;
That, you see, makes two.

Here is a bud,
That makes a flower;
Watch it bloom for you!

THE CLOVER

Here's a green petal,
Here's a second green petal,
And another one makes three.
Put them all together
And a green clover you will see.

120

RECIPES

GREEN PEPPER TREAT

YOU'LL NEED

Several green peppers
Several types of hard cheese
Rounded toothpicks

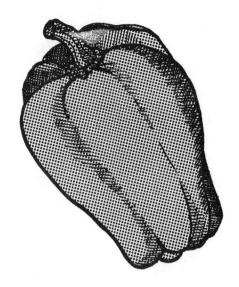

TO MAKE: Wash the green peppers. Cut the cheese into small sections. Poke a toothpick into each piece of cheese and then slide the other ends of the toothpick into the green peppers. Serve on green paper plates or napkins.

   After the children have eaten several pieces of cheese, cut up the green peppers and give each child a taste.

FIELD TRIPS

• Take a *'Green Walk.'* Bring a piece of green construction paper and a green marker on the walk. Have the children look for green objects. When someone finds one he should tell you and you write it down on the green paper. When you return to the classroom read the list to the children. Hang it low on the door. Encourage the children to keep looking for green. Add more objects to the list each day.

LANGUAGE GAMES

THINK GREEN   Bring a piece of light green posterboard and a wide-tipped marker to circle time. Have the children name things they know that are green such as: things which they see in the room, toys, clothes, foods, things from nature, and so on. Write down their ideas.

121

GREG AND GERTA GREEN

Before circle time make the twins, Greg and Gerta Green. (They can be felt board characters or finger puppets.)

Bring Greg and Gerta to circle time. Introduce them to your children. Tell the children that Greg and Gerta are going for a springtime walk to look for green things. They want the children to come along and play a game with them. When the twins see something green, they are going to describe it to the children and the twins want the children to call out what they think the twins are looking at. Are you ready? Open the door and breathe in the springtime air.

"Oh," said Greg, *"I see something green already! It is flying in the sky just above the trees. There is a long string hanging from it. On the ground, a child is holding onto the other end of the string and making the object in the sky do twists and turns."*

(Let children guess.) Continue the walk describing other springtime things that would be familiar to the children.

EXTENSION: Depending on the children's language abilities, you might let them describe some green things and have Greg and Gerta guess their riddles.

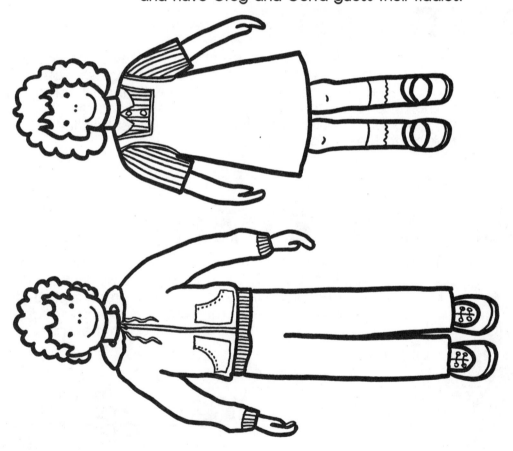

BEING GREEN

Get a copy of the song *'It Isn't Easy Being Green'* by Kermit the Frog or Frank Sinatra. Have the children quietly listen to the music and sway to the beat. After the song, pass out a small piece of green cellophane or construction paper to each child and talk about how it might feel to be green.

122

LOOK FOR THE GREEN

Collect objects from around the room, some of which have green in them and some of which do not. Have at least one object for each child. Put the objects in a bag. Walk to each child and have him pull out one object, look at it, and try to find green on the object. After everyone has explored his object, have each child tell the others if his object has green on it and where the green is.

Lay a piece of green posterboard on the floor. Those children who had green on their objects should bring them up and lay them on the green posterboard. Those who did not have any green on their objects should come up and put their objects back in the bag. EXTENSION: Put the green posterboard and objects on the Discovery Table for further examination.

ACTIVE GAMES

ARM DANCING

Collect enough shades of green crayons so that each child can have two. Lay a long piece of white or light green butcher paper on the floor. Have a record player and a record which the children enjoy.

Have the children sit around the butcher paper. Pass the crayons around having each child take two. Tell the children that when the music begins, they should hold the crayons up in front of them and pretend that they are coloring a piece of paper to the beat of the music.

Now have them kneel around the paper. This time when you start the music, have the children 'arm dance' right on the paper. When the song is over, they should stop dancing. Talk about the different shades of green and the different types of lines the children made. Hang the 'Arm Dancing Mural' on a wall for everyone to enjoy.

GO FOR THE GREEN

Collect a variety of green collage materials (bows, paper, yarn, string, fabric) for an art activity. Save one of each thing. Hide the rest around the room. Show the children the different green objects that they will be looking for. Have a green box in the middle of the circle time area. When you say "Go for the green," all of the children should begin searching throughout the room for the green materials. As the children find them, they should put the materials in the green box. When all of the materials have been found, have a child take the box to the art area to use later.

BOOKS

VALRIE M. SELKOWE – ***SPRING GREEN***
THOMAS ZACHARIAS – ***BUT WHERE IS THE GREEN PARROT***

TURTLES AND FROGS

FOR OPENERS

MAKE THREE TO FIVE TURTLES AND LET THE CHILDREN RACE THEM. TO MAKE, CUT TURTLE SHAPES OUT OF GREEN POSTERBOARD. NUMBER OR NAME EACH ONE. PUNCH A HOLE JUST ABOVE THE CENTER OF EACH TURTLE AND PUT A FIVE TO EIGHT FOOT LONG PIECE OF STRING THROUGH IT. GET ONE CHAIR FOR EACH TURTLE. TIE ONE END OF EACH PIECE OF STRING TO ONE OF THE LEGS OF A CHAIR. LINE UP THE CHAIRS ALONG THE FINISH LINE.

HAVE THE CHILDREN WHO ARE RACING THEIR TURTLES STAND IN A ROW AT THE *'STARTING LINE.'* EACH CHILD SHOULD HOLD THE LOOSE END OF ONE OF THE STRINGS. BEGIN THE RACE WITH THE TURTLES NEAR THE CHILDREN'S HANDS.

WHEN YOU SAY, "GO!" THE CHILDREN WHO ARE RACING SHOULD START JIGGLING THEIR PIECES OF STRING SO THAT THE TURTLES BOUNCE TOWARD THE FINISH LINE. THE OTHER CHILDREN SHOULD PICK A TURTLE AND CHEER FOR IT. WHICH TURTLE MADE IT TO THE END FIRST? WHICH ONE WAS LAST? RACE AGAIN.

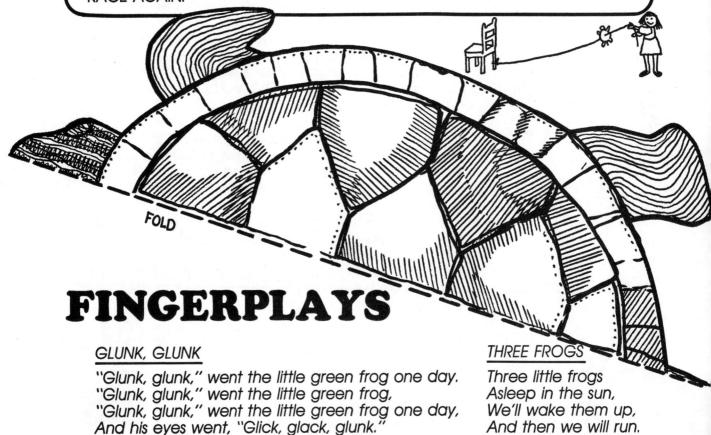

FINGERPLAYS

GLUNK, GLUNK

"Glunk, glunk," went the little green frog one day.
"Glunk, glunk," went the little green frog,
"Glunk, glunk," went the little green frog one day,
And his eyes went, "Glick, glack, glunk."

THREE FROGS

Three little frogs
Asleep in the sun,
We'll wake them up,
And then we will run.

LITTLE TURTLE

There was a little turtle,
He lived in a box.
He swam in a puddle,
He climbed on the rocks.

He snapped at a mosquito,
He snapped at a flea,
He snapped at a minnow,
He snapped at me.

He caught the mosquito,
He caught the flea,
He caught the minnow,
But he didn't catch me.

RECIPES

Have the children pretend that they are turtles and frogs as they taste-test different types of water such as tonic, seltzer, club soda, tap, distilled, and/or flavored. To vary the *'waters'* even more, add a *'squeeze'* of lemon or lime in each small cup before pouring the water.

FIELD TRIPS

- Take a trip to a nearby pet store. Watch the turtles and frogs. Have an employee explain how the turtles and frogs are cared for and what they eat. Maybe the employee could feed the animals while the children are there.

LANGUAGE GAMES

TURTLE OR
FROG

Divide the children into two groups, *'turtles'* and *'frogs.'* The *'turtles'* have very short legs and move ever so slowly. The *'frogs'* have long legs and leap up and down. Tell the *'turtles'* and *'frogs'* that you are going to say things which relate to either turtles or frogs or sometimes both. When you say something that relates to turtles, the children who are pretending to be turtles should blink their eyes and make snapping noises. When you say something that relates to frogs, the *'frog children'* should leap up and down and croak. When you say something that relates to both of them, all of the children move and make noise.

- *"Many of us have hard shells on our backs."* (turtle)
- *"We usually move slowly."* (turtle)
- *"We like water."* (both)
- *"We are very difficult to catch."* (frog)
- *"We have long legs."* (frog)
- *"We have big eyes."* (frog)
- *"Many of us hide under our shells."* (turtle)
- *"We are partially green."* (both)
- *"We lay eggs."* (both)

TOBY TURTLE AND FREDDI FROG

Cut a pond shape from a large piece of construction paper. Make stick puppets or felt characters of Toby Turtle and Freddi Frog. Bring them to circle time and introduce them to the children. Then bring out the construction paper pond.

Tell the children that Toby and Freddi are going for a walk around their favorite pond. Before they go, however, the animals would like the children to write down all of the things that they think Toby and Freddi will see on their walk. (Have the children name everything that they can imagine would be around the real pond. Write down the children's ideas on the construction paper pond.)

After the children have made their list, Toby and Freddi can begin their walk.

"One of Toby and Freddi's favorite things to do is to walk around their pond and see who is home and what is going on. They started out near the sand pile. There were several children digging tunnels in the sand for their cars and trucks. Maybe they would build roads later. 'We'll come back after our walk and see if the children are still there,' said Toby."

Continue the story from this point, letting Toby and Freddi see many of the things which your children mentioned and adding others. (Check off the children's ideas as Toby and Freddi see them and add their new sightings.) Conclude the story.

"'That was such a nice walk. It looked like everything was just fine on the pond. Look, the children are still playing in the sand. I'm glad they enjoy our pond too. Maybe we could walk again tomorrow!'" (Talk about what Toby and Freddi did and did not see on their walk.)

126

LOOK CAREFULLY	Make three felt turtles and three frogs. Bring them and your felt board to circle time.

Put a turtle and a frog next to each other on the board. Tell the children that the turtle and frog are going for a walk. Have the children look carefully at who is going. Then cover up the felt animals with a piece of cardboard. Say to the children, *"Name the first animal who is going for a walk."* The children answer, *"Turtle."* Then say, *"Name the second animal."* (*"Frog."*) Take the piece of cardboard down and have the children look once again. Were they right? Take the two animals off of the board. Put up a new sequence using from two to six turtles and frogs. Say to the children, *"Name the order in which the animals are taking their second walk."* (Point to each animal and have the children call out, *"Turtle"* or *"Frog."*) Cover up the animals and see if the children can remember the sequence. Uncover the animals. Did the children remember? Repeat with a new sequence for a third walk.

FROG TALK — Have one child be a frog and 'croak' a message to his frog friends. While he is 'croaking', encourage him to use gestures and facial movements relating to his 'message.' When he is done 'croaking', have his friends guess what he might have said. After several guesses, have the 'frog' tell his friends in regular talk what he said. Continue by choosing another 'frog' to 'croak' a message to the group.

ACTIVE GAMES

LEAP FROG — Choose several children to be 'frogs' leaping over each other as the rest of the 'frogs' sun themselves on rocks and chant:

> *Leap frog, leap frog*
> *Easy as can be.*
> *I'll leap frog you,*
> *Then you leap frog me.*
> Dick Wilmes

TURTLE, TURTLE, FROG — Have the children sit in a circle. Pick one child to be the frog. He starts leaping around the outside of the circle tapping each child on the head saying, *"Turtle,"* to each one. When he gets to the one he wants to chase him, he says, *"Frog."* That child gets up and starts leaping after his frog friend, trying to catch him before he gets back to his place.

BOOKS

FRANK ASCH – *TURTLE TALE*
ROBERT AKLAN – *JUMP, FROG, JUMP*
MARY BLOUNT CHRISTIAN – *DEVIN AND GOLIATH*

BACKWARDS DAY

FOR OPENERS

ABOUT A WEEK BEFORE 'BACKWARDS DAY,' SEND A NOTE HOME TO THE PARENTS INFORMING THEM OF THE SPECIAL DAY. SUGGEST THAT THEY LET THEIR CHILDREN WEAR SOME OF THEIR CLOTHES BACKWARDS, SUCH AS A BELT, HAT, SWEATER, SWEATSHIRT, SKIRT, OR SCARF. WHEN YOU GREET THE CHILDREN AT THE BEGINNING OF 'BACKWARDS DAY' SAY, "MORNING, GOOD; LEAH, HI; GENE, DAY GOOD" AND SO ON. THEN HAVE THE CHILDREN TELL YOU WHAT THEY WORE BACKWARDS AND WALK INTO THE ROOM BACKSIDE FIRST.

FINGERPLAYS

BACKWARDS MONKEY

A little monkey likes to do,
Just the opposite of you.

When you sit up very tall,
Monkey won't sit up at all.

When you pretend to throw a ball,
Monkey pretends to let it fall.

When you try to touch your toes,
Monkey tries to touch his nose.

When you try to be quiet,
Monkey tries to start a riot.

When you jump up in the air,
Monkey sits down in a chair.

RECIPES

Serve breakfast foods for lunch.
Encourage the children to eat their 'lunch'
with the opposite hand they normally do.

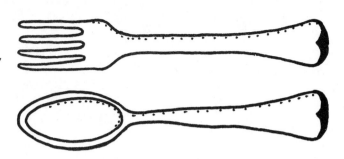

FIELD TRIPS

- Take a short 'Backwards Walk' around the neighborhood. Once everyone is outside, start walking backwards. After a short distance, turn around and walk forwards for awhile. Reverse and walk backwards again. Continue changing from backwards to forwards until you're back in the classroom. Talk about how it felt to walk backwards. Would the children like to walk backwards? Why?

129

LANGUAGE GAMES

BACKWARDS STORIES

Tell the children short stories which have three to five major events in them. After you tell each story in the correct order, have the group try to tell it backwards, beginning with the conclusion and ending with the beginning. For example:

> "Bobby jumped out of bed and got dressed. Then he ate breakfast. After breakfast he helped his dad feed the chickens and cows."

After talking with the children about the sequence in which the different events happened, they might retell the story like so:

> "Bobby helped his dad feed the cows and chickens. Then he ate breakfast. After breakfast he got dressed, and then jumped out of bed."

UPSIDE-DOWN PICTURES

Gather several very simple pictures which you are sure the children will be able to recognize and discuss. Bring them to circle time.

Show the children the pictures right-side up. Turn the first one upside-down and show it to the children. Discuss what it looks like now. Have several children bend over, look through their legs and describe the picture. Turn the picture right-side again. Look at and briefly discuss it. Pick the second picture and repeat the activity.

BACKWARDS MEMORY

Say two words to the children, such as "*red, yellow.*" They repeat it back to you reversing the order, so they would say, "*yellow, red.*" After they can reverse two words, increase the sequence to three or four words: "*truck, hose, clock*" becomes "*clock, hose, truck.*"

130

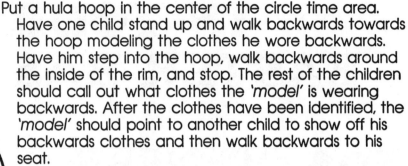

BACKWARDS STYLE SHOW

Put a hula hoop in the center of the circle time area. Have one child stand up and walk backwards towards the hoop modeling the clothes he wore backwards. Have him step into the hoop, walk backwards around the inside of the rim, and stop. The rest of the children should call out what clothes the *'model'* is wearing backwards. After the clothes have been identified, the *'model'* should point to another child to show off his backwards clothes and then walk backwards to his seat.

EXTENSION: Make a video recording of this activity and show it at your next parent meeting.

ACTIVE GAMES

COUNTING BACKWARDS

Enjoy a variety of exercises (arm twirls, head rolls, waist bends, leg kicks, etc.) with the children. When you count the repetitions for each one, count backwards. For example, the children are going to jump up and down five times. Instead of counting from 1 to 5, you would count *"5, 4, 3, 2, 1."* The children should stop jumping when you say *"1."* Continue, changing the exercise and the number of repetitions.

WATCH MY HAT

Wear a baseball cap to circle time. Have the children stand in front of you. Give them a direction such as walk, crawl, hop, skate, slide, etc. Then have them look at your cap. If you are wearing the cap frontwards, they should move towards you. If you are wearing your cap backwards, they should move backwards, going away from you. Once the children understand the idea, try to *'trick'* them by changing your cap while they are moving.

BOOKS

MOLLY BANG – *TEN, NINE, EIGHT . . . . .*

IN YOUR EASTER BASKET

FOR OPENERS

BEFORE CIRCLE TIME FILL AN EASTER BASKET WITH ARTIFICIAL GRASS AND COLORED HARD-BOILED EGGS.

TELL THE CHILDREN TO WASH THEIR HANDS AND THEN MEET YOU AT THE SNACK TABLE. WHEN THEY ARRIVE, BRING OUT THE BASKET WHICH YOU FILLED AND TELL THE CHILDREN THAT THEY ARE GOING TO USE ALL OF THEIR SENSES TO EXAMINE THE BASKET AND THE EGGS WHICH ARE NESTLED INSIDE.

PASS THE BASKET AROUND THE TABLE AND HAVE THE CHILDREN **LOOK** AT IT. GIVE EACH CHILD THE OPPORTUNITY TO SAY ONE THING ABOUT THE BASKET. NEXT HAVE EACH CHILD WIGGLE HIS 'BUNNY NOSE' AND SNIFF THE EASTER BASKET AS IT GOES AROUND THE TABLE AGAIN. HOW DOES IT **SMELL**? PASS THE BASKET AROUND THE TABLE AGAIN, THIS TIME HAVING EACH CHILD TELL HOW THE BASKET OR ITS CONTENTS **FEELS.** FINALLY, HAVE EACH CHILD CHOOSE AN EGG FROM THE BASKET. HE SHOULD CRACK AND PEEL IT. HOW DOES IT **SOUND**? NOW IT'S TIME FOR EACH CHILD TO **TASTE** HIS EGG. ENJOY EATING THE EASTER EGG SNACK.

FINGERPLAYS

FIVE LITTLE EASTER EGGS

Five little Easter eggs,
Lovely colors wore:
Mother ate the blue one.
Then there were four.
Four little Easter eggs,
Two and two, you see;
Daddy ate the red one,
Then there were three.
Three little Easter eggs;
Before I knew,
Sister ate the yellow one,
Then there were two.
Two little Easter eggs,
Oh, what fun!
Brother ate the purple one.
Then there was one.
One little Easter egg;
See me run!
I ate the last one.
And then there were none.

IN MY EASTER BASKET

Red eggs, yellow eggs,
Green eggs too.
So many colors
I'll share some with you.
(Point to a friend.)
        Dick Wilmes

WHERE'S MY EASTER BASKET

A tisket, a tasket
The bunny hid my basket.
I wish he would have left a clue,
Oh! There it is . . . . . YAHOO!
(Let each child tell where
his basket is hiding.)
        Vohny Moehling

RECIPES

YOU'LL NEED

Easter eggs
Celery
Onion
Carrot
Mayonnaise
Party rye bread

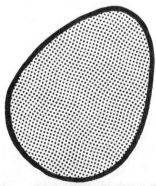

TO MAKE: Peel the eggs. Dice them and put them in a bowl. Clean and peel the vegetables. Cut them into small pieces. Put them in the bowl with the eggs. Add mayonnaise and stir until well mixed. Spread the egg salad on party rye bread. Enjoy with a glass of milk.

FIELD TRIPS

• Have an Easter egg hunt using real eggs which the children have colored. After all of the eggs have been collected, crack, peel, and enjoy them for a snack with carrot sticks.

LANGUAGE GAMES

WHAT'S MISSING?

On a large magnetic cookie sheet, use washable markers to draw an outline of an Easter basket. Collect boxes, wrappers, and pictures of things that might go into an Easter basket. Glue a piece of magnetic tape on the back of each one. Bring the items and the cookie sheet to circle time.

Show the children the drawing of the Easter basket. Pass out all of the 'goodies.' One at a time, let the children fill the basket and tell the others what they are adding. After all of the 'goodies' are in the basket, point to each one and have the children name it.

Now have the children close their eyes. Take one 'goodie' away. Have the children open their eyes, look at the Easter basket, and figure out what treat is missing. After guessing, show the children the one you took away. Put it back in the basket and play again. After several times, you might let the children take turns removing a 'goodie' from the basket.

FILL THE BASKET

Collect a variety of objects, some of which are appropriate for an Easter basket and some of which are not. Put all of the objects in a bag. Have an empty Easter basket.

Tell the children that you've brought lots of things in your bag and you want them to decide which ones should go in the Easter basket. Pull out one item and have the children look at it. If they want it in the basket have them call out "Yes," if not call out "No." Put the 'Yes' objects in the basket and the 'No' objects off to the side.

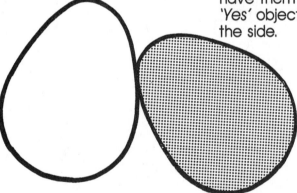

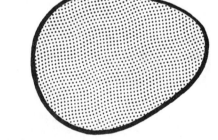

EGG MATCH

Get several dozen colored plastic Easter eggs which divide in two pieces. Put all of the halves in an Easter basket. Pass the basket around and have the children each take out one half. Continue passing the basket around until all of the halves are taken.

Tell the children to look at their halves and pick one up. Then have all of the girls stand. See if they can match egg halves of the same color. If so, have them put the matching halves together, set the whole eggs back into the basket, and then sit back down. Any children unable to match their halves should remain standing. Pick another group, such as those wearing belts, to join the group already standing and continue to let the children match halves and fill the basket.

| HIDE THE BASKET | Bring a piece of pastel colored posterboard and a marker to circle time. Have the children pretend that they are *'Easter bunnies'* who have gotten together to plan where they should hide the Easter baskets. Write their ideas down and hang the list on the classroom door. Add to the list when the *'bunnies'* have more ideas. |

ACTIVE GAMES

| BUNNY BUDDIES | Before circle time, make a headband for each child. Using different colors of construction paper, cut one bunny for every two children. Cut each bunny vertically in half. Hide all of the bunny halves around the room. |

When you say, *"Hunt for your bunny,'* the children should search for a bunny half. When each child finds a half, have him return to the circle time area. After everyone is back, have each child look at his bunny half, find the child who has the other half, and stand together. Those two children can be *'bunny buddies.'* They can enjoy activities together such as holding hands and hopping outside together, painting at the same easel, and sitting next to each other at snack. Staple the bunny halves to the headbands.

VARIATION: Instead of hunting for *'bunnies'* hunt for eggs cut from wallpaper.

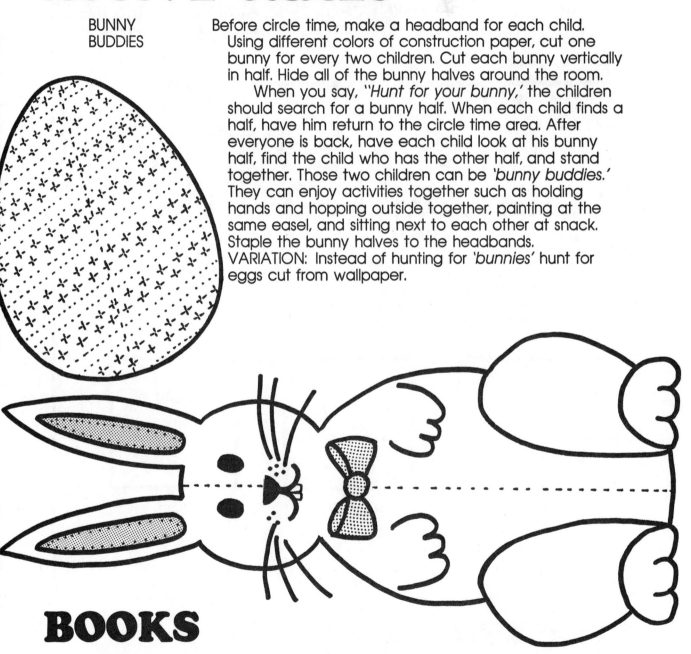

BOOKS

CAROL CARRICK – ***A RABBIT FOR EASTER***
DuBOSE HEYWARD – ***COUNTRY BUNNY AND THE LITTLE GOLD SHOES***
JAMES STEVENSON – ***GREAT BIG ESPECIALLY BEAUTIFUL EASTER EGG***
ALIKI – ***MY FIVE SENSES***
TASHA TUDOR – ***FIRST DELIGHTS***

ANIMAL HOMES

FOR OPENERS

TALK WITH THE CHILDREN ABOUT THE DIFFERENT TYPES OF HOMES IN WHICH THEY LIVE. THEN ASK THEM WHO HAVE ANIMALS LIVING WITH THEM. WHAT KINDS OF ANIMALS? WHERE DO THE ANIMALS LIVE? WHAT DO THE ANIMALS DO? YOU MIGHT MAKE A CHART OF WHAT ANIMALS LIVE IN THE DIFFERENT CHILDREN'S HOMES. HANG IT LOW ON A WALL. YOUR CHART MIGHT LOOK LIKE THIS ONE.

DOG	**CAT**	**FISH**	**BIRD**
Dick	Dawn	Taba	Mary
Helen	Judy	Jose	Matt
Greg			

RABBIT	**HAMSTER**	**OTHER**
Doreen	Mary Ann	Rick - snake
Miguel		Judy - sheep

FINGERPLAYS

SOFT KITTY

Soft kitty, warm kitty,
Little ball of fur.
Lazy kitty, pretty kitty,
"Purr, purr, purr."

HOUSES

This is the nest for Mrs. Bluebird,
This is the hive for Mr. Bee,
This is the hole for Mrs. Rabbit,
And this is the house for me.

MY PETS

I have five pets
That I'd like you to meet.
They all live together
On Mulberry Street.

This is my chicken,
The smallest of all.
He comes running
Whenever I call.

This is my duckling.
He says, "Quack, quack, quack,"
As he shakes the water
Off of his back.

Here is my rabbit,
He runs from his pen,
Then I must put him
Back again.

This is my kitten,
Her coat is black and white,
She loves to sleep
On my pillow at night.

Here is my puppy,
Who has lots of fun.
He chases the others
And makes them all run.

THE PUPPY

Call the puppy,
Give him some milk.
Brush his coat
Till it shines like silk.

Call the dog
And give him a bone.
Take him for a walk,
Then put him in his home.

RECIPES

PINECONE TREATS
(for birds only)

YOU'LL NEED

Peanut butter
Birdseed
Pinecones

TO MAKE: Put peanut butter in a large bowl. Have each child add a spoonful of birdseed to the peanut butter. Stir until the ingredients are well mixed. Using popsicle sticks, spread the peanut butter mixture onto the pinecones. Hang them in nearby trees and bushes so that you can watch the birds eat the treat you made for them.

FIELD TRIPS

• Visit an animal shelter in your area. Note all of the different types of animals. Depending on the policy of the shelter, make a date for one of the caretakers to bring an animal to your classroom and talk about it in a little more detail.

LANGUAGE GAMES

ANIMAL
HOMES

Before circle time, cut out pictures of water, trees, houses, and barns for all of the children. Pass out the pictures so that each child has at least one type of home. Call out an animal name. Any child who has a picture of a home which he thinks matches the animal you named should hold it up. Talk about the pictures the children are holding up. Remember they may be holding up the same picture or several different ones. For example, if you say, *"Fish,"* children might hold up pictures of water and houses. Continue naming different animals and talking about their homes.

ANIMAL
SEARCH

Talk with the children about the animals which live in their homes. Then ask them what animals they see outside. After listing the animals, talk about where they might live.

Take a walk with the children and look for animals and their homes. Check out the trees. Any bird nests, spider webs, cocoons, holes, etc? Look on the sidewalk and the ground. Any ant hills? Look in people's yards for animal homes people might have built such as doghouses or birdhouses.

EXTENSION: Have the children bring in photos of their animals. Hang them in a special place in the room.

IF I WERE A
WORM

Have the children close their eyes. Name an animal. Have the children pretend to be that animal. Where do they live? How do they move? What do they eat? Do they watch television? What programs? Do they move fast or slowly? Tell the children to open their eyes. Talk about the animal. Then have the children move around the room like that animal. Repeat with other animals.

138

BIRD NESTS Collect a variety of materials which birds use to make their nests, such as string, straw, sticks, stones, yarn, and leaves. Have a large container about one-quarter filled with dirt, a pitcher of water, a sturdy spoon, and a cookie sheet. Bring all of these items to circle time.

Show the children all of the materials. Tell them that birds use these different things to build their nests. Now have the children pretend to be birds who are going to build a springtime nest. First have several children pour a little water into the dirt and stir it to make a thick mud. Now let the other 'birds' add more materials. Continue mixing. Once all of the ingredients are in the container, stir several more times. Then pour the mixture onto a cookie sheet. Shape the mixture into a bird nest. Set it in the sun to dry.

ACTIVE GAMES

IN THE WATER-ON THE LAND Have a clothesline laying in a straight line on the floor. Have all of the children stand on one side of the rope. That side is the 'land.' The other side is the 'water.' You name an animal. If the animal lives in the water, the children step over the line and start swimming. Name another animal. If that animal lives in the water, the children continue to swim. If the animal lives on land, the children step back over the line and begin running in place. Keep naming different animals. Let the children move to where each animal lives.

VISIT A TREE Take a walk to a tree that is near your school. Look at it carefully; feel it; smell the bark; listen for noises coming from the tree. Now look even more closely. Can you find any animal homes? What are they? Where are they? Who do you think lives in them? If you have a classroom camera, take photographs of your tree. Revisit your tree every couple of days. Note things which are the same and things which have changed. Do you see any animals near the tree? (Remember safety.)

BOOKS

MARY ANN HOBERMAN – *HOUSE IS A HOME FOR ME*
ANNE ROCKWELL – *I LOVE MY PETS*
LIESEL SKORPEN – *ALL THE LASSIES*
CHRIS DEMAREST – *BENEDICT FINDS A HOME*
JOAN NODSET – *WHO TOOK THE FARMER'S HAT*
JAN PIENKOWSKI – *HOMES*
LEO LIONNI – *INCH BY INCH*
JANICE MAY UDRY – *A TREE IS NICE*

DUCKS

FOR OPENERS

SING THE SONG *'FIVE LITTLE DUCKS'* WITH THE CHILDREN.

FIVE LITTLE DUCKS

*FIVE LITTLE DUCKS THAT I ONCE KNEW,
FAT ONES, SKINNY ONES, TALL ONES, TOO.
BUT THE ONE LITTLE DUCK WITH THE FEATHER ON HIS BACK,
HE LED THE OTHERS WITH A "QUACK, QUACK, QUACK."*

*DOWN TO THE RIVER THEY WOULD GO,
WIBBLE WOBBLE, WIBBLE WOBBLE, TO AND FRO.
BUT THE ONE LITTLE DUCK WITH THE FEATHER ON HIS BACK,
HE LED THE OTHERS WITH A "QUACK, QUACK, QUACK."*

*UP FROM THE RIVER THEY WOULD COME,
HO, HO, HO, HO; HUM, HUM, HUM.
BUT THE ONE LITTLE DUCK WITH THE FEATHER ON HIS BACK,
HE LED THE OTHERS WITH A "QUACK, QUACK, QUACK."*

ONCE THE CHILDREN KNOW IT, HAVE THEM STAND IN A LINE, SQUAT DOWN, PUT ONE HAND BEHIND THEIR BACKS FOR FEATHERS, AND PRETEND TO BE DUCKS.

BEGIN SINGING THE SONG AGAIN, THIS TIME WITH THE CHILDREN WADDLING AROUND THE ROOM. WHEN THEY SING THE LINE, *"BUT THE ONE LITTLE DUCK WITH THE FEATHER ON HIS BACK,"* ENCOURAGE THEM TO REALLY WAVE THEIR FEATHERS AND SHOUT, *"QUACK, QUACK, QUACK!"*

FINGERPLAYS

FIVE LITTLE DUCKS

*Five little ducks
Swimming in the lake,
The first one said,
"Watch the waves I make."
The second duck said,
"Swimming is such fun."
The third duck said,
"I'd rather sit in the sun."
The fourth duck said,
"Oh, let's stay."
Then along came a motor boat
With a PUTT, PUTT, PUTT!
And five little ducks swam away.*

QUACKING DUCKS

*Five little ducks went out to play,
Over the hills and far away.
Mama Duck said, "Quack, quack, quack."
Four little ducks came waddling back.*

*Four little ducks went out to play,
Over the hill and far away.
Mama Duck said, "Quack, quack, quack."
Three little ducks came waddling back.*

*Three little ducks went out to play,
Over the hill and far away.
Mama Duck said, "Quack, quack, quack."
Two little ducks came waddling back.*

*Two little ducks went out to play,
Over the hill and far away.
Mama Duck said, "Quack, quack, quack!"
One little duck came waddling back.*

*One little duck went out to play,
Over the hill and far away.
Mama Duck yelled, "Quack, quack, quack!"
Five little ducks came running back.*

RECIPES

Have a *'Bread Taste Testing'* party. Get a variety of breads and cut them into small pieces. Have the children pretend that they are *'ducks'* as they sample the different breads. After tasting each one have those *'ducks'* who liked the bread quack loudly and those *'ducks'* who did not like the bread quack softly.

FIELD TRIPS

- Visit a duck sanctuary in your area. If allowed, bring bread to feed the ducks. Have the children watch how the ducks move and talk. If possible, have one of the caretakers talk with the children about the ducks and the facility.

LANGUAGE GAMES

DUCK FUN

Make duck stick puppets for all of the children. To make them, cut out duck shapes in a variety of colors to represent real ducks (white, gray, brown, tan, black). Glue a popsicle stick to each one.

Talk with the children about all of the things that they think ducks do throughout the day. Think about how they live and have fun.

Pass the duck shapes to the children. Have each child look at his duck and think of one thing he knows that his duck really likes to do. Have a child stand, hold up his duck, and tell the others what that one thing is. Write the key action word on the child's duck. As you're writing, have the next child stand up ready to tell the group about his duck.

Have the children take their ducks home and tell their parents what their ducks and the other children's ducks like to do all day.

DUCK CALLS   One child pretends to be the *'leader duck'* and gives a *'duck call'* such as, "Quack, quack, honk." The rest of the *'ducks'* echo the call. Let another child be the *'leader duck'* give another *'call'* ("Quack, honk, honk, quack"), and have the *'flock'* echo his *'call'* back to him. Continue with other *'leader ducks,'* creating different *'duck calls'* which the *'flock'* echoes back.

GO FISHING   Cut out fish from different colors of construction paper. Mark off a pond in your circle time area. Put the fish in the pond.

Have the children sit around the pond. Say to a child, "Tabatha, dive for a yellow fish." Tabatha should fly around the pond and then catch the yellow fish and fly back to her place. Continue with one or more children until all of the fish have been caught.

FLY AND SPY   Have the children *'flap their wings'* and pretend to be *'ducks'* flying around the *'lake.'* When you say, "Stop ducks," they should stop where they are and look around the *'lake.'* Ask the ducks, "What do you see?" Have several ducks tell you what they are looking at. Then say, "Fly on, ducks." After awhile, have them stop again and talk about what they see. (Continue in this manner.)

ACTIVE GAMES

DUCK, DUCK, GOOSE   Play this game according to the traditional rules, except encourage the children to waddle on short legs like a duck and longer legs like a goose.

TEACH THE DUCKLINGS   Pretend that you are the *'Mother Duck'* and you are teaching all of your *'ducklings'* (the children) to do duck-like things. Have the *'ducklings'* close to you and follow your instructions:

- *"Baby ducks, quack as loudly as you can."*
- *"Baby ducks, waddle around the room."*
- *"Baby ducks, dive for fish."*
- *"Baby ducks, follow me down the river."*
- *"Baby ducks, swim around the pond."*
- *"Baby ducks, eat the bread people have left."*
- *"Baby ducks, fly to the island in the middle of the river."*

BOOKS

RON ROY – ***THREE DUCKS WENT WANDERING***
MIRRA GINSBURG – ***CHICK AND THE DUCKLING***
MARJORIE FLACK – ***ANGUS AND THE DUCKS***
ROBERT McCLOSKEY – ***MAKE WAY FOR DUCKLINGS***

PUDDLIN' AROUND

FOR OPENERS

PUT DAMP SAND IN A CHILD'S WADING POOL. PAIR OFF THE CHILDREN AND HAVE THEM STAND AROUND THE POOL. GIVE ONE CHILD IN EACH PAIR A SMALL GLASS OF WATER. LET THE OTHER CHILD USE HIS FINGERS TO DIG A HOLE IN THE SAND. AFTER THE HOLE HAS BEEN DUG, HAVE THE CHILD WITH THE GLASS OF WATER POUR THE WATER INTO THE HOLE TO MAKE A PUDDLE. HAVE EACH PAIR WATCH THEIR PUDDLE. WHEN THE PUDDLE DRIES UP, HAVE THE PAIR RAISE THEIR HANDS. AFTER AWHILE ASK, *"WHOSE PUDDLE HAS NOT DRIED UP?" WHY DO THE CHILDREN THINK THERE IS WATER IN SOME OF THE PUDDLES BUT NOT IN OTHERS?*

FINGERPLAYS

PUDDLE MAGIC

The trees and sky are overhead
Until the raindrops fall,
The trees and sky are underfoot
And, oh! I feel so tall.

So splash along in puddles,
And then just wait and see.
You'll walk among the treetops, too,
And feel sky-high, like me.
(When you take 'puddle walks,' see if you can see reflections of clouds and trees in the puddles.)

LITTLE FROG

I'm a little frog in the pond,
Hippity, hippity, hop.

I can jump high in the air,
Hippity, hippity, hop.

I can jump from rock to rock,
Hippity, hippity, hop.

I am very tired,
No more hippity, hippity, hop.
Liz Wilmes

RECIPES

Read the book 'Rain Makes Applesauce' by Julian Scheer and Marvin Bileck. Then make applesauce with the children.

YOU'LL NEED

3 apples
1/4 cup honey
A little water

TO MAKE: Wash and core the apples. Chop them into small pieces. Put them into a blender with the honey and just enough water to create applesauce. Enjoy the snack right after you make it.

FIELD TRIPS

- Take a 'Puddle Walk' after a Springtime rain. Look for puddles. Where are they? Bend over and look in the puddle. What do you see? Can you see your reflection? What other reflections do you see? Touch the water. How does it feel?

LANGUAGE GAMES

PUDDLE DETECTIVES

During a rainstorm put out several clean buckets to collect rainwater. When the rain stops, bring the buckets inside. Bring this special water to circle time. Have several clear plastic glasses.

Dip the glasses into the water, filling them a quarter to half full. Pass the glasses to the children. Have them look at the rainwater. What do they see? Do they think the water is clean? Dirty? Do they see anything on the bottom of the glasses?

EXTENSION: Go outside and find a puddle. Fill a different glass with 'puddle water.' Put a piece of masking tape on the glass and label it 'puddle water.' Now, remembering that this water also came from the rain, does it look the same or different? How? Why?

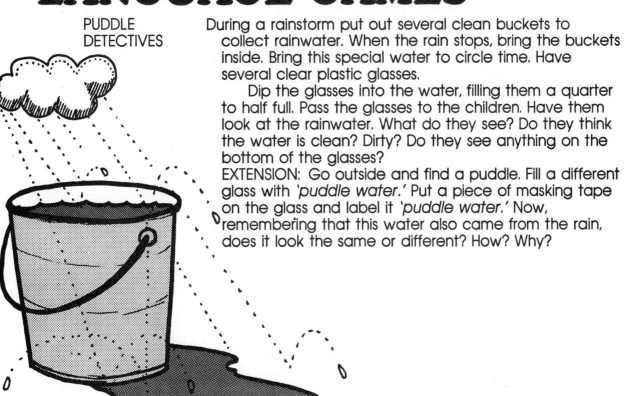

145

PUDDLE FUN

Find a picture of a child splashing in puddles. Back the picture with felt. Bring the picture and felt board to circle time.

Put the picture on the board. Talk about what the child in the picture is doing. Is he having fun? How do you know? Say the *'Rainy Day Fun'* rhyme with the children.

RAINY DAY FUN

Slip on your raincoat,
Pull on galoshes,
Wading in puddles
Makes splishes and sploshes.

Have the children pretend to put on their raincoats and galoshes. What would they like to do in puddles?

WHAT'S IN THE PUDDLE?

After the children have had the opportunity to explore and play in different puddles around the school, talk about all of the things they have found in the puddles, such as leaves, grass, worms, stones, sticks, etc.

Cut a puddle shape from a piece of posterboard. Cut magazine pictures (or draw simple ones) of the different things that the children found in puddles. Put a paper clip on each picture. Make several fishing rods with magnets and strings. Lay the posterboard puddle in the middle of the circle time area and put all of the pictures on it.

Have several children get fishing rods and go fishing. When they catch something, have them take it off of the magnet and tell the others what they caught. Switch the children. Continue until the children have cleaned the puddle.

RAIN, RAIN GO AWAY

Before circle time cut out lots of large raindrops from different colors of construction paper. Bring the raindrops and a marker to circle time.

First have the children think of activities that they like to do when it is raining. As they say each one, write the activity on a raindrop. Next have the children think of activities they like to do when the rain has stopped. Turn the raindrops upside-down and write all of these activities on more raindrops.

When all of the ideas are on raindrops, mix all of them up. Have a child come up and pick a raindrop. Read what the activity is. If the activity is something the children like to do when it is raining, have them say this rhyme:

Rain, rain, we're having fun
We'll do this 'til the rain is done.

If it is an activity that they like to do when the rain has stopped, have them say this rhyme:

Rain, rain, go away
Come again another day.

ACTIVE GAMES

PUDDLIN'
AROUND

All of the children stand in a circle and pretend to be *'dancing raindrops'* falling and splashing to the ground. After it has been raining for awhile, have the children pretend to make different size puddles. Say, *"Raindrops with brown hair dance to the middle and form a puddle."* When the *'raindrops'* are in the middle, ask the other *'raindrops'* if the ones in the middle are making a big or small puddle. (Answer.) Have the *'raindrops'* dance back to the circle. Have another group of *'raindrops'* (wearing red shoes, wearing belts, all of the *'raindrops'*) form a new puddle. Is it a big one or a small one? Continue in this manner.

EXTENSION: Go for a walk with boots on. Look for big and small puddles. Stomp and splash in them.

ME AND MY
PUDDLE

Cut puddle shapes out of construction paper. Give one to each child. Have the children move in relationship to their puddle. For example:

- *"Step on your puddle."*
- *"Walk over your puddle."*
- *"Hop around your puddle."*
- *"Stand next to your puddle."*
- *"Run away from your puddle."*
- *"Come back to your puddle."*

BOOKS

CHARLOTTE POMERANTZ – *PIGGY IN THE PUDDLE*
MIKE THALER – *IN THE MIDDLE OF THE PUDDLE*

RAINBOWS

FOR OPENERS

ON A LARGE PIECE OF BUTCHER PAPER, DRAW SEVEN ARCS FOR A
RAINBOW. CUT OUT THE ARCS SO THAT YOU HAVE INDIVIDUAL ONES. MIX
PAINT SO THAT YOU HAVE RED, ORANGE, YELLOW, GREEN, BLUE, INDIGO,
AND VIOLET. PUT EACH COLOR IN A DIFFERENT CONTAINER WITH SEVERAL
BRUSHES. PLACE THE LARGEST ARC WITH THE RED PAINT, THE NEXT LARGEST
WITH THE ORANGE PAINT, AND SO ON.

HAVE THE CHILDREN MEET IN THE ART AREA. TELL THEM ABOUT RAINBOWS,
EMPHASIZING THE DIFFERENT COLORS. DIVIDE THE CHILDREN INTO SEVEN
GROUPS. HAVE EACH GROUP PAINT AN ARC. LET THE ARCS DRY AND THEN
HANG THE LARGE RAINBOW ON A WALL OR BULLETIN BOARD FOR
EVERYONE TO SEE.

FINGERPLAYS

RAIN

Rain on green grass,
And rain on the tree,
Rain on the roof top,
But not on me.

RAINBOW GAY

From big black clouds
The raindrops fell,
Drip, drip, drip, one day;
Until bright sunlight
Changed them all into a rainbow gay.

RAINBOW RECIPE

First some rain or a little mist.
Then out comes the sun.
And arcs of colored light,
Make a rainbow for everyone.
Vohny Moehling

148

RECIPES

Eat foods that are the colors of the rainbow:

RED–Red pepper slices topped with a
    little cream cheese
ORANGE–Carrot coins
YELLOW–Pears
GREEN–Honeydew melon slices
BLUE–Hard boiled eggs with the shells
    dyed blue
INDIGO–Blueberries topped with a little
    cottage cheese
VIOLET–Grape juice finger gelatin

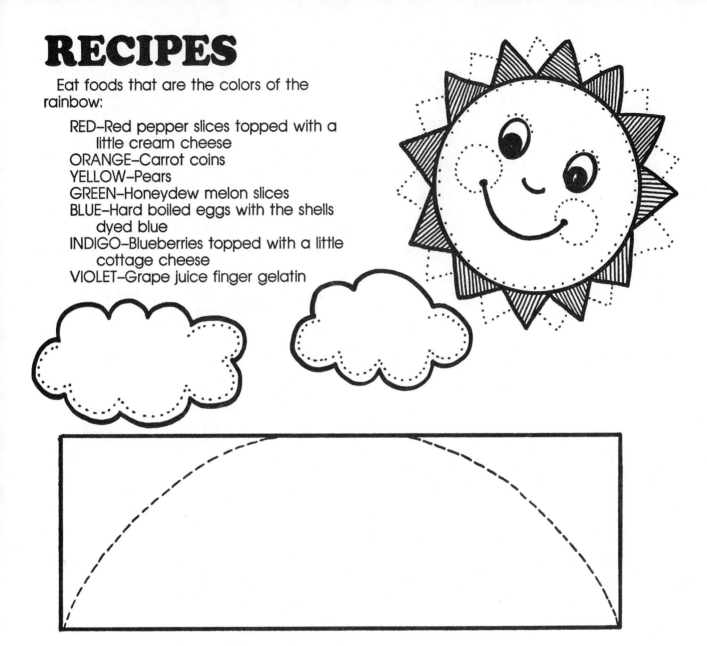

LANGUAGE GAMES

BUILD A
RAINBOW

Using the seven basic rainbow colors, cut several sets of 6" x 2" construction paper strips. Round each end to give the impression of an arc.

Pass the strips to the children. Call out 'red,' the first color of the rainbow. If a child has a red strip, he should hold it up. Call on one of the children holding up 'red' to come up to the front. Call out 'orange.' Children with orange should hold up that color. Have one of them come up to the front and hold his strip under the red strip. Continue until the children have built a rainbow. Repeat the activity, reversing the colors and letting a second group of children build another rainbow from the bottom to the top.

FLASH A RAINBOW

Have several plastic prisms. Gather the children around a sunlit window. Talk with them about the sun shining into the classroom through the window. Pass the prisms around. Explain that a prism can be used to refract the sun's light and break it up into its seven basic colors.

Flash the prism so it makes a rainbow on a nearby wall. Have the children look at it and call out the colors they see. Have several children come up and try to flash a rainbow. Talk about their rainbows. Continue with several other children.

EXTENSION: Leave the prisms on the window ledge and encourage the children to flash rainbows when the sun is shining into the classroom.

I WANT TO BE A RAINBOW

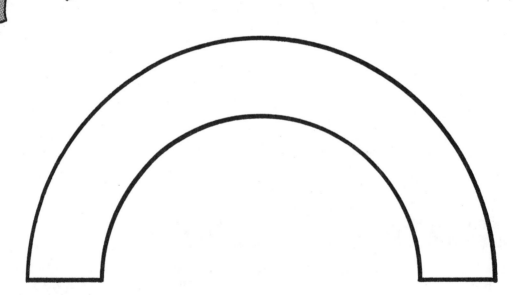

Cut several arcs out of appropriate colors of construction paper. Punch holes at the ends of each arc and string pieces of yarn through them to make necklaces. Bring the arcs to circle time.

Ask each child which color arc is his favorite. As each child names his favorite color, have him come up, get an arc, and put it around his neck. Now have the children think of something they like that is the same color as their arcs. For example, *"I have a red arc and I like to eat tomatoes."* Continue until all of the children have shared ideas. Let them wear their arcs all day and then take them home.

RAINBOW SUNCATCHERS

Bring a commercial rainbow suncatcher to circle time. Hold it up so that all of the children can see the colors. Point to the top color in the rainbow. Have the children call out what color it is. Then have them look at one of the bulletin boards and find things on it that are that color. Point to the next color, have the children name it, and then look at one of the adults and name anything s/he is wearing that is the same color. Continue with the rest of the colors. Then hang the rainbow in a sunny window.

ACTIVE GAMES

COLOR SEARCH

Cut out about ten construction paper squares of each of the seven colors in the rainbow. Hide the squares all over the room. Put a picture of a rainbow on the floor in the circle time area. Point to each color in the rainbow and have the children call out the color.

Now the children are ready to play 'Color Search.' Tell them that you have hidden squares of the rainbow colors all over the room and when you say, "Color search," they are going to try to find them. When they have found a square they should come over to the rainbow and lay it on or next to the matching arc.

BE A RAINBOW

Have the children wear their rainbow necklaces. (See 'I Want To Be a Rainbow.') Get a recording of 'We All Live Together, Volume II' by Millang and Scelesa. Play the song, 'The World Is A Rainbow' and have the children move gently to the rhythm.

BOOKS

PETER SPIER — *PETER SPIER'S RAIN*
DON FREEMAN — *RAINBOW OF MY OWN*

GOOD-BYE OLD FRIENDS

FOR OPENERS

BRING THE CLASSROOM SCRAPBOOK TO CIRCLE TIME. *(FALL SECTION—'HELLO NEW FRIENDS')* HAVE THE CHILDREN PUT ON THEIR 'THINKING CAPS,' LOOK AT THE PICTURES, AND REMEMBER MANY OF THE FUN THINGS THAT THEY HAVE DONE THROUGHOUT THE YEAR. IF YOU HAVE WRITTEN DESCRIPTIONS UNDER THE PHOTOS, TAKE TIME TO READ THESE TO THE CHILDREN.

FINGERPLAYS

GOOD-BYE

<u>GOOD-BYE OLD FRIENDS</u>
(Tune: Good Night Ladies)

*Good-Bye Todd,
Good-bye Kris,
Good-bye Katie,
We'll see you soon again.*

*We have had lots of fun,
Lots of fun,
Lots of fun,
We have had lots of fun,
And now we're saying, "Good-bye."*

Good-bye. . . . . (Name three more children
and repeat as above.)

<u>FRIEND OF MINE</u>
(Tune: Mary Had A Little Lamb)

*(Child's name) is a friend of mine,
Friend of mine, friend of mine.
(Child's name) is a friend of mine,
Good-bye, (child's name).*

<u>GOOD-BYE</u>

*Wave your hand
And give a sign.
It's the end of school,
Good-bye! Good-bye!*

RECIPES

BREAD DOUGH INITIALS

YOU'LL NEED

Refrigerator biscuits

TO MAKE: Prepare the dough according to the directions. Give each child a piece of the dough, have him roll it out, and then shape it into the first letter of his name or one of his favorite shapes. Bake and enjoy with a glass of juice.

FIELD TRIPS

• Take a variety of 'Memory Walks' to different places which the children have enjoyed. For example: a nearby park, a special grocery store, an ongoing construction site, a neighbor's garden, a shady tree, etc.

LANGUAGE GAMES

MEMORIES

For several days during free choice time, have the children tell you what they liked best about school. Write down what they say on individual pieces of construction paper. After they have dictated their memories, have them add a picture to their page/s. When everyone has completed his page/s, punch holes along one side and bind all of the pages together with colored yarn. Now the children have a classroom scrapbook of their favorite activities.

Bring the book to circle time and read it to the children. Then put it on the book shelf for the children to 'read' again and again.

EXTENSION: Put the scrapbook on a special table for parents to enjoy while visiting the classroom.

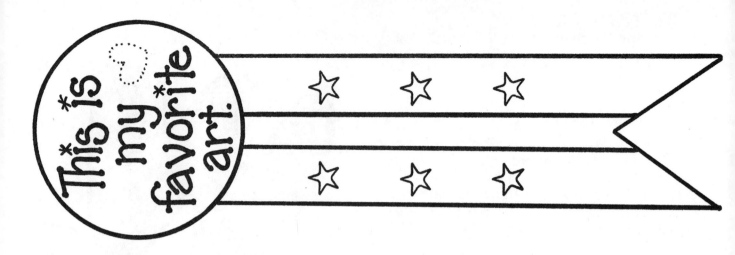

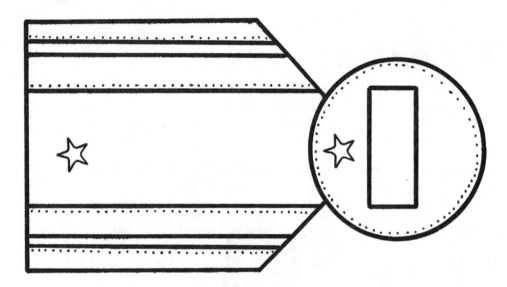

ART GALLERY
For several weeks before the end of school, save all of the children's artwork. Designate a special place low on a large wall (hallway) for each child's work. Let each child decide what art he wants to display and what he wants to take home.

After all of the children's art has been hung, take a walk with them through the Art Gallery. Talk with them about the different works they have done. Note the different media, collage materials, and colors.

Give each child a blue ribbon with a loop of tape on the backside. Have him go back through the Art Gallery and look at all of the art he chose to display. Have him choose his favorite one and put a blue ribbon on it.

FAVORITE
ACTIVITIES
Have all of the children think of things that they like about school. Call on three children and have them stand in a row. Each one should tell the group of children one thing he likes about school. Then lay your hand on the first child's head. The group should call out what the child said he liked. Repeat with the second and third child. Continue in this manner using three or more different children each time.

IF I KNEW YOU WERE COMING

Call on a child to stand in front of the group. Have all of the others sing the first verse and do actions to the song 'If I Knew You Were Coming I'd A Baked A Cake.'

"If I knew you were coming I'd a baked a cake,
Baked a cake, baked a cake.
If I knew you were coming I'd baked a cake,
Howdy-do, howdy-do, howdy-do."

After singing, have the child who is standing point to another child. That child stands up and the first one sits down. Ask the children what they would do if they had known that (child's name) was coming to visit (gotten dressed up, poured the milk, dusted the furniture, gotten out the toys, etc.). Sing the song again substituting the new words and adding different actions. Continue substituting new words for each new child who comes to visit.

ACTIVE GAMES

FAVORITE GAMES

Have the children choose active games they especially liked doing during the past year. Enjoy playing all of their suggestions.

FOLLOW THE LEADER

Call on a child, have him stand up and tell the others what his favorite exercise is. Give everyone time to get ready and then let the child lead the group in the exercise. Repeat with different children leading their favorite exercises.

MARCHING BANDS

FOR OPENERS

CALL YOUR LOCAL JUNIOR OR SENIOR HIGH SCHOOL MUSIC DEPARTMENT AND MAKE ARRANGEMENTS FOR SEVERAL STUDENTS TO VISIT YOUR CLASSROOM. HAVE THE MUSICIANS BRING THEIR INSTRUMENTS WITH THEM. WHEN THE MUSICIANS ARRIVE, HAVE THEM TELL YOUR CHILDREN ABOUT THEIR PARTICULAR INSTRUMENT AND PLAY THE INSTRUMENT INDIVIDUALLY FOR THE CHILDREN.

TALK WITH THE CHILDREN ABOUT HOW THE DIFFERENT INSTRUMENTS LOOK, HOW BIG THEY ARE, HOW THEY SOUND, ETC. IF POSSIBLE, DIVIDE THE CHILDREN INTO AS MANY SMALL GROUPS AS THERE ARE MUSICIANS. LET THE CHILDREN SEE THE INSTRUMENTS UP CLOSE. THE CHILDREN MIGHT EVEN HAVE THE OPPORTUNITY TO PLAY SEVERAL OF THEM, SUCH AS THE CYMBALS OR DRUMS.

FINGERPLAYS

THE FINGER BAND
(Tune: Here We Go 'Round the Mulberry Bush)

The finger band is coming to town,
Coming to town, coming to town.
The finger band is coming to town,
So early in the morning.

This is the way they wear their hats,
Wear their hats, wear their hats.
This is the way they wear their hats,
So early in the morning.

This is the way they wave their flags,
Wave their flags, wave their flags.
This is the way they wave their flags,
So early in the morning.

This is the way they beat their drums,
Beat their drums, beat their drums.
This is the way they beat their drums,
So early in the morning.

This is the way they blow their horns,
Blow their horns, blow their horns.
This is the way they blow their horns,
So early in the morning.

The finger band is going away,
Going away, going away.
The finger band is going away,
So early in the morning.

TOWN PARADE

The people are beside the street,
All standing in the sun.
I hear the noon whistle blowing,
The parade has just begun.

First I hear police cars,
Sirens going "Vrrum, Vrrum!"
Driving slowly up the street,
Trying to make some room.

Next there comes the ambulance,
Yellow as it can be,
With the paramedics ready,
In case of an emergency.

Followed by the fire trucks,
The horns and whistles scream,
And hanging all along the rail,
Is the proud firefighting team.

Now there comes the color guard.
Scouts are marching proud,
Carrying the flags we all know,
Presenting them to the crowd.

The motorcycle troop is next,
You can hear them roar and zoom.
As they weave and turn about,
There's hardly any room.

Soon we see a tiny car,
Putting up the street.
Out jump fourteen clowns,
Each with great big feet.

Don't forget the bands and such,
Making music fine.
Drums and horns and cymbals play,
All marching in a line.

There are floats that carry people,
A car to drive the queen,
People riding horseback,
And a street sweeping machine.

Finally comes the last police car.
The music starts to fade.
We had a fine afternoon,
Watching the town parade.
Dick Wilmes

LANGUAGE GAMES

LISTEN TO THE INSTRUMENTS

Have four to seven rhythm instruments hidden in a bag. Pull each one out, name it, play it, and then lay the instrument on the floor in front of you so that all of the children can see it. Have the children cover their eyes. Pick up one instrument, play it, and put the instrument down. Have the children uncover their eyes and point to the instrument which they think you were playing. Pick up the instrument they are pointing to, name it, and play it. Ask the children if it sounds like the one you were originally playing. If so have the children clap for themselves and repeat the game with another instrument; if not, pick up the instrument you had played and play it again for the children. Have the children name it and clap for themselves.

NAME THAT INSTRUMENT

Put all of the instruments on a tray. Point to each one and have the children call out its name. Have the children cover their eyes and take one instrument away. Have the children uncover their eyes, look at the instruments left on the tray, and decide which one isn't there. Have them keep their ideas secret. Then say, *"Name that instrument."* Have all of the children call out which one they think is missing. Repeat.

TRAVELIN' BAND

Have the children bring a utensil from home which they can use in a band. (Have extras for those who forget.) Get a recording of *'This Little Cow'* by Fred Koch. Play the song *'Travelin' Band'* for the children. Then have them show, talk about, and demonstrate the *'travelin' instrument'* which they brought.

Now have each child choose to be one of the musicians in the travelin' band. Play the song again and let the children march around the room and play their instruments when their musician plays in the travelin' band.

PLAY YOUR
INSTRUMENTS

Get a recording of *'Play Your Instruments and Make a Pretty Sound'* by Ella Jenkins. Pass out musical instruments which match the ones in the song. Have the children practice with their instruments. Then play the recording and have the children listen carefully for when their particular instrument is played. Play the recording again and march around as you play the instruments. Repeat, this time encouraging the children to play their instruments a little quieter. Try again being even more quiet.

ACTIVE GAMES

BAND
PRACTICE

The big town parade is only days away and the band needs to practice with their instruments. Pick a child to be the *'drum major'* who leads the band. Give him/her a baton. Let all of the other children choose instruments. Have the children in the band line up and have the *'drum major'* face the band.

When everyone is ready to begin, the *'drum major'* should swing his baton back and forth signaling the musicians to play their instruments. When he wants the band to *'stop,'* he should hold his baton straight up in front of him. The *'drum major'* can also use his baton to signal different sections of the band. When he points to a specific section, only that section should play and the other musicians should be quiet. That section should continue playing until the *'drum major'* gives them the *'stop signal.'* The children should continue practicing, always watching the signals that the 'drum major' is giving them.

After awhile, switch *'drum majors'* and continue practicing. After the band members know how to play their instruments, they can march in place as they play.

PRACTICE
MARCHING

Have the children form several rows like a marching band. Get a drum. Beat out a slow rhythm. Have the children march to that rhythm while standing in place. Change the beat and have the children change their marching rhythm. Once they get used to marching and listening to the beating drum, have them march as if they were in a parade.

BOOKS

DONALD CREWS – ***PARADE***
MIRIAM STECHER – ***MAX THE MUSIC MAKER***

VEGETABLE GARDEN

FOR OPENERS

LAY A PIECE OF LIGHT BLUE BUTCHER PAPER IN THE ART AREA AND HAVE THE CHILDREN PAINT THE BOTTOM HALF BROWN. WHEN DRY, TACK IT TO A BULLETIN BOARD. CUT OUT PICTURES OF DIFFERENT VEGETABLES, SOME OF WHICH GROW ABOVE THE GROUND AND SOME OF WHICH GROW BELOW THE GROUND. (GARDENING MAGAZINES AND SEED CATALOGUES ARE GOOD SOURCES.) BRING THE PICTURES TO CIRCLE TIME ALONG WITH TACKS.

HOLD UP EACH PICTURE AND HAVE THE CHILDREN NAME THE VEGETABLE. PASS OUT THE PICTURES. SAY TO THE CHILDREN, *"IF YOU ARE HOLDING A PICTURE OF A TOMATO, STAND UP. (CHILDREN DO.) THE TOMATO GROWS ABOVE THE GROUND. COME UP AND I'LL HELP YOU TACK IT ON THE BULLETIN BOARD."* (DO IT.) CONTINUE WITH THE REST OF THE PICTURES.

ABOVE GROUND VEGETABLES

TOMATOES	*BEANS*
LETTUCE	*BROCCOLI*
CAULIFLOWER	*CORN*
PEPPERS	

BELOW GROUND VEGETABLES

CARROTS	*RADISHES*
POTATOES	*ONIONS*
BEETS	*TURNIPS*
PEANUTS	

FINGERPLAYS

<u>FARMER PLOWS THE GROUND</u>
(Tune: Here We go 'Round the Mulberry Bush)

First the farmer plows the ground,
Plows the ground, plows the ground.
First the farmer plows the ground,
Then he plants the seeds.

This is the way he plants the seeds,
So that they will grow.

The rain and sun will help them grow,
Right up through the ground.

Now the farmer picks the beans,
And we have vegetables to eat.

(Repeat the song using another vegetable.)

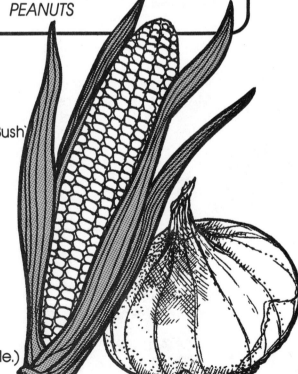

MAKE A GARDEN

Dig! Dig! Dig! Rake just so.
Plant the seeds, watch them grow.
Chop! Chop! Chop! Pull out weeds.
Warm rain and sun, my garden needs.
Up! Up! Up! Green stems climb.
Open wide, it's vegetable time!

I DIG, DIG, DIG

I dig, dig, dig,
I plant some seeds.
I rake, rake, rake,
I pull some weeds.
I wait and watch
And soon I know
Vegetables sprout
And start to grow.

RECIPES

NOISY DAY TREAT

YOU'LL NEED

Carrots
Radishes
Celery
Green pepper

TO MAKE: Wash and clean the vegetables. Cut them into bite-size pieces and put them on a plate. Pass the plate and let each child take one of each vegetable. As the children eat, encourage them to listen to their vegetables. Which vegetable is the loudest?

Quiet Day Treat: Tomatoes, cucumbers, peas. Listen carefully. Can the children hear these vegetables as they chew?

CLASSROOM VISITORS

• Ask a parent who likes to garden to visit your classroom and tell the children how s/he prepares his/her garden for planting, what kinds of foods s/he plants, and how long it takes the plants to grow.

LANGUAGE GAMES

NAME THAT
VEGETABLE

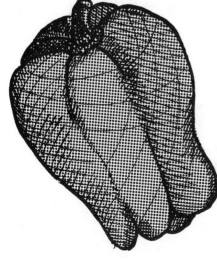

Fill a basket with real vegetables. Have pictures backed with felt of the same vegetables. Bring the real vegetables, the pictures, and the felt board to circle time.

Pass out the real vegetables and the pictures. Have the felt board and the basket near the front. Choose a child holding a real vegetable to stand up. Have all of the children with pictures look at their pictures. The child with the picture of that vegetable should stand up also.

The two children should hold their vegetables together so everyone can see the real vegetable along side of the picture of that vegetable. Everyone in the group call out the name of the vegetable. The child with the real vegetable should put it back into the basket and the child with the picture should put it on the felt board. Continue with the rest of the vegetables.

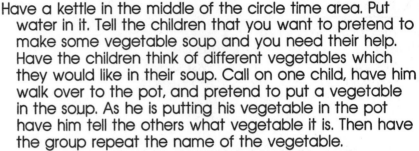

VEGETABLE SOUP

Have a kettle in the middle of the circle time area. Put water in it. Tell the children that you want to pretend to make some vegetable soup and you need their help. Have the children think of different vegetables which they would like in their soup. Call on one child, have him walk over to the pot, and pretend to put a vegetable in the soup. As he is putting his vegetable in the pot have him tell the others what vegetable it is. Then have the group repeat the name of the vegetable.

Call on a second child, have him add another vegetable. Have the group of children call out the names of the two vegetables that are in the soup. Let a third child add another vegetable. Have the children call out the three vegetables. Continue until the vegetable soup has all of the vegetables in it. EXTENSION: Read 'Stone Soup' and make soup with the children.

ABOVE AND BELOW THE GROUND

Have the children sit so they can all see the vegetable bulletin board. (See the 'For Openers' activity.) You name a vegetable. Have the children look at the bulletin board and find the picture of the vegetable you named. If it grows above the ground the children should stand up. If it grows below the ground the children should curl up into a ball. Name another vegetable, and have the children stand or curl up. Continue with the other vegetables.

PLANTING

Get a variety of vegetable seeds. Gather at least one small pot with soil in it for each child. Bring the pots and seeds to circle time.

Tell the children that each of them will have the opportunity to plant one type of seed. Tell them to think about the type of seed they want to plant.

Hold up one seed packet. Let the children look at the picture and guess what type of seeds are in the packet. Then open the packet and pour a few seeds into your hand. Walk around and show the children the seeds. Pour the seeds back into the packet. Repeat with the other seeds.

Hold up the first type of seed. Have those children who want to plant that type sit together in a small group. Continue, dividing the children into small groups according to the type of seed they want to plant. Help the children plant the seeds, put the pots in the window, water them, and care for them on a regular basis. You may want to put a small pennant with the child's name and what type of vegetable seed he planted in each pot.

162

WHAT COLOR IS IT?	Have a grocery bag full of different vegetables. Have a child come up, look into the bag, pick a vegetable, and tell the others what it is, such as lettuce. The group should call out what color they think lettuce is. After they have answered, the child should pull the vegetable out of the bag. Is it the color they thought? Continue with the rest of the vegetables in the bag. EXTENSION: Make a tossed salad for lunch or snack.

ACTIVE GAMES

HOW DOES YOUR GARDEN GROW?	Bring a hoe, rake, shovel, watering can, toy wheelbarrow, and toy truck to circle time. Display all of the items. Choose a child to go into the middle of the circle. Have the rest of the children say to him, "*How does your garden grow?*" He should then pretend to use one of the items you have displayed. He should continue to pantomime the action until the rest of the children guess which item he is using. When the children have guessed correctly, the child should stop his action, go over and pick up the item he was pretending to use. Continue letting other children pantomime how their gardens grow.
ONCE THERE WAS A BUNNY	Have the children pretend to be '*bunnies*' hopping around the room looking for vegetables to eat. When one of the '*bunnies*' finds a vegetable, he should say, "*Stop, I have found some carrots.*" All of the '*bunnies*' should stop and pretend to eat carrots. When they have finished, they should continue hopping until another '*bunny*' finds a vegetable to eat. EXTENSION: Enjoy this rhyme with the children.

<u>ONCE I SAW A BUNNY</u>

Once there was a bunny
And a green, green cabbage head.
"I think I'll have some cabbage."
The little bunny said.

So he nibbled and he nibbled.
And he perked his ears to say,
"Now I think it's time
I should be hopping on my way."
(Let the children choose another
vegetable for the bunny to eat and
then repeat the rhyme.)

BOOKS

MARCIA BROWN – *STONE SOUP*
LOIS EHLERT – *GROWING VEGETABLE SOUP*
RUTH KRAUSS – *CARROT SEED*
BRUCE McMILLAN – *GROWING COLORS*
NADINE WESTCOTT – *GIANT VEGETABLE GARDEN*

WHEELS AND TIRES

FOR OPENERS

BRING A VARIETY OF TOYS WHICH HAVE WHEELS TO CIRCLE TIME (TRIKES, CARS, TRUCKS, AIRPLANES, SCOOTERS, PULL TOYS, ETC.). SHOW THEM TO THE CHILDREN. TALK ABOUT WHICH ONES HAVE THE LARGEST WHEELS AND SMALLEST WHEELS.

HAVE A CHILD GET ON ONE OF THE TRIKES AND VERY SLOWLY *DRIVE* IT AROUND IN A CIRCLE. AS HE IS RIDING, HAVE THE CHILDREN ROLL THEIR ARMS AT THE SAME SPEED AS THE WHEELS ON THE TRIKE. HAVE THE CHILD GET OFF OF THE TRIKE. LET ANOTHER CHILD PICK A SMALL CAR. HAVE HIM *DRIVE* IT AROUND THE CIRCLE. THE CHILDREN SHOULD ROLL THEIR ARMS THE SPEED AT WHICH THE CHILD IS *DRIVING* THE CAR. LET SEVERAL MORE CHILDREN *DRIVE* VEHICLES AND HAVE THE CHILDREN MOVE THE SPEED AT WHICH THE CHILD IS DRIVING.

VARIATION: INSTEAD OF ROLLING THEIR ARMS TO THE SPEED AT WHICH THE CHILD IS *DRIVING* HIS VEHICLE, HAVE THEM MOVE THEIR LEGS OR NOD THEIR HEADS.

FINGERPLAYS

AUTO, AUTO

Auto, auto, may I have a ride?
Yes, sir; yes, sir; step inside.
Pour in the water, turn on the gas.
Chug-away, chug-away, but not too fast.

MY BICYCLE

One wheel, two wheels on the ground;
My feet make the pedals go 'round and 'round.
Handle bars help me steer so straight,
Down the sidewalk, through the gate.

THE ENGINE

Here is an engine
That runs on this track,
It whistles—"Toot Toot,"
And then it runs back.

RECIPES

WHITE WALLS

YOU'LL NEED

Dried prunes
Cream cheese

TO MAKE: Cut each prune in half. Put a dab of cream cheese in the center of each one. Serve with round crackers.

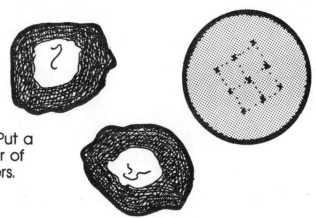

FIELD TRIPS

• Take a *'Tire Walk.'* Before going outside, talk with the children about different places where they might see tires, such as in parking lots, on playgrounds or streets, and at gas stations, tire stores or bike dealers. You might take paper and pencil along to keep a record of all of the places at which the children saw tires.

LANGUAGE GAMES

AROUND THE TOWN

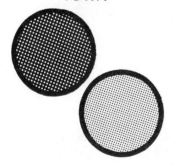

Have the children sit down. Give each one a paper plate to use as a steering wheel. Have a red and green construction paper circle. When you hold up the *'green sign,'* the children should pretend to be driving around the town. When you hold up the *'red sign,'* all of the drivers should stop. Ask several of them where they are going, what they have seen, what type vehicle they are driving, how many wheels does it have, and so on. Hold up the *'go sign'* and drive to your next destination. Hold up the *'stop sign,'* talk about it, and then continue on your trip around town.

**WHEELS ON
MY TRIKE**

Sing the following song to the tune *'The Wheels On the Bus.'* After the first several verses, have the children think of their own tricycles, now let them add more verses to the song.

*The wheels on my trike go 'round
    and 'round,
'Round and 'round, 'round and
    'round.
The wheels on my trike go 'round
    and 'round
All through the town.*

*The bell on my trike goes ring, ring,
    ring,*

*The pedals on my trike go up and
    down,*

*The basket on my trike goes squeak,
    squeak, squeak.*

**DRIVING
ALONG**

Get a strip of rubber garden edging. Cut two strips, each six to eight feet long. Collect several types of model vehicles, such as a truck, tractor, motorcycle, car, van, motor home, and bicycle. Bring the vehicles and *'roads'* to circle time.

Lay the *'roads'* down in the middle of the circle time area. Park the vehicles at the beginning of each *'road.'* Say to a child, *"Choose the tractor and drive it down the road."* Continue until the children understand the game. Then begin to vary the instructions, such as:

- *"Pick the bicycle and ride it backwards down the road."*
- *"Pick your favorite vehicle and drive it very slowly down the road."*
- *"Choose the tractor and drive it halfway down the road, turn around and come back. You forgot your hoe."*

EXTENSION: Set up the *'roads'* in the Block Center. You might bend them to make tunnels and bridges. Add several more *'roads'* and build an interstate highway.

166

BUILDING A CAR WHEEL	Go to an auto repair shop and ask an employee if you could borrow all of the parts used to construct a car wheel (tire, hubcap, lug bolts, rim, etc.). Bring them to circle time.

Lay all of the parts out so the children can see them. Talk about the wheels of their family cars. Then point to each part and name it. Show the children the order in which the parts are used to put the wheel together.

Now mix up the parts. Say, *"If I was going to make a wheel for a car, which part would I begin with?"* (Answer.) Put that one first. Now say, *"Which part would I use next?"* (Answer.) Put that next to the first part. Continue until the sequence is complete.

ACTIVE GAMES

ROLLING TIRES

Bring several tires to circle time. Divide the children into two or more small groups and have the children in each group stand in a line behind each other. Give the first child in each group a tire. When you say, *"Start,"* have the children roll the tires along the line of children until they get to the last child in their groups. Reverse the direction and roll the tires back to the front. Have the first child run to the end of his line. Repeat with each child. When the last child gets to the front of his group, the children should form a small circle around their tire to indicate that they are finished.

CHOO-CHOO

Show the children how to move their arms like train wheels, make the *'All-aboard'* arm motion, and toot the whistle. Then put on *'Rock-A-Motion, Choo-Choo'* by Millang and Scelesa from their album *'We All Live Together, Volume I,'* and have the children chug around the room.

ROADS FOR WHEELS

Make roads inside using masking tape or outside using chalk. Choose three or four children to ride their vehicles along the roads. The other children chant, *"Where are your wheels taking you?"* The riders chant back:

> *Over, under, up and down,*
> *Under, over, all around.*
> *(Each tells where he's going.)*

Switch drivers and continue.

BOOKS

BYRON BARTON – ***WHEELS***
STAN BERENSTAIN – ***BEARS ON WHEELS***
RAFFI – ***WHEELS ON THE BUS***
GAIL GIBBONS – ***TRAINS***
ANNE ROCKWELL – ***THRUWAY***

SAFETY FIRST

FOR OPENERS

MAKE A 'SAFETY SAM' STICK PUPPET OR USE ANOTHER PUPPET.
INTRODUCE HIM TO THE CHILDREN AND THEN SAY, *"I'M NEW HERE AND I
NEED TO LEARN ALL OF YOUR SAFETY RULES. I HOPE THAT YOU CAN HELP
ME. TELL ME, HOW CAN I BE SAFE WHILE PLAYING OUTSIDE?* (LET THE
CHILDREN RESPOND.) *I WANT TO TAKE A WALK AROUND THE
NEIGHBORHOOD. WHAT SHOULD I REMEMBER?* (RESPOND.) *ARE THERE ANY
SPECIAL SIGNS I NEED TO LOOK FOR?"* (RESPOND.) THEN HAVE *SAFETY
SAM* GET A PHONE CALL AND TALK TO SOMEONE. *"A FRIEND JUST CALLED
AND MY MOM IS GOING TO TAKE ME OVER TO HIS HOUSE TO PLAY.
WHAT SHOULD I DO IN THE CAR?"* TALK ABOUT CAR SAFETY AND ANY
OTHER SAFETY RULES THE CHILDREN THINK THAT *SAFETY SAM* SHOULD KNOW
ABOUT. LET HIM GO OFF TO A FRIEND'S HOUSE TO PLAY.
EXTENSION: PUT *SAFETY SAM* IN THE LANGUAGE CENTER FOR THE
CHILDREN TO USE DURING FREE CHOICE.

FINGERPLAYS

SIRENS

When the siren blows,
It seems to say,
"Clear the street.
Get out of the way."
    Dick Wilmes

STOP, DROP, AND ROLL

Clothes on fire,
Don't get scared.
STOP!
DROP!
And ROLL!

RED LIGHT

Red says STOP!
Green says GO!
Yellow says CAUTION!
Be sure you know.

168

STOP, LOOK AND LISTEN

Stop, look, and listen,
Before you cross the street.
Use your eyes and ears,
And then use your feet.

RECIPES

STOP LIGHTS

YOU'LL NEED

Rectangular crackers
Cream cheese
Cherry tomatoes
Yellow cheese slices
Green olives

TO MAKE: Cut the tomatoes, olives, and cheese slices into circles. Spread the cheese on the crackers and then add the *'red, yellow, and green lights.'*

FIELD TRIPS

• Visit a local hospital. Try to arrange a tour of the Emergency Room and an ambulance. Have one of the attendants explain to the children what happens when people have accidents and are brought to the Emergency Room for treatment.

• Take a *'Safety Walk'* with the children. As they are going around the neighborhood have them look for safety signs. Talk about what each one means. Have them also look for potentially dangerous situations such as a broken bottle on the ground, a tree branch across the sidewalk, or entrances and exits to and from parking lots and driveways.

LANGUAGE GAMES

SAFETY
NUMBERS

Get two telephones. Keep one and give the other one to a child. Say to the child, *"It is an emergency. What number would you dial for help?"* (Have the child tell you and then have the others repeat it.) Have the child hand the phone to another child. Say to that child, *"If you were playing at a friend's home and wanted to call your house, what number would you dial?"* (Response.) Have that child hand the phone to a third child. Say to that child, *"The person in the office wants to know your phone number. What would you tell her?"* (Response.) Continue on other days with other children and different situations.

SPIN FOR SAFETY

Make a Safety Spinner Board. Cut a large circle out of posterboard or use a pizza board. Divide the board into six to eight equal sections. Glue a picture onto each section. Cover the board with clear Contact®. Fasten a spinner in the middle.

Lay the Safety Spinner Board on the floor so that all of the children can see it. Let one child flick the spinner and tell the others what picture it stopped at. Have another child tell what safety rule the child in the picture is remembering. Talk about times when the children have been safe, just like the child in the picture. Spin again and remember another safety rule.
EXTENSION: Put the Safety Spinner Board in the Manipulative Center.

SAFETY EQUIPMENT

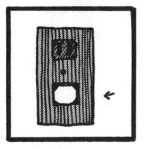

Put a variety of safety devices, such as a fire alarm, safety caps for electrical outlets, life preservers, reflective tape, a key, a seat belt, safety goggles, masks, and a hard hat in a box.

Show the children the box and tell them that you have some things in the box which help people be safe. Pull out the items one at a time, identify what they are, and talk about when to use them. Ask the children if they have ever used any of them or know someone who has.

WHAT WOULD YOU DO?

Present safety problems to the children and let them think about and express ideas about what they could do in each one. Here are a few for starters:

- You are playing with toy cars in your bedroom. All of a sudden someone yells, "*Juan, fire! Get out of the house!*" What would you do?

- Your family is going to the beach for the day. While there everyone is going for a ride in your uncle's boat. What should each member of the family remember while riding in the boat?

- You're outside riding a bike. You go around the corner too fast and fall off. You look down and your knee is bleeding. What would you do?

- You go to the park. How do you know what equipment is safe for you to play on?

- You are walking down the sidewalk with several friends. A car stops and someone in the car asks you and your friends if you'd like a candy bar. What would you and your friends do?

ACTIVE GAMES

STOP AND GO

Make a *'stop and go'* sign. Cut out a red and green circle. Glue the circles to the opposite sides of a paint stir stick.

Have all of the children stand up. Tell them to do a specific movement, such as hop on one foot, run in place, leap like a frog, or whatever. When they see the *'green sign'* they should begin doing the movement. When they see the *'red sign'* they should stop. Twist the sign back to *'green'* and they should go again. Continue with other movements.

RED LIGHT-GREEN LIGHT

Have the children stand in a straight line at one end of the room. Tell them that you are going to turn your back to them and say, "*Green light.*" When you do, they should begin sneaking towards you. Soon you'll turn around and say, "*Red light.*" They should freeze. Play until all of the children have reached you.

SING FOR SAFETY

Sing the song *'Safety First'* to the tune *'Here We Go 'Round the Mulberry Bush.'*

SAFETY FIRST

This is the way that we are safe,
We are safe, we are safe.
This is the way that we are safe,
Everyday of the year.

This is the way we cross the street
Look to the left, then to the right,
This is the way we cross the street,
Look left then right for safety.

This is the way we ride in the car,
Sit up straight, buckle our belts.
This is the way we ride in the car
Buckle our belts for safety.

This is the way we phone for help,
Dial 911, dial 911. (Use '0' in some locations.)
This is the way we phone for help,
Dial 911 for safety.

This is the way that we are safe,
We are safe, we are safe.
This is the way that we are safe,
Everyday of the year.
        Liz Wilmes

BOOKS

*VIRGINIA POULET — **BLUE BUGS SAFETY BOOK***
*JUDITH VIORST — **PLAY IT AGAIN SAM***
*DOROTHY CHLAD — **STRANGERS***

SUMMER COLORS

FOR OPENERS

HELP THE CHILDREN DECIDE WHICH COLORS ARE 'SUMMER COLORS' BY PLAYING A RIDDLE GAME. DESCRIBE OBVIOUS SUMMER SIGHTS IN NATURE. LET THE CHILDREN GUESS WHAT YOU ARE DESCRIBING. THEN TALK ABOUT THE COLORS. FOR EXAMPLE:

- *"WHAT IS BIG, HAS A CIRCULAR SHAPE, AND IS OFTEN FOUND IN THE SKY? IT CAUSES US TO BE HOT IN THE SUMMER."* (SUN)

- *"NOW I'M THINKING OF SOMETHING THAT FLIES, HAS DIFFERENT COLORS ON ITS WINGS, HAS ANTENNAE, AND LIKES TO REST ON FLOWERS."* (BUTTERFLY)

- *"I GROW IN DIRT. BECAUSE I USUALLY GROW VERY FAST, PEOPLE ARE ALWAYS CUTTING ME. IT IS OK THOUGH FOR THEM TO CUT ME. I JUST WISH THAT THEIR MACHINE DID NOT MAKE SO MUCH NOISE."* (GRASS)

- *"I AM BIG AND ROUND AND BRIGHTLY COLORED. PEOPLE ROLL ME, THROW ME, KICK ME, PUNCH ME, AND SOMETIMES EVEN USE ME FOR A PILLOW. MANY PEOPLE TAKE ME TO THE BEACH WITH THEM."* (BEACHBALL)

EXTENSION: MAKE A LIST OF THE THINGS WHICH YOU DESCRIBED. AFTER CIRCLE TIME DRAW A SMALL PICTURE OF EACH THING NEXT TO THE WORD. TAKE SMALL COLORED DOTS OR CONSTRUCTION PAPER CIRCLES AND GLUE THEM NEXT TO EACH PICTURE TO INDICATE THEIR COLOR/S. HANG THE CHART LOW ON A WALL FOR EVERYONE TO *READ.*

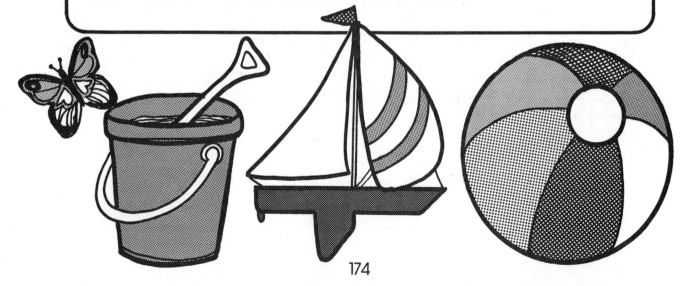

FINGERPLAYS

FRUIT STAND

A rainbow full of colors you will see,
When you visit the fruit stand today with me.
Cases full of oranges stacked so high.
Then bushels of red apples will catch your eye.

Yellow bananas, grapes that are green,
Pineapples, melons, and peaches between.
Berries in colors, red, black, and blue.
Cherries, pears, and tangerines too.
      Dick Wilmes

(Pass real fruit to the children. Read the rhyme slowly and have them listen for the names of the fruits which they are holding. When you name each child's fruit have the him show it to the others. Make a fruit salad later.)

THE COLOR GARDEN

Red is the apple,
Up in the tree,
Hiding behind a green leaf,
Winking at me.

Blue is the little bird,
Sitting in her nest,
Who just caught a big brown worm,
And is now taking a rest.

Orange is the butterfly
Floating near the brook.
Amid the purple violets,
Think I'll take a look.

Yellow is the sun up high
Warming up the day.
With colors all around me,
I'm a lucky girl (boy) I'd say.

Black is the little animal,
Who isn't far away.
The stripe of white upon his back,
Tells me not to stay.
      Dick Wilmes

(Read this rhyme to the children. Leave off the last word in each stanza and let the children fill in the rhyming word.)

WHAT COLOR ARE YOU WEARING

Leader: *Red, red, red, red,*
      Who is wearing red today?
      Red, red, red, red,
      Who is wearing red today?

All of the children wearing red say:
      I am wearing red today.
      Look at me and you will say
      Red, red, red, red,
      I am wearing red.

(Continue with other colors.)

THE FLOWER

Here's a green leaf
And here's a green leaf,
That, you see, makes two.
Here is a red bud,
That makes a flower.
Watch it bloom for you.

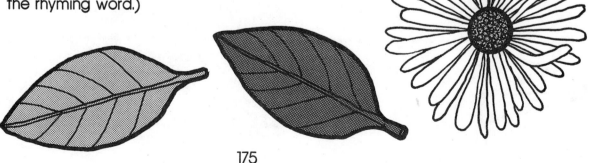

175

RECIPES

YOGURT SUNDAES

YOU'LL NEED

Yogurt
Assortment of fruit
    (berries, bananas, apples, apricots,
    peaches, pineapple, raisins, dates,
    coconut)
Assortment of nuts
    (walnuts, pecans, peanuts)
Assortment of seeds
Granola

TO MAKE: Set out an assortment of the fruit, nuts, and seeds. Have cups of yogurt ready. Let each person create his own sundae by topping his yogurt with an assortment of goodies.
from COME AND GET IT
by Kathleen Baxter

FIELD TRIPS

• Walk to a nearby park or grassy area. After playing, lie on the grass and look up in the sky. Look around. What colors do you see? Are you looking at the clouds? At trees? Buildings? Birds?

• Take a slow walk around the neighborhood. Look for flowers that are blooming. What colors are they? Are any of the flowers the same color? What color is most popular?

LANGUAGE GAMES

SUMMER SPIN

Make a color wheel. Cut a large circle out of white posterboard. Cut eight equal triangles to fit on the circle from different pieces of colored construction paper. Glue the triangles to the circle. Attach a spinner. Have colored pictures or plastic models of fruits and vegetables.

Hold up each fruit and vegetable and have the children name it. Pass the produce to the children. Then have one child flick the spinner and call out what color it stopped at. Have the children look at their fruits and vegetables and if theirs matches the color on the wheel they should put it near that color. Flick again and match the next color. Continue flicking and matching until all of the produce is around the color wheel.

COLORFUL BOUQUET	Bring a bouquet of freshly cut flowers to show the children. Pass the bouquet around. Let the children smell the flowers and look carefully at them to find all of the colors. Make a list of the colors as the children call them out.
THINK ABOUT COLORS	Cut a large square of felt for each of the summer colors. Hold each one up and have the children name it. Then put one color on the felt board, say pink. Have the children think of as many pink things as they can that are related to summer. Continue with the remaining colors.

LOOK AT THE BUBBLES	Get a bottle of commercial bubble solution. Dip the wand into the solution and blow a bubble or two. Have the children watch the bubble/s float away. What colors are in the bubble/s? Blow another bubble in a different direction. What colors are in that bubble? Are the colors in the bubbles the same or different? Which colors are the same? Different?

ACTIVE GAMES

MUSICAL COLORS	Have one of the children's favorite records available. Cut one large piece of construction paper for each 'summer color.' Lay the pieces in a large circle on the floor.
	Have the children form a circle around the outside of the pieces of construction paper. Have the children look at their clothes and then the pieces of paper. Begin the music. Have the children walk around the colored paper as the music plays. When you stop the music, each child should quickly walk to the color which matches something he is wearing. Have each child tell what the match is.

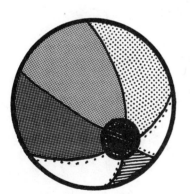

Now have each child think of his favorite summer color. Start the music and have the children walk again. When you stop it this time, each child should quickly walk to the piece which matches his favorite summer color. Continue with other types of matches.

BEACHBALL BOUNCE	Give several children blown-up beachballs. Talk about all of the different colors. Then say, "If you are holding a beachball which has 'red' on it, call out a friend's name and roll it to him." Continue.

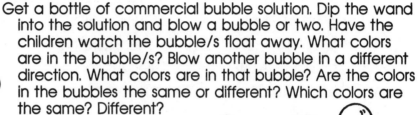

BOOKS

TANA TOBAN - ***IS IT RED?***
BILL MARTIN - ***BROWN BEAR, BROWN BEAR, WHAT DO YOU SEE?***
JOHN REISS - ***COLOR***

BOUNCING BALLS

FOR OPENERS

GATHER ENOUGH DIFFERENT TYPES OF BALLS (LARGE TO SMALL, SOFT TO FIRM, VARIETY OF TEXTURES) TO GIVE EACH CHILD AT LEAST ONE. PUT ALL OF THE BALLS IN A LARGE BASKET OR BAG. BRING THEM TO CIRCLE TIME.

TELL THE CHILDREN THAT YOU HAVE BROUGHT LOTS OF DIFFERENT BALLS FOR THEM TO EXAMINE. WALK AROUND AND HAVE EACH CHILD RANDOMLY TAKE A BALL OUT OF THE BASKET/BAG. TELL THEM TO CAREFULLY LOOK AT THE BALLS THEY'RE HOLDING, FEEL THEM, SMELL THEM, SHAKE THEM, AND SO ON. LET EACH CHILD TELL THE OTHERS ONE THING ABOUT HIS BALL.

NOW HAVE THE CHILDREN WHO THINK THEY ARE HOLDING SMALL BALLS STAND UP. HAVE THEM DROP AND CATCH THEIR BALLS. WHICH BALLS BOUNCED? HAVE THE CHILDREN WHOSE BALLS BOUNCED PUT THEM BACK INTO THE BASKET/BAG. HAVE THE CHILDREN WHOSE BALLS DID NOT BOUNCE PUT THEM IN THE BASKET/BAG. NOW HAVE THE CHILDREN HOLDING THE LARGER BALLS STAND. HAVE THEM DROP AND CATCH THEIR BALLS. TALK ABOUT WHICH ONES BOUNCED. HAVE THE CHILDREN WHOSE BALLS BOUNCED PUT THEM BACK INTO THE BASKET/BAG. HAVE THE REST OF THE CHILDREN PUT THEIR BALLS BACK INTO THE BASKET/BAG.

FINGERPLAYS

HERE'S A BALL

Here's a ball,
And here's a ball,
And a great big ball I see.

Shall we count them?
Are you ready?
One! Two! Three!

I'M BOUNCING

I'm bouncing, bouncing everywhere.
I bounce and bounce into the air.
I'm bouncing, bouncing like a ball.
I bounce and bounce, and then down I fall.

RECIPES

PEANUT BUTTER BALLS

YOU'LL NEED

1/2 cup peanut butter
1/2 cup honey
3/4 to 1 cup of powdered milk
Coconut, chopped nuts, seeds,
   dried parsley (optional)

TO MAKE: Put the peanut butter and
honey in a bowl and mix well. Add the dry
milk and stir again until well mixed. (Add
more dried milk if necessary.) Divide the
mixture into small pieces and roll it into
balls. Roll the balls in a variety of toppings.
Serve with juice and bread sticks.

FIELD TRIPS

- Take a *'Ball Walk'* around the neighborhood with the children. Have
them look for and watch people who are using balls either in their play or
work. What kind of balls are they using? How are they using them? Do they
look like they are having fun?

CLASSROOM VISITORS

- Ask a parent who juggles for a hobby to come and show your children
several juggling routines. Ask him/her to juggle balls as well as other things
s/he might like to use. Let the children try their skill at juggling, by tossing
one or two balls into the air and then catching them.

LANGUAGE GAMES

HOW BIG
IS IT?

Bring a variety of different sized balls to circle time. Pass
out three or four of them to different children. Have the
children hold up the balls for everyone to see. Have all
of the children look at the balls and pick out the largest
one. The child holding that ball should lay it on the floor
for everyone to see. Have the children holding balls
hold them up high again. Have the children look at
them and pick out the next largest one. Have the child
with that ball lay it next to the biggest one. Continue
with the remaining balls. Talk about the different sizes.
   Pick up the balls, put them back in the bag and
then pull out several more. Play the game again.

BOUNCING BALL

Before circle time put a styrofoam ball on a pencil or short dowel rod. Bring it to circle time and tell the children that you have brought a special *'bouncing ball'* to show them. As you are talking, move the ball up and down as if it were bouncing. Hand the *'bouncing ball'* to several children and let them *'bounce'* it around.

Then give the *'bouncing ball'* to a child and tell him to pick a spot in the room where he would like the *'ball'* to land after it has *'bounced'* around. (He should keep the spot a secret.) After the child has chosen his spot tell him to walk towards his secret spot *'bouncing'* the ball. As he is *'bouncing'* the *'ball'* the other children should chant:

> *Bouncing, bouncing, bouncing, ball,*
> *Where will you land? Where will you fall?*
> *Up and down you bounce along.*
> *Where will you be at the end of our song?*

When the children have finished chanting, the child with the *'bouncing ball'* should let it land and the children call out where it is resting. Continue in this manner letting other children take turns *'bouncing the ball'* around the room.

BALL TALK

Bring the variety of balls which you used at the *'For Opener'* activity to circle time. Use them to talk about opposites. For example pass around a ball which has a rough coating and let the children feel it. Then pass around a ball which has a smooth coating. Talk about the different textures. You could pass around a large beach ball and a small ping pong ball. You could pass a ball that is very soft and one that is very hard.

Now let the children do *'opposite'* activities with the balls. Give two children each the same type of ball. Tell one child to hold the ball very still and the other child to bounce his ball as fast as he can. Talk about what the children are doing with the balls. Give two more children identical balls. Tell one child to bounce his ball high and the other one to bounce his ball low. Talk. Have two children roll a ball to each other slowly, then fast. Have a child hold a ball close to his body and another child hold it as far away from his body as possible. Continue with other opposites.

YES OR NO

Play a 'yes-no' game with the children. You say different things, some of which pertain to balls and some of which do not. The children should pretend that their heads are balls. If the children think that what you said is about a ball then they should bounce their heads up and down as if to say yes. If they do not think it pertains to balls, then they should roll their heads side to side as if to say no. For example:

- "You can bounce balls." (yes)
- "Most balls are round." (yes)
- "Balls grow in the ground." (no)
- And so on.

ACTIVE GAMES

BE A BALL

Tell the children that they are going to be great big bouncing balls. Have them begin by bouncing their heads around. After their heads are bouncing tell them to bounce their shoulders too. Continue adding different body parts all the way down to their feet. As the children are bouncing all around the room, have them say this rhyme:

<u>BOUNCING BALLS</u>

We're just great big bouncing balls,
Bouncing, bouncing, bouncing all.
Bouncing, bouncing everywhere.
Up and down in the air.

HERE'S A BALL

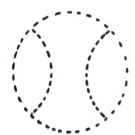

Teach the children the rhyme below. Then give one child a ball. Have everyone say the rhyme stopping after the word "*to*" in the second line. The child with the ball should name a person and roll the ball to that child. Then that child should roll it back again while everyone finishes the rhyme. Then the first child gives the ball to a child sitting next to him and everyone can repeat the game.

Here is a ball,
I'll roll it to _____.
Please catch it and roll it,
Right back to me.
                          Dick Wilmes

BOOKS

BARBRO LINDGREN – *SAM'S BALL*
NANCY TAFURI – *BALL BOUNCED*

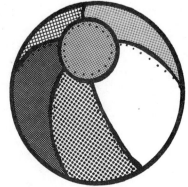

SUMMER BREEZES

FOR OPENERS

BLOW UP A COLORED BALLOON FOR EACH OF THE CHILDREN. ATTACH A SHORT STRING TO EACH BALLOON AND THEN TIE A RUBBER CANNING RING TO THE OTHER END OF EACH STRING. BRING THE BUNCH OF BALLOONS TO CIRCLE TIME.

WALK AROUND THE CIRCLE AND GIVE EACH CHILD A BALLOON. HAVE HIM SLIP THE CANNING RING AROUND HIS WRIST OR SIMPLY HOLD IT IN HIS HAND. TELL THE CHILDREN TO HOLD THEIR WRISTS/HANDS AS STILL AS THEY POSSIBLY CAN. THEN ASK THEM WHY THEY THINK THEIR BALLOONS ARE MOVING. AFTER TALKING ABOUT IT, ASK THEM TO THINK OF DIFFERENT WAYS THAT, STILL SITTING IN ONE PLACE, THEY COULD MAKE THEIR BALLOONS MOVE EVEN MORE. (TALK ABOUT AND LET EVERYONE TRY THE DIFFERENT IDEAS.) WHICH IDEA MOVES THE BALLOONS THE MOST? LEAST?

GO OUTSIDE AND LET THE CHILDREN FLY THEIR BALLOONS LIKE KITES.

FINGERPLAYS

BALLOONS

This is the way we blow our balloons,
Blow, blow, blow.

This is the way we fly our balloons,
Look at them go!

WIND TRICKS

The wind is full of tricks today.
It blew my daddy's hat away.
It chased our paper down the street.
It almost blew me off my feet.
It makes the trees and brushes dance.
Just listen to it howl and prance.

OCEAN BREEZE

Ocean breeze blowing,
Feet kick and splash,
Ocean waves breaking
On rocks with a crash.

RECIPES

COOL AS A BREEZE

YOU'LL NEED

Fruit juice
Ice cube trays
Popsicle sticks

TO MAKE: Pour the fruit juice into the ice cube trays and put the trays in the freezer. Once the fruit cubes are slightly firm, push a popsicle stick into each one. When the juice is frozen, pop the cubes out of the tray and enjoy eating them in the shade. Can you feel a breeze?

FIELD TRIPS

• Visit a local airport to watch the small airplanes land and take off. Look for the windsocks. Which way is the wind blowing? Are the airplanes taking off into the wind, with the wind behind them, or are the pilots using all of the runways?

LANGUAGE GAMES

RHYMES
WITH BREEZE

Have the children think of words which rhyme with breeze such as: please, squeeze, trapeze, cheese, seize, tease, ease, skis, these, sneeze, etc.

Encourage the children to each choose a rhyming word and think of how to use it in a sentence. Have one of the children whisper his sentence to you. You whisper the sentence to a child next to you. The children should keep passing the sentence until you say, *"Stop."* Then have the last child repeat what was just whispered to him.

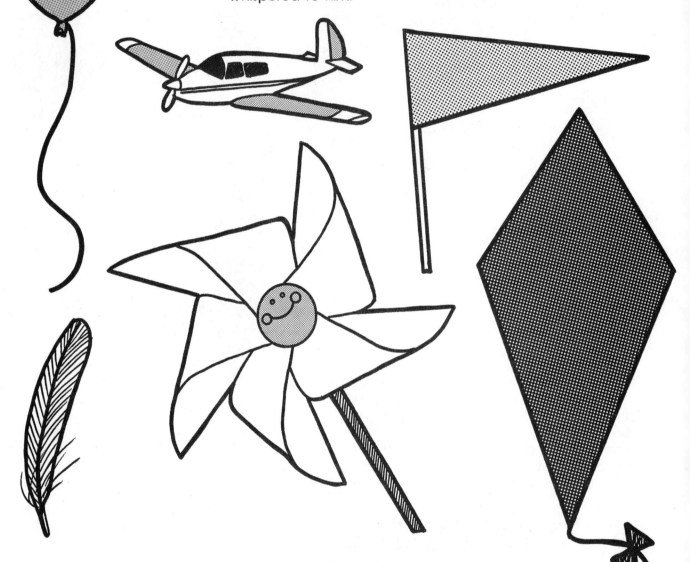

BREEZE CHAT

Cut out felt shapes (balloon, kite, feather, plane, pennant, pinwheel) of things which move in the breeze. Bring these and the felt board to circle time.

Lay the pieces on the floor so that all of the children can see them. Have a child pick one of the shapes, name it, and put it on the felt board. Encourage everyone to talk about times when he might have played with the object in the wind. After each child relates an incident, clap for him. Continue with the other pieces.

BREEZING ALONG	Use the balloons from the *'For Openers'* activity or blow up more balloons. Give one to each child. Walk outside with the children. Spread out several picnic blankets and have the children sit down with plenty of room between each other. Tell the children to look up in the sky. What do they see? Now have the children lie down holding their balloons by the rubber rings and imagining that they are floating in the breeze. What do they see? How does it feel? Where would they like the breeze to blow them? What would they take with them? How will they get back home?
MAKING SUMMER BREEZES	Have the children make a breeze by taking a deep breath and blowing out. Now encourage them to think of other ways to make breezes. Try each of their ideas.

ACTIVE GAMES

BLOWING IN THE BREEZE	Put batteries in your tape recorder and bring it outside along with several of the children's favorite instrumental tapes. Have various colors of crepe paper streamers for the children. Pass them out and begin the music. Encourage the children to dance all around the playground holding their streamers so that they blow in the summer breeze.

BREEZE ALONG	Have a basket or large tote bag filled with frisbees, kites, wooden airplanes, plastic lids, pinwheels, and feathers. Take the bag outside each nice day and have the children play with the different toys. Talk about the breezes and how they effect each toy.

BOOKS

DOUGLAS FLORIAN – *A SUMMER DAY*
ARTHUR GETZ – *TAR BEACH*
HOWARD KNOTTS – *SUMMER CAT*
GENE ZION – *THE SUMMER SNOWMAN*

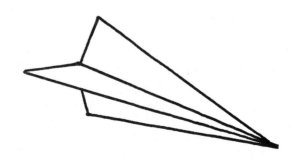

FIREWORKS

FOR OPENERS

SAY TO THE CHILDREN, "*LET'S PRETEND THAT IT IS THE NIGHT OF THE FOURTH OF JULY. WE'RE SITTING ON A BIG BLANKET WAITING FOR THE FIREWORKS DISPLAY TO BEGIN. WHO IS WITH YOU?* (ANSWERS) *WHAT ARE YOU GOING TO SEE?* (ANSWERS) HOW DOES IT SOUND? (ANSWERS) *WHAT SAFETY PRECAUTIONS WERE TAKEN BEFORE, DURING, AND AFTER THE FIREWORKS?"* (ANSWERS)

EXTENSION: AT THE END OF THE DISCUSSION BRING OUT A PIECE OF POSTERBOARD AND A MARKER. WRITE AT THE TOP *'FIREWORKS TONIGHT.'* HAVE THE CHILDREN DICTATE A STORY TO YOU ABOUT WATCHING FIREWORKS. WRITE DOWN WHAT THEY SAY. HANG THE STORY IN THE LANGUAGE CENTER. READ IT OFTEN AND ADD ANY OTHER COMMENTS THE CHILDREN MIGHT WANT TO MAKE.

FINGERPLAYS

BOOM BANG!

Boom, bang, boom, bang!
Rumpety, lumpety, hump!
Zoom, zam, zoom, zam!
Clippety, clappety, clump!

Rustles and bustles
And swishes and zings!
What wonderful noises
Fireworks bring!

BIRTHDAY FIREWORKS

Red, white and blue,
Happy birthday to you.
Way up high,
Lighting up the sky.
Happy Birthday to you!
Vohny Moehling

RECIPES

RED, WHITE, AND BLUE KABOBS

YOU'LL NEED

Strawberries
Pineapple
Blueberries
Cocktail toothpicks

TO MAKE: Clean and slice the fruit. Have the children place a blueberry, strawberry, and a piece of pineapple on each toothpick. Take the kabobs outside and pretend there are fireworks in the sky as you enjoy the snack.

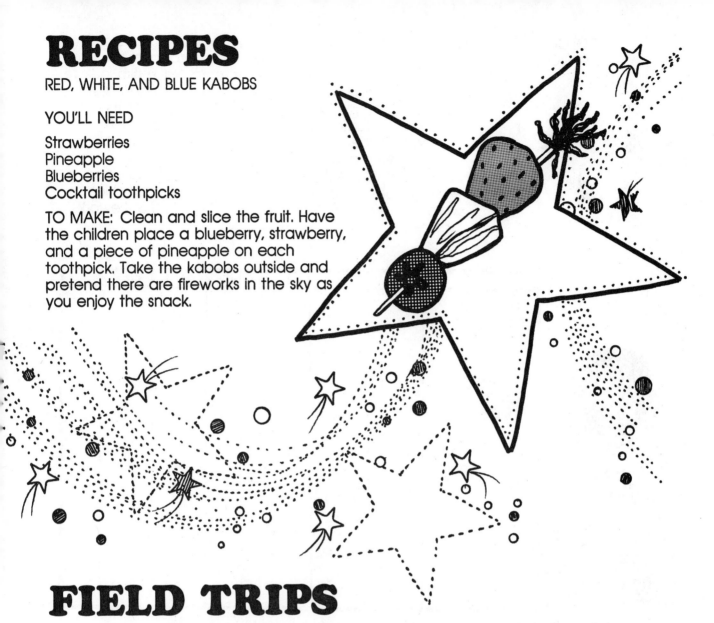

FIELD TRIPS

• Bring a wide variety of colors of construction paper to circle time. Ask each child what his/her favorite color of fireworks is. Cut a strip of construction paper to match that color and then give it to him/her.

Now take a *'Fireworks Walk.'* Have the children bring their strips of color and look for things on the walk that are that color. After the walk, during the free choice time, talk to each child about the things s/he saw on the walk. Write down on his/her strip what s/he saw. Encourage the children to take their strips home.

LANGUAGE GAMES

BANG OR FIZZLE

Tell the children to think about fireworks. Then say, *"I'm going to say a word. After I say it, you say, 'Bang' if the word reminds you of fireworks and 'fizzle' if it does not."* (Here are some firework words to get you started: noisy, night, colorful, kaboom, bright, sky, big, red, green, etc.)

COLORFUL FIREWORKS

Before circle time find and cut out colorful pictures of fireworks. Glue each picture to a piece of construction paper. Hand the first picture to a child. Have him look at the fireworks and name one color he sees and pass it to a child sitting next to him. That child looks at the picture and names another color in it. Keep passing it around until the children have named all of the colors. Continue with another picture.

EXTENSION: Make a chart to keep track of the colors in each picture. Look at the chart and figure out which were the most and least popular colors in the fireworks pictures.

	red	green	blue	white	gold	pink	
Amy	/				/	/	
John		/	/				
Kristin			/		/		
Chris		/					
Jose		/			/		
Danny							
Beth	/			/			
Kate						/	

FELT BOARD FIREWORKS

Cut different lengths of colored felt to use in making a variety of fireworks. Bring the felt board and strips to circle time.

Using the strips, make a fireworks display on the board. Point to each color and have the children name it. Have a child come up and take one strip off. As he is doing it have the others call out what color it is. Continue until the entire display has fizzled. Have the children cover their eyes while you 'shoot off' another display on the felt board and play again. Repeat the game.

FIRECRACKER FEELINGS

Have the children think about why they like and do not like fireworks. Then encourage them to share their feelings by having them say, "*I like fireworks because* _____" or "*I do not like fireworks because* _____."

ACTIVE GAMES

FIRECRACKER
DANCE

Before circle time have the children make 'firecrackers' by gluing different colors of crepe paper streamers to toilet paper rolls. Gather a variety of patriotic recordings such as 'Stars and Stripes Forever,' 'Yankee Doodle Dandy,' 'You're a Grand Old Flag,' etc.

Have the children bring their 'firecrackers' to circle time. Play a variety of songs and let the children wave, shake, and snap their 'firecrackers' while dancing to the music.

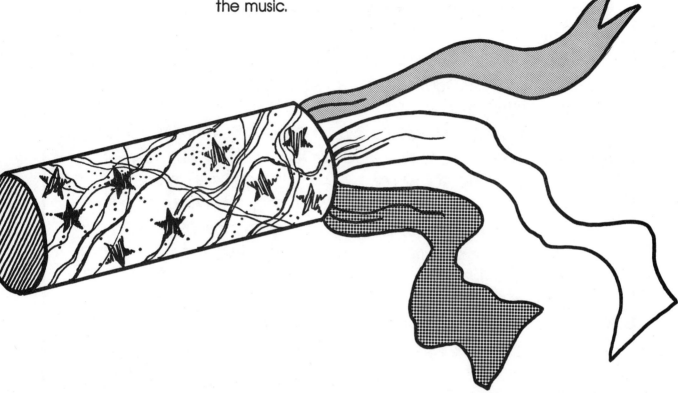

BOOM,
BANG, FIZZLE

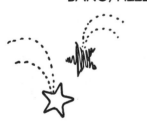

All the children should stand. You start slowly and emphatically saying words which refer to fireworks bursting in the sky (boom, bang, zam, zing, zap). As you say the words, the children should use their whole bodies to pretend to be fireworks. When you say, "Fizzle," they should slowly fade to the ground. Let the children rest and then shoot off more fireworks by saying another series of words. Continue until the colorful display is over.

BOOKS

PETER SPIER – **CRASH! BANG! BOOM!**
BARBARA JOOSSE – **FOURTH OF JULY**
HOLLY KELLER – **HENRY'S FOURTH OF JULY**
DOROTHY CHLAD – **MATCHES, LIGHTERS AND FIRECRACKERS ARE NOT TOYS**

PICNICS

FOR OPENERS

BEFORE CIRCLE TIME PACK A BASKET WITH PAPER NAPKINS, FINGER GELATIN (RECIPES) CUT INTO INDIVIDUAL SERVINGS, A PICNIC BLANKET OR SHEET, AND THE BOOK, *'THE BEARS PICNIC'* BY STANLEY AND JAN BERENSTAIN.

BRING THE BASKET TO CIRCLE TIME AND SAY TO THE CHILDREN, *"WE'RE GOING TO WALK AROUND THE ROOM AND LOOK FOR THE PERFECT SPOT TO HAVE AN INSIDE PICNIC SNACK. I'VE ALREADY PACKED THE BASKET AND I'VE BROUGHT A BLANKET, SO LET'S GO. MAKE A 'TRAIN' BEHIND ME. KEEP YOUR EYES OPEN AS WE CHUG AROUND THE ROOM.* (WEAVE SLOWLY AROUND THE ROOM ELIMINATING UNACCEPTABLE SPOTS.) *I THINK IT WOULD BE TOO WARM HERE IN THE SUN. THIS SPOT MIGHT BE TOO BUMPY. WOULD THIS SPOT BE BIG ENOUGH FOR ALL OF US TO PICNIC?* (CONTINUE UNTIL YOU'VE REACHED YOUR CIRCLE TIME AREA.) *DOES THIS LOOK LIKE THE PERFECT SPOT?* (ANSWER.)

"HELP ME SPREAD OUT THE BLANKET SO THAT WE CAN SIT DOWN AND SEE WHAT'S IN OUR PICNIC BASKET. (WHEN EVERYONE IS SITTING ON THE BLANKET, HOLD UP THE NAPKINS.) *WHAT ARE THESE?* (ANSWER.) *WHAT SHOULD WE DO WITH THEM?* (DISCUSS AND DO IT. HOLD UP THE SNACK.) *WHAT DID I PACK FOR US TO SNACK ON?"* (DISCUSS AND PASS THE SNACK.)

WHILE EVERYONE IS EATING TALK ABOUT HOW PICNICING INSIDE IS DIFFERENT THAN PICNICING OUTSIDE. (FOR EXAMPLE: IS THERE A BREEZE? ARE THERE ANTS? IS THE SUN SHINING ON THEM? ARE THERE CLOUDS FLOATING OVERHEAD?)

AFTER YOU HAVE FINISHED WITH THE SNACK, READ THE BOOK YOU TUCKED INTO THE BOTTOM OF THE BASKET.

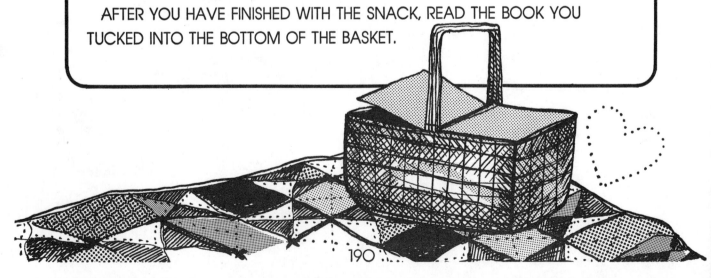

FINGERPLAYS

THERE'S A BUG ON ME

1, 2, 3, there's a bug on me.
Where did he go?
I don't know.
(Talk with the children about bugs
they might see at a picnic.)

TEETER-TOTTER

Up and down and up and down,
On my teeter-totter.
Up and down and up and down,
Oh my it's getting hotter.
Up and down and up and down,
Over grass and trees and water.

OUR PICNIC

Good morning, Mr. Sunshine,
How are you today?
We're going to have a picnic
And laugh and sing and play.

RECIPES

FINGER GELATIN

YOU'LL NEED

3 envelopes unflavored gelatin
1-12 oz. can frozen grape juice concentrate
16 oz. water

TO MAKE: Unthaw the concentrate and pour it into a bowl. Add the gelatin to the concentrate. Bring the water to a boil, pour it in the bowl, and stir until the gelatin is dissolved.

Pour the mixture into a lightly greased dish (9" × 13") and set it in the refrigerator for several hours until firm. Cut the gelatin into individual size squares and store in an airtight container.

FIELD TRIPS

• Take opportunities to go on various picnics. Have a playground picnic, park picnic, indoor picnic, etc. Take along special pieces of equipment such as a parachute, kite, or rhythm instruments to play with while at the picnic.

191

LANGUAGE GAMES

PICNIC
PICTURES

Using the shapes provided, make cards for each of the children, representing partial pictures of different things associated with picnics.

At circle time pass out the pictures and have the children look at them carefully. Call on a child and have him show his picture to the others. As he is holding it up have him say what he thinks the picture is. Continue with the other children. Mix up the cards and play again.

PICNIC
BASKET

Point to a child and have him say one thing he would put in a picnic basket. Point to another child and have him repeat the first item and add another one. Continue until your pretend picnic basket is full.

WHAT'S
MISSING?

Bring a picnic basket filled with picnic goodies. Take two things out of your basket and show them to the children. Have the children close their eyes. Hide one object behind your back. Tell the children to open their eyes and call out which one is missing. Play again. Increase the number of objects as the children master the game.

PICNIC MEMORIES

Enjoy this activity after one of the class picnics. Bring a plastic tablecloth and permanent markers to circle time. Have the children sit around the cloth. Talk about the picnic. Then pass out the markers. Have the children draw on the plastic tablecloth what they ate, played, or remember about the picnic. When finished ask the children to give the picnic a title and print it in the middle of the cloth. Let it dry, fold it up, and use it at your next picnic.

ACTIVE GAMES

ON A PICNIC WE WILL GO

Before circle time make one felt picnic basket and a variety of felt picnic pieces for the children.

Put the picnic basket on the felt board. Let each child choose a picnic piece. Tell the children that they are going on a pretend picnic, but first must fill the basket.

Have the children stand up and hold hands. (Keep picnic pieces.) Teach them the picnic song to the tune of *'The Farmer In The Dell.'* As they sing the first verse of the song have them walk around in a circle. Stop. Call on a child to add his piece to the basket. As he does, have the group sing the second verse. Continue, always changing the verse to match the new child and his object.

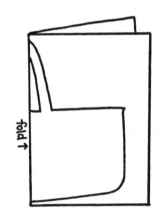

ON A PICNIC WE WILL GO

On a picnic we will go.
On a picnic we will go.
Let's fill our basket up.
On a picnic we will go.

(Child's name) brings a blanket.
(Child's name) brings a blanket.
Let's fill our basket up.
On a picnic we will go.

PICNIC GAMES

Play different picnic-type games, such as frisbee toss with plastic lids, peanuts in the grass, rope games, hide-and-go-seek, water balloon toss, and so on.

BOOKS

CINDY WHEELER – **MARMALADE'S PICNIC**
ERIC HILL – **SPOT'S FIRST PICNIC**
EMILY ARNOLD McCULLY – **PICNIC**
VINCENT GABRIELLE – **ERNEST AND CELESTINE'S PICNIC**
AILEEN FISHER – **ONCE WE WENT ON A PICNIC**

BLAST-OFF

FOR OPENERS

TAKE AN IMAGINARY TRIP TO THE MOON WITH THE CHILDREN. SAY, "TODAY WE ARE GOING TO PRETEND THAT WE ARE GOING TO THE MOON. IT IS 240,000 MILES AWAY. THAT IS VERY FAR!! USUALLY IT WOULD TAKE US ABOUT FOUR DAYS IN A SPACESHIP TO GET THERE, BUT TODAY WE ARE GOING TO MAKE A VERY FAST TRIP.

"WHILE WE ARE SITTING DOWN LET'S PUT ON OUR SPACESUITS. (DO IT.) NOW OUR BOOTS, GLOVES, AND HELMETS. WE MUST FASTEN OUR SEAT BELTS BEFORE THE FINAL COUNTDOWN. (DO IT.) LET'S COUNTDOWN TO BLAST OFF, 10, 9, 8, 7, 6, 5, 4, 3, 2, 1 . . . . LIFT OFF. (COUNT TOGETHER.) NOW THAT OUR SHIP IS OUT OF THE EARTH'S ATMOSPHERE WE CAN TAKE OFF OUR SEAT BELTS AND FLOAT IN THE AIR. THERE IS NO GRAVITY IN SPACE SO WE DON'T WEIGH ANYTHING. WE ARE WEIGHTLESS. WE CAN PUSH OFF ONE WALL OF THE SPACESHIP AND WE'LL CONTINUE MOVING THROUGH THE AIR UNTIL WE TOUCH ANOTHER WALL. (DO THIS WITH THE CHILDREN.)

"WE BETTER BUCKLE UP AGAIN BECAUSE THE MOON IS IN SIGHT. LOOK OUT OF YOUR WINDOW AT THE BEAUTIFUL VIEW OF THE STARS ABOVE AND THE EARTH BELOW. (DO IT.) PREPARE FOR LANDING. WE'RE DOWN. BEFORE WE TAKE A WALK ON THE MOON, WE'LL HAVE TO MAKE SURE THAT THERE ARE NO LEAKS IN OUR SPACESUITS, OR WE COULD BOIL OR TURN TO ICE WHEN WE STEP OUT OF THE SHIP. WE MUST EACH STRAP OXYGEN TANKS ON OUR BACKS SO THAT WE HAVE AIR TO BREATHE.

"NOW WE ARE ON THE MOON. (PRETEND TO WALK ON THE MOON.) SCOOP UP SOME MOON ROCKS TO TAKE BACK WITH YOU. (DO IT.) OVER THERE IS THE UNITED STATES FLAG LEFT BY NEIL ARMSTRONG, THE FIRST PERSON TO WALK ON THE MOON. WE BETTER HEAD BACK TO THE SHIP, IT'S TIME TO GO. GOOD-BYE MOON. (WAVE GOOD-BYE. GET BACK IN THE SHIP. TALK ABOUT SPACE AS YOU GET CLOSER TO PLANET EARTH.)

"PREPARE FOR LANDING ON PLANET EARTH. WE MADE IT TO THE MOON AND BACK. AFTER YOU TAKE OFF YOUR SPACESUIT I'LL GIVE YOU EACH A MOON MEDAL TO COMMEMORATE YOUR TRIP."

EXTENSION: DECORATE THE STAR AT THE ART TABLE.

FINGERPLAYS

MOON RIDE

Do you want to go up with me to the moon?
Let's get in our rocket and blast-off soon!
Faster and faster we reach to the sky.
Isn't it fun to be able to fly?

BEND AND STRETCH

Bend and stretch, reach for the stars,
Here comes Jupiter, there goes Mars.
Bend and stretch, reach for the sky.
Stand on tip-e-toe, oh, so high.

STARS

I watch the stars come out at night,
I wonder where they get their light.
I don't think they'll ever fall,
So, I'll reach up and pick them all.

BLAST-OFF

3, 2, 1, blast-off!
Up and up and up we go.
In our rocketship,
Very fast not slow.

RECIPES

ASTRONAUT BARS

YOU'LL NEED

2 T. butter
1/4 cup peanut butter
1/2 cup honey
1/8 cup chopped nuts
1-1/2 t. cinnamon
1 t. vanilla
1/2 cup raisins
2 cups whole bran cereal

TO MAKE: Heat the butter, peanut butter, and honey until the mixture is hot, but not boiling. Add chopped nuts, cinnamon, and vanilla. Stir until blended. Stir in raisins and bran cereal. Spoon the mixture into a lightly greased eight inch square dish. Press the mixture firmly into the pan. Chill and cut into squares.

You might eat this on one of your flights to the moon.

195

LANGUAGE GAMES

STAR SEARCH

Cut a star out of white or yellow paper and bring it to circle time.

Give it to a child to hide someplace in the room, while the others cover their eyes. After the star is hidden, have the children uncover their eyes and begin guessing where the star is. As they guess closer to where the star is hidden, the child can say, *"The star is getting brighter."* When the guesses are getting farther away, the child can say, *"The star is getting dimmer."* Encourage the child to give the other children clues to where the star is hiding, but not to tell the exact location. After the star is found have the children sing *'Twinkle, Twinkle Little Star.'*

SPACE TALK

Introduce your children to space terms:

Oxygen tanks
Experiments
Rockets
Launch pad
Moon rover
Parachutes
Space shuttle
Satellite

Astronaut
Space walk
Countdown
Blast-off
Splashdown
Booster rockets
Orbit

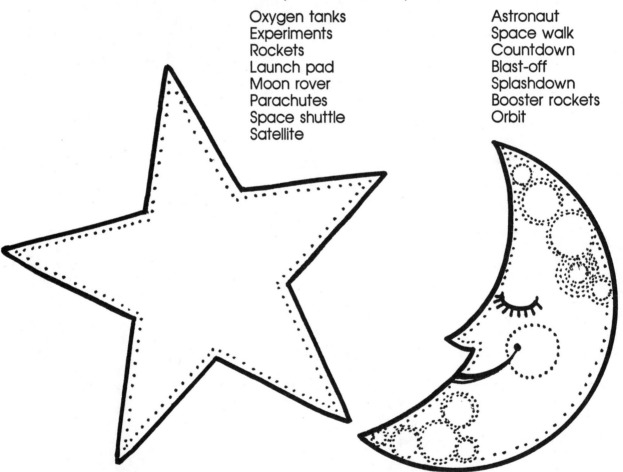

WHERE'S THE STAR?

Cut out a felt star and moon. Bring them to circle time along with the felt board.

Put the moon on the board. Call on a child to come up to the board. Hand him the star and whisper to him where he should put the star in relation to the moon. (On, next to, under, over, far away from, on top of the moon.) Let him put the star where you've said and then turn to the other children. They should call out where the star is. Take the star off of the board and give it to another child and continue to play.

| FAVORITE THINGS | Cut out a large rocketship from posterboard. Bring it and a marker to circle time. |

Ask the children, *"If you were going on a trip to the moon and could only take one thing with you, what would you bring?"* Write the child's name and what he would take in the rocketship.

Hang the rocketship on the door so that parents can easily read it when they come to school. After a while cut it up and give each child the piece of the rocketship with his name on it. Have him take it home and tell his family about his trip to the moon.

ACTIVE GAMES

LAUNCHING PADS

Each child should have a carpet square for a personal launching pad. Have the children stand on the *'pads'* and practice different maneuvers, such as:

- Have the children squat down and when you say, *"Blast-off,"* jump as high as they can.

- Have the children stand on the *'launching pads'* and countdown to blast-off.

- Have the children squat down preparing for the lift-off. You countdown. Stop before you get to the blast-off number. Have the children relax and talk about the possible reasons you might have had for stopping the countdown.

- Have the children stand on their *'pads.'* Call out the different parts of a spacesuit. Each child should check to see that he is wearing everything. Then blast-off.

ASTRONAUTS IN TRAINING

Set up an obstacle course for the children to go through so that they become familiar with space travel.

- Begin by walking down a masking tape strip as if boarding a space vehicle.

- Walk the balance beam as if on a tethered space walk.

- Bounce on a bouncer to experience weightlessness.

- Ride a trike pretending it is the moon rover.

- Rock in a rocking boat to experience a splashdown.

- Climb over a climber to exit the space craft.

BOOKS

JILL MURPHY – ***WHAT NEXT, BABY BEAR!***
ERICH FUCHS – ***JOURNEY TO THE MOON***
EZRA JACK KEATS – ***REGARDS TO THE MAN IN THE MOON***

ON THE ROAD

FOR OPENERS

BRING THE CHILDREN'S FAVORITE PUPPET AND A SUITCASE TO CIRCLE TIME. TELL THE CHILDREN THAT (PUPPET'S NAME) IS GOING TO TAKE A TRIP. INCLUDE WHERE HE IS GOING AND SOME OF THE THINGS THAT HE MIGHT DO WHILE HE IS AWAY. THEN BRING OUT THE SUITCASE. TELL THE CHILDREN THAT (PUPPET'S NAME) WANTS THE CHILDREN TO HELP HIM PACK.

PUT THE SUITCASE IN THE MIDDLE OF THE FLOOR AND OPEN IT UP. HAVE A CHILD CALL OUT SOMETHING THAT HE THINKS (PUPPET'S NAME) SHOULD TAKE ON THE TRIP. LOOK AT THE PUPPET. IF THE PUPPET WANTS TO TAKE IT ON THE TRIP HE SHOULD SHAKE HIS HEAD 'YES' AND IF HE DOES NOT WANT TO TAKE IT HE SHOULD SHAKE HIS HEAD 'NO.' CONTINUE UNTIL THE SUITCASE IS ALL PACKED. CLOSE IT UP AND WISH (PUPPET'S NAME) A GOOD TRIP.

FINGERPLAYS

HELPING MOTHER DRIVE

Open the car door,
Climb inside.
I get to help my mother drive!
Fasten the seat belt,
Shut the door,
Start the motor.
Hear it roar?
Brrr! Brrr! Brrr!

WHEELS ON THE BUS

The wheels on the bus go 'round and 'round,
'Round and 'round, 'round and 'round.
The wheels on the bus go 'round and 'round,
All through the town.

The people on the bus go up and down,

The wipers on the bus go swish, swish, swish,

The driver on the bus says, "Move on back,"

The door on the bus goes open and shut,

The babies on the bus go, "Wa, wa, wa,"

RECIPES

ROAD SNACK

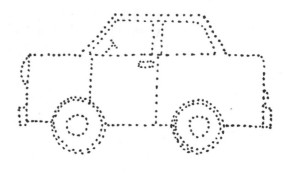

YOU'LL NEED

Several types of nutritious cereals
Pretzel bits
Raisins
Small paper plates

TO MAKE: Mix all of the above ingredients together. Put them in a closed container.

At snack time gather all of the children and give them each a paper plate to use for a steering wheel as they 'drive' outside to the playground. When you get to a shady spot, take a break. Pass the snack around and let each child take a handful and put it on his plate. After snack read or tell a story and then continue your 'pretend drive' back to the classroom.

FIELD TRIPS

• Make arrangements to visit a car dealership in your area. Have the children see the new cars and trucks on the lot and then get a tour of the service department. Have one of the employees tell the children what the mechanics are doing to the different vehicles that are in for servicing.

• Have the children sit on the sidewalk looking at the street. As each vehicle goes by, talk about it. What was it? What color was it? How many people were in it?

CLASSROOM VISITORS

• If one of your children's parents is an auto mechanic, have him/her visit the class and tell the children what s/he does. Maybe s/he could bring some of his/her tools to show the children.

LANGUAGE GAMES

BEEP, BEEP

Read a book about transportation, stopping now and then to substitute "Beep, beep," for the key word/s in the story. After you say this the children should fill in the word/thoughts they think would be appropriate to the storyline. Continue reading and see if the children's ideas agreed with the author's.

VEHICLE WATCH

Cut out a large posterboard car shape. Bring it and a marker to circle time.

Ask the children to close their eyes and picture a road. Have them think about the different types of vehicles they have seen going along the road. Now have them open their eyes and name all of the vehicles they thought of. Write their ideas on the large car shape. Hang the car on a wall or the classroom door.

EXTENSION: Have the children look for pictures of different vehicles and paste them next to the words which name those vehicles.

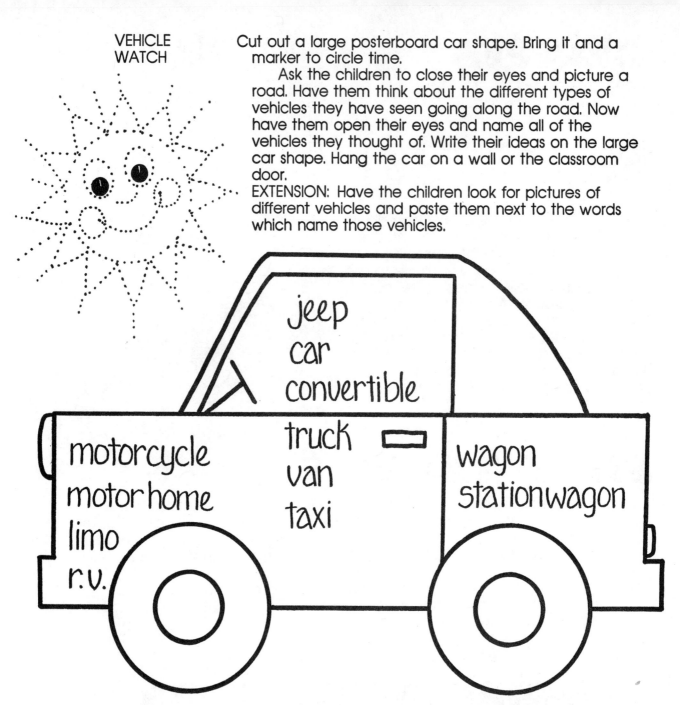

jeep
car
convertible
truck
van
taxi
motorcycle
motorhome
limo
r.v.
wagon
stationwagon

DRIVE THROUGH TOWN

Make a simple neighborhood map with the children or use the one you made during 'In Your Neighborhood.' Bring the map and several miniature vehicles to circle time.

Line the vehicles up in a 'parking lot' or 'parking spaces' designated on the map. Have the children take turns choosing a vehicle and driving it along the roads of the map. While each child is driving his vehicle, have him tell the others what he is driving past, where he is going, if the road is bumpy or smooth, when he needs to stop, and so on.

TALK ABOUT

Name a vehicle and let the children talk about times when they have ridden in that type of vehicle. Name another one and discuss it.

ROAD
STORIES

Create the beginnings of different *'road stories'* and let the children complete them. Here are some with which to start:

- *"I paid my toll and I'm driving onto the expressway. It seems crowded today. I wonder what color cars I will pass. There goes a red one. Now . . . . . "*

- *"I filled my tractor with gas. Now I'm . . . ."*

- *"The suitcases are loaded in the car and we are ready for vacation. Mom is the first driver. She is backing out of the driveway. We . . . . . "*

ACTIVE GAMES

TRAFFIC JAM

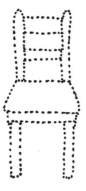

Cut out posterboard circles about nine inches in diameter for each of the children. Find pictures of different vehicles. Glue one picture on each circle. Bring the circles to circle time.

Pass the circles to the children and have each child name the vehicle pictured. Tell the children you are going to play some travel music (*'On the Road Again,'* *'Around the World in Eighty Days,'* *'She'll Be Comin' Around the Mountain'*) and that they can use the circles as *'steering wheels'* to drive along the road to the rhythm of the music. When you stop the music however, they should *'put on their brakes'* and stop steering for there is a traffic jam ahead. Wait until the jam is cleared and then begin the music again. After the song is over, have the children switch circles, name their new vehicles, and play again with a different song.

MUSICAL
CHAIRS

Get a recording of *'The Wheels On the Bus.'* Set up the chairs so that each player has a chair. Have the children walk around the chairs while the song is playing. When you stop the music everyone should find a seat.

Take one chair away, play the music and have the children begin walking. Stop the music again. This time all of the children should scamper for a chair. The child who does not have a chair should sit on someone's lap. Now take another chair away and play again. This time when the music stops, two children will sit on laps. Continue, until there is one chair left. By now the children will have figured out how they can all sit on one chair.

BOOKS

HELEN OXENBURY – **CAR TRIP**
NANCY WHITE CARLSTROM – **THE MOON CAME TOO**
HUCK SCARRY – **ON THE ROAD**
SUSAN HOGUET – **I UNPACKED MY GRANDMOTHER'S TRUNK**

ME AND MY SHADOW

FOR OPENERS

ENLARGE THE *'SHADOW CARDS'* PROVIDED AND MAKE MORE OF YOUR OWN. BRING THEM TO CIRCLE TIME. TALK ABOUT SHADOWS WITH THE CHILDREN. THEN HAVE THEM STAND UP. HOLD UP ONE OF THE CARDS. TALK ABOUT WHAT THE SHADOW ON THE CARD IS DOING AND THEN HAVE THE CHILDREN MIMIC THE SHADOW. HOLD UP ANOTHER SHADOW AND HAVE THE CHILDREN MIMIC THAT ONE. ONCE YOU HAVE GONE THROUGH ALL OF THE CARDS, REPEAT THE GAME, ONLY THIS TIME GOING THROUGH THE CARDS A LITTLE FASTER. DEPENDING ON YOUR CHILDREN PLAY A THIRD TIME WITH EVEN MORE SPEED.

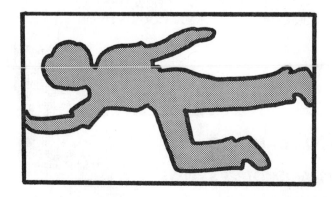
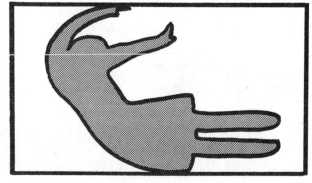

FINGERPLAYS

ME AND MY SHADOW

We're best friends,
My shadow and me.
Wherever I go,
My shadow will be.
        Vohny Moehling

SHADOW WALK

I'm taking my shadow for a walk,
We'll be very quiet, he doesn't talk.
With the sun overhead and the sidewalk below,
We'll walk very fast or tiptoe really slow.
        Vohny Moehling

RECIPES

SHADOW CRACKERS

YOU'LL NEED

Crackers
Peanut butter
Spreadable cheese

TO MAKE: Give each child two crackers.
Have the peanut butter and spreadable
cheese on the table. Have the children
make a design on one cracker by
spreading cheese on it. Then have them
make the *'shadow cracker'* by spreading
the identical design with peanut butter on
the other cracker. Have fun eating the
crackers with glasses of milk.

FIELD TRIPS

• Take a *'Shadow Walk'* with the children. Go outside on a sunny day.
Talk with the children about the bright sunlight and how to make shadows
on the sidewalk. As you walk along encourage the children to watch their
shadows. Stop along the way and have the children do specific motions
and watch thei shadows do them back. For example, have them wave,
twirl their arms jump up and down, and so on.

LANGUAGE GAMES

**SILLY
SHADOWS**

During the free choice time set up a *'shadow-making corner.'* On a table have a projector or spot (flood) light, which shines against an empty wall. Have large sheets of butcher paper available. Hang a sheet of light colored butcher paper on the wall. Have a child come over and stand whichever way he wants in front of the light making a silly shadow. Trace around it. Write his name and what his body is doing under the shadow. For example, *"Eric is showing his muscles."* He can paint or color it if he wants.

After all of the children have had an opportunity to make silly shadows, bring the shadows to circle time. Have a child stand up while you hold his shadow next to him as he tells the others what his shadow is doing. Repeat with the other children and their shadows.

Hang all of the silly shadows in the hallway.

SHADOW CHAT	Talk with the children about what is needed to make shadows (object, surface for the shadow to lie on, light of some type).
	Gather several different light sources such as a flashlight, projector, and spotlight and several distinct objects such as a ball, pencil, banana, and drinking glass. Set up the different light sources. Put one of the objects in front of a light source. Have the children identify it. Now put that same object in front of the other light sources. Can they still recognize what it is? Which is the best light for 'shadow-making?' Repeat with the other objects.

SHADOW PARTNERS	Pair off the children. Designate one child to be the 'shadow-maker' and the other one to be his 'shadow.' The 'shadow-maker' moves his body in a specific way and freezes. Then the 'shadow' mimics the 'maker' and freezes. You clap for all of the children. Then they switch roles and repeat. Continue for several more shadows.

ACTIVE GAMES

SHAKEY SHADOWS	Do the traditional 'Hokey-Pokey' dance outside in the bright sunlight. As the children are dancing have them watch the shadows their different body parts are making.
BE MY SHADOW	Have the children stand where they can easily see you. Tell them that you are going to do some exercises and that they should be your shadows, so that they need to watch carefully and move just like you do. For example, you could march, jump up and down or side to side, bob your head, stand at attention, do hip twirls, etc.

BOOKS

DICK GACKENBACH – *MR. WINK AND HIS SHADOW*
TARO GOMI – *SHADOWS*
ANNO MITSUMASA – *IN SHADOWLAND*
MARGARET MAHY – *BOY WITH TWO SHADOWS*
KEIKO NARAHASHI – *I HAVE A FRIEND*

SHOES

FOR OPENERS

BRING A VARIETY OF PAIRS OF SHOES AND BOOTS PLUS A LARGE BAG TO CIRCLE TIME. GIVE ONE PAIR TO EACH CHILD. HAVE THE CHILDREN LOOK AT THE PAIR OF SHOES WHICH YOU GAVE THEM. TALK ABOUT WHO MIGHT WEAR THE DIFFERENT SHOES, WHEN A PERSON WOULD WEAR THEM, AND WHY SOMEONE WOULD WEAR THAT PARTICULAR PAIR.

AFTER THE DISCUSSION WALK AROUND THE CIRCLE AND HAVE EACH CHILD PUT ONE SHOE/BOOT IN A BAG AND KEEP THE MATE. AFTER YOU HAVE COLLECTED THE FOOTWEAR, PULL ONE SHOE OUT OF THE BAG AND HOLD IT UP. HAVE THE CHILD WHO HAS THE MATE BRING IT UP. PUT THE PAIR TOGETHER AND SET IT ON THE FLOOR. CONTINUE UNTIL YOU HAVE PAIRED ALL OF THE FOOTWEAR.

FINGERPLAYS

I AM A COBBLER

I am a cobbler
And this is what I do.
Rap-tap-a-tap
I mend your shoe.

TYING MY SHOE

I know how to tie my shoe,
I take the loop and poke it through.
It's very hard to make it stay,
Because my thumbs get in the way.

ONE, TWO - BUCKLE MY SHOE

One, two - buckle my shoe.
Three, four - knock at the door.
Five, six - pick up sticks.
Seven, eight - lay them straight.
Nine, ten - a good, fat hen.

SHINY SHOES

First I loosen mud and dirt.
My shoes I then rub clean,
For shoes in such a dreadful sight
Never should be seen.

Next I spread the polish on,
And then I let it dry.
I brush and brush, and brush, and brush.
How those shoes shine! Oh, my!

RECIPES

FRUIT LEATHER

YOU'LL NEED

5 cups fresh fruit
Cinnamon and other spices (optional)

TO MAKE: Peel and core the fruit. Blend it
in a blender. Add spices. Heat the mixture
in a saucepan. Blend again.
   Put Saran Wrap® over a cookie sheet.
Pour the fruit puree on top. Spread it out
as thin as possible. Bake in the oven at 150
degrees for 8 hours.
from SUPER SNACKS
by Jean Warren.

FIELD TRIPS

• Take several *'Shoe Walks'* with the children. First take a walk around the
immediate area of the center. Have the children look at the shoes that the
people they pass are wearing. When you return to the center talk about
the different types and colors which the children saw. On another day take
a walk to different area, say a nearby park. Note the shoes again. Talk
about them. Compare them to the shoes the children saw during their first
walk.

CLASSROOM VISITORS

• Ask a firefighter to visit the children. During his/her visit have him/her
show the children his/her complete uniform. Ask him/her beforehand to
bring all of the different types of footwear s/he wears on the job. As s/he is
explaining his/her uniform, have him/her focus on the different types of
footwear.

LANGUAGE GAMES

SHOE MATCH   Find pictures of different types of shoes, cut them out and back them with pieces of felt. Gather pairs of shoes to match each type of shoe in the pictures. Have the felt board available.

Bring the felt board, shoes, and pictures of shoes to circle time. Pass out all of the pictures of the shoes. Line the real shoes up so the children can easily see them. Call on a child. Have him tell the others about the picture he is holding. Have that child call on another child to pick out the pair of real shoes which matches the picture. Have the first child put his picture on the felt board and have the other child put the pair of shoes behind him for later.

After all of the shoes have been matched with the pictures, have the children with the shoes bring them out from behind their backs. Have each child tell the others what type of shoe he is holding and then return it to the front.

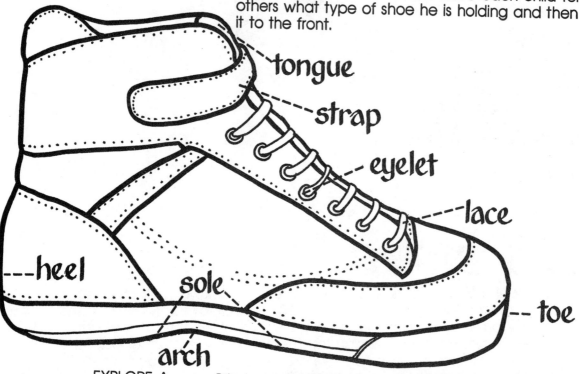

tongue

strap

eyelet

lace

heel

sole

toe

arch

EXPLORE A SHOE   Bring several different types of shoes to circle time. Pass them around and tell the children to look at them carefully. Then hold up one of the shoes. Point to one part of the shoe such as the 'heel' and ask the children to name the part you're touching. Continue with the other parts (buckles, toe, lace, eyelet, tongue, sole, arch, etc.). Pick up another shoe and repeat. Do both shoes, have some parts that are similar? Different? Same?

NAME THAT SHOE   Put a wide variety of shoes in a bag. Bring the bag to circle time. Have a child pull one shoe out of the bag and hold it up. Have the group quietly call out the name of the shoe. Put the shoe off to the side. Have another child pull out a second shoe and repeat. Continue until the bag is empty.

STEPPING OUT

Say to the children, *"I'm going to the grocery store and I'm going to wear my boots."* Have the children take turns telling where they are going and what shoes/boots they are going to wear. Encourage them to go to as many different places and wear as many different types of footwear as possible.

ACTIVE GAMES

SHOE HUNT

Have all of the children take off one of their shoes and put them in a bag. Now have them cover their eyes. You quickly hide all of the shoes around the room.

After all of the shoes have been hidden, have the children uncover their eyes. Tell them that you have hidden their shoes all over the room and that when you say, *"Hunt for the shoes,"* they should get up and begin looking for a shoe. When each child finds a shoe he should return to the circle time area. After everyone has returned, they should sit with their legs straight out. Have them examine the shoe they found and look at all of their friends' shoes to find the mates. When everyone thinks he knows who belongs to the mates, have the children return the shoes to their owners.

FEET FEELINGS

Prepare a *'texture trail'* for the children to walk along. One way you can do this is to get about ten plastic tubs and put a different type of material (flour, rice, beans, sand, water, dirt, buttons, styrofoam bits, yarn pieces, rounded pebbles) in each one. Lay the tubs in a trail with the water last.

Have the children take off their shoes and socks. Beginning with the first tub have the children slowly walk the *'texture trail.'* Be sure to hold the hands of those children who are a little unsure of the experience. At the end have the children wash and dry their feet.

Repeat the activity (eliminating the tub of water) letting the children wear their shoes. Talk about the difference.

BOOKS

PETER SPIER – *NEW BLUE SHOES*
DOROTHY COREY – *NEW SHOES!*
NIKI DALY – *NOT SO FAST, SONGOLOLO*
BEATRICE SCHENK DeREGNIERS – *WHAT CAN YOU DO WITH A SHOE?*
RON ROY – *WHOSE SHOES ARE THESE?*

HOLES

FOR OPENERS

HAVE THE CHILDREN HOLD UP THEIR HANDS AND WIGGLE THEIR FINGERS, THEN TWIRL THEIR ARMS, TWIST AT THEIR WAIST, AND FINALLY SHAKE ALL OVER. NOW THAT THE CHILDREN ARE ALL LOOSENED-UP, SAY TO THEM, *"HOLD UP ONE OF YOUR POINTER FINGERS AND ONE THUMB. MAKE A SMALL CIRCLE WITH THEM."* THEN SAY, *"PUT YOUR NOSE THROUGH THE HOLE YOU JUST MADE."* HAVE THEM THINK OF OTHER THINGS THAT WOULD FIT THROUGH THE HOLES THEY'VE CREATED. THEN SAY, *"MAKE A BIGGER HOLE BY PUTTING THE TIPS OF BOTH OF YOUR POINTER FINGERS TOGETHER WHILE TOUCHING YOUR THUMBS TO EACH OTHER."* AFTER EACH CHILD HAS MADE A BIGGER HOLE SAY, *"TRY FITTING YOUR KNEE THROUGH YOUR NEW HOLE."* (DO IT.) THEN SAY, *"NOW MAKE AN EVEN BIGGER HOLE BY PUTTING ONE OF YOUR HANDS ON A HIP. (DO IT.) TURN TO A PERSON NEXT TO YOU AND SEE IF THAT PERSON CAN PUT HIS HEAD THROUGH THE VERY BIG HOLE WHICH YOU'VE MADE."* (HAVE THE CHILDREN TAKE TURNS PUTTING THEIR HEADS THROUGH EACH OTHERS HOLES.)

FINGERPLAYS

THE DOUGHNUT

*Here's the doughnut
Big and round and fat.
Here's the hole.
Now don't eat that.*

I STUCK MY HEAD IN A LITTLE SKUNK'S HOLE

*I stuck my head in a little skunk's hole,
And the little skunk said, "Why bless my soul.
Take it out, Take it out, Take it out.
Remove it."*

*I didn't take it out, and the little skunk said,
"You better take it out or you'll wish you had.
Take it out, Take it out, Take it out."
Sh-h-h, I removed it, too late.*

FIVE LITTLE MICE

Five little mice on the pantry floor;
This little mouse peeked behind the door;
This little mouse nibbled at the cake;
This little mouse not a sound did make;
This little mouse took a bite of cheese;
This little mouse heard the kitten sneeze.
"Ah-choo!" sneezed kitten, and "Squeak!" they cried,
As they found a hole and ran inside.

RECIPES

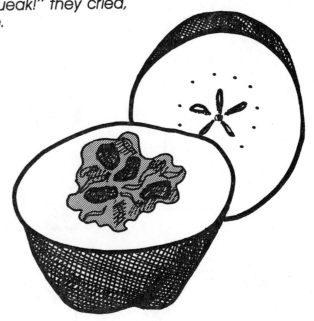

STUFFED APPLES

YOU'LL NEED

Apples
Peanut butter
Raisins
Carrots

TO MAKE: First make the peanut butter mixture: Clean and shred the carrots. Put the carrots, raisins, and peanut butter in a bowl and mix. Next wash the apples, cut them in half horizontally, core the halves, and fill each hole with the peanut butter mixture.

FIELD TRIPS

• Take a very slow walk down the sidewalk in front of your center. Look carefully for holes in the concrete. When you've reached the corner, turn around and walk back. As you're returning, try to determine which are the largest and smallest holes.

• If there is a construction site near the center, walk over to it and note all of the holes in the ground, materials, and equipment.

LANGUAGE GAMES

I'M THINKING
OF A HOLE

Have the children sit in an area of the classroom where they can easily see most of it. Then walk over to a part of the classroom and say to the children, *"I'm thinking of a small hole close to where I'm standing."* (Let them make several guesses. If they haven't guessed it, then give them a few clues.) Walk over to another section and repeat the game. Continue with different size holes.

PEEK-A-HOLE

Find ten to twenty magazine pictures of objects with holes in them. Fold the same number of 9" x 12" sheets of construction paper in half. Glue one of the magazine pictures to the inside right-hand page of each piece of folded construction paper. Cut a 'peek hole' in each left-hand page revealing only a portion of the picture.

Bring the 'Peek-A-Hole Cards' to circle time. Hold up one card, let the children carefully look at the clue through the 'peek hole' and then guess what the picture is. After they have guessed, have one child open the card revealing the whole picture to the children. Talk about it.

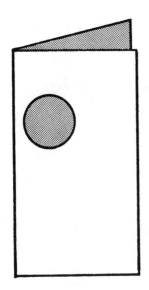

HOLES EVERYWHERE

Get a large sheet of butcher paper. Cut different size holes in it, leaving enough room to write words between and around the holes. Bring the paper and a marker to circle time.

Tell the children to think of things that have holes in them. As they think of objects have them call out their ideas. You write them down on the paper. When finished, read all of their ideas back to them and then hang the paper up. Add to it when children have more thoughts.

SAY "HOLES"

Read the book 'Holes' by Joan Elma Rahn and/or 'The Very Hungry Caterpillar' by Eric Carle. Hold the book so that the children can see the pictures. Have the children say, "Hole" everytime they see a hole pictured on one of the pages. Point to all of the holes on a page they have identified. When you have finished the book, encourage the children to share all of the types of holes they remember from the story. They may want to add these to the list of holes in the previous activity.

ACTIVE GAMES

OBSTACLE COURSE

Before circle time set up an outside obstacle course using pieces of equipment which have holes in them such as, ladders, hula hoops, tires, wash tubs, etc. Have the children step through the rungs of the ladders, hop around the hula hoops, crawl over the tires, and walk in and out of the big wash tubs.

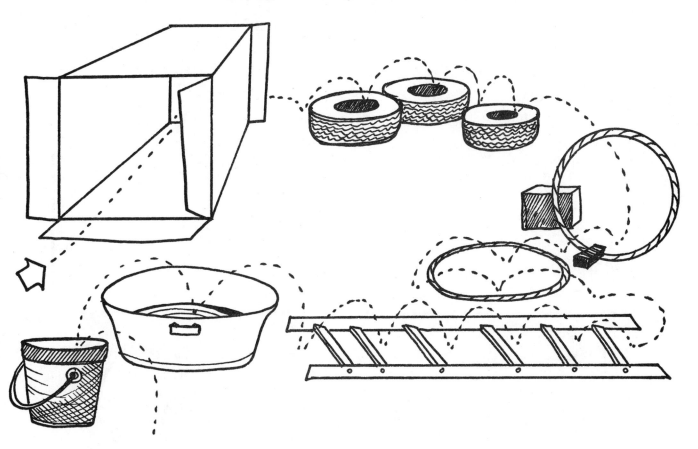

HOOP FUN

Bring a hula hoop to circle time. Pretend that it is a variety of things:

- The hoop is a bubble wand and each child becomes a bubble as you blow him through. Let the children be bubbles floating around the room.

- The hoop is a circus hoop. Hold it up and let the children be circus animals doing tricks through the hoop.

- The hoop is a giant soup bowl and the children are the vegetables in the soup.

BOOKS

RUTH KRAUSS – *A HOLE IS TO DIG*
BEVERLY CLEARY – *REAL HOLE*
ANN JONAS – *HOLES AND PEEKS*

IT'S IN THE BAG

FOR OPENERS

COLLECT A VARIETY OF BAGS AND BRING THEM TO CIRCLE TIME. LAY THEM ON THE FLOOR SO THAT THE CHILDREN CAN EASILY SEE THEM. POINT TO EACH BAG, TELL ITS RELATIVE SIZE AND WHAT MATERIAL IT IS MADE OF. FOR EXAMPLE, *"THIS IS A SMALL PLASTIC BAG; HERE IS A LARGE NYLON BAG; THIS ONE IS A MEDIUM SIZE MESH BAG,"* AND SO ON.

SAY A SENTENCE ABOUT HOW YOU MIGHT USE ONE OF THE BAGS AND HAVE THE CHILDREN FIGURE OUT WHICH BAG YOU ARE DESCRIBING. ONCE THEY HAVE NAMED IT, TAKE THAT BAG AWAY FROM THE GROUP. TELL THE CHILDREN ABOUT HOW YOU COULD USE ANOTHER BAG AND HAVE THEM NAME IT. CONTINUE UNTIL THERE IS ONE BAG LEFT. HOLD THAT BAG UP AND LET THE CHILDREN THINK OF AS MANY WAYS AS THEY CAN TO USE THE LAST BAG.

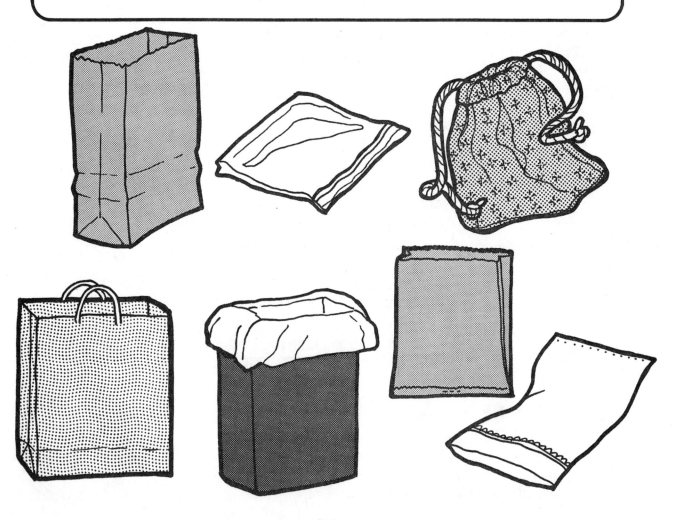

FINGERPLAYS

POP THE BAG

Hold the bag up to your mouth,
And blow, and blow, and blow.

Hold it out and clap your hand,
And hear your bag go bam!

RECIPES

SNACK IN A BAG

Serve snacks each day in a different type of bag.

FOR EXAMPLE:
- Popcorn in popcorn bags
- Small sandwiches in sandwich bags
- Bags of raisins
- Juice in drink bags
- Bring all of the snacks in one large bag

FIELD TRIPS

- Take a *'Bag Walk'* around your neighborhood. Look for all types of bags and note what they are used for.

LANGUAGE GAMES

BAGS, BAGS, AND MORE BAGS

Have the children close their eyes. Name one of the rooms in their homes, such as the kitchen. Encourage the children to think about the different kinds of bags that they can find in that room. Have the children open their eyes, tell what bags are in that room, what they are used for, and where they are placed. Continue by naming another room, maybe the garage.

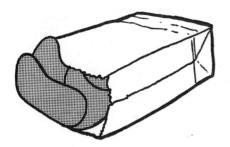

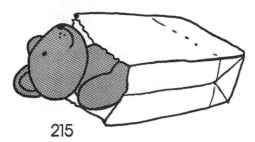

IT'S IN THE BAG

Bring a marker and a variety of sizes of paper bags to circle time. Hold up one of the bags and ask the children, "*What could you put in this bag?*" As they name things, write their ideas on the bag. Hold up another bag and continue the game in the same manner.

Hang the different bags in the language center.

WHO'S HIDING IN THE BAG?

Cut out eye, nose, and mouth holes in a bag to comfortably fit over your children's heads.

Have the children sit in a circle so that they can see each other. Have them cover their eyes with their hands. You walk around the outside of the circle. Tap one of the children on the shoulder, have him quietly walk to the center of the circle, sit down, and put the bag over his head. Have the children uncover their eyes and look at the child in the middle. Say the '*In the Bag*' rhyme and guess who is hiding in the bag. When the child in the middle hears his name, he should take off the bag and stand up. Play again.

<u>IN THE BAG</u>

Friend in the bag,
Friend in the bag,
Who is that
Friend in the bag?

IT'S A SECRET

During the first several days of the week have the children bring something in a bag that they want to share with the others. Make sure that the bags are closed and have the children's names written on them. Put the '*secret bags*' in a special place.

Each day have several children hold up their bags and tell the others about the objects while trying not to name them. After each child has talked a little bit about his object, have him take it out of the bag, and hold it up. Have everyone call out what it is. Then have the child pass it around for everyone to see.

ACTIVE GAMES

SACK GAMES

At the beginning of the week send a note home asking each child to bring an old pillowcase to school.

On nice days have the children take their pillowcases outside and enjoy different types of movement activities on the grass or other soft surfaces.

- Slip the pillowcase over one or two legs and stand up straight, holding onto the top edge. Jump up and down slowly. Jump side to side.

- Lie down on the ground. Slip the pillowcase over your legs and roll around.

- Draw a start and finish line. Stand behind the start line, slip your pillowcase over one or two legs, and shuffle slowly to the finish line.

- Using a clothesline, wiggle a line around the grassy part of the playground. Slip the pillowcase over one or two legs and walk along the line.

DO AS I DO

Have the children slip their pillowcases over one or two legs. Have one child lead the others in different movements. Periodically change leaders.

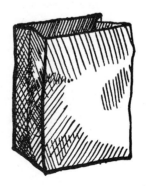

BOOKS

DICK GACKENBACK – *BAG FULL OF PUPS*
JAY WILLIAMS – *BAG FULL OF NOTHING*

IN YOUR NEIGHBORHOOD

FOR OPENERS

TELL THE CHILDREN THAT THEY ARE GOING TO BE THE *'NEIGHBORHOOD PATROL'* AND GO FOR A LONG, SLOW WALK AROUND THE BLOCK THAT THE SCHOOL IS ON. YOU ARE GOING TO BRING ALONG A TABLET OF PAPER AND A PENCIL, A CAMERA, AND THE TAPE RECORDER. WHILE THEY ARE WALKING THE CHILDREN CAN TALK INTO THE TAPE RECORDER AND RECORD WHAT THEY SEE AND FEEL. HAVE THE CHILDREN POINT OUT THINGS THAT THEY WANT YOU TO TAKE PHOTOGRAPHS OF. ENCOURAGE THEM TO TELL YOU ABOUT THE NEIGHBORHOOD. WRITE DOWN WHAT THEY SAY. STOP AT A STORE AND BUY A SNACK. PICK A SPOT TO EAT IT AND THEN RETURN TO THE CLASSROOM.

EXTENSION: HAVE THE CHILDREN CONSTRUCT A NEIGHBORHOOD OF THEIR OWN WHICH THEY CAN PUT IN THE PLAYGROUND AREA. HAVE THEM PAINT LARGE APPLIANCE BOXES TO REPRESENT THE DIFFERENT HOMES AND BUILDINGS. ADD OTHER DETAILS SUCH AS BIKES FOR THE CARS, POTTED PLANTS FOR THE GARDENS, AND LARGE CHALKED OR TAPED-OFF AREAS FOR PARKING LOTS.

FINGERPLAYS

THE BAKERY

Down around the corner
In the Bakery Shop,
There were ten little doughnuts,
With sugar on top.
Along came (child's name) all alone.
She bought a (color chosen) one and then ran home.

To use the above fingerplay as a game, put red, blue, green, etc. paper doughnuts in the center of the circle. Each child has a turn to come to the *'Bakery,'* walk around the circle once, and then choose a colored donut as the children say the above rhyme.

MY HOUSE AND TOM'S

This is my house,
Cozy and neat;
This is Tom's house
Across the street.

Everyday
My door opens wide,
And away I go
To play outside.

Soon Tom's door
Flies open too,
And he comes out,
Calling, "How are you?"

We talk and play,
And jump and run;
Our mothers call
And we stop our fun.

Then in we go—
The doors close tight,
But we wave from our windows,
To say, "Goodnight!"

RECIPES

REFRESHMENT STAND

YOU'LL NEED

A simple snack each day:
    Cheese and crackers
    Cereal Mix
    Raisins
    Muffins
    Pretzels

TO MAKE: Using a puppet stage, large box, or some other prop, set up a refreshment stand outside. At snack time, have the children get their snack from the attendants behind the stand.
    At other times serve glasses of water and *'pretend food'* from the stand.

FIELD TRIPS

• Pick different places in the neighborhood which are appropriate to play and/or have snack at. Each day walk to a different place and enjoy it.

• Visit special parks which are close to your school.

CLASSROOM VISITORS

- Invite someone from the local park district to visit your class. Have the person tell the children about the different types of parks and activities that the children and their families can do at each one.

LANGUAGE GAMES

PATROL
DATA

Bring the tape recording, notes, and photographs which you and the children compiled during the walk explained in the 'For Openers' activity.

Listen to the tape, read the notes, and show the children the photographs. Talk about the neighborhood using all of the data which the children collected. EXTENSION: Using the information which the children gathered, write a group experience story about the neighborhood. Include the story in your next parent newsletter.

NEIGHBORHOOD
MAP

Make a map of the neighborhood or simply the block around the school. You'll need a piece of posterboard, pencil, eraser, and a marker.

Tell the children that you want them to help you make a map of the buildings and other areas surrounding the school. Draw a large rectangle to represent the sidewalk around the school. Using pencil mark the school. Now say to the children, "Let's go outside and see what is next to the school and across the street." (Go outside, look, and then mark off the areas which you see. Continue walking and marking the major buildings and areas.)

When you return to the center, talk about the map. Add anything else that the children suggest. Tell the children that you are going to retrace the pencil lines with marker, so that they will be able to 'read' the map better. (Do it with the children during free choice time.) When the map is finished, bring it to circle time and talk about the neighborhood.

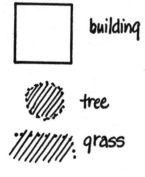

building

tree

grass

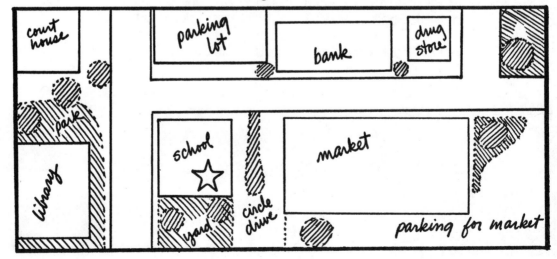

NEIGHBORHOOD MYSTERIES Have the children close their eyes. Begin describing something in the neighborhood. When a child thinks he knows what you are describing, have him open his eyes. When several children have opened their eyes, call on one of them to tell the others what his guess is. Ask the others if they agree. Play again describing something else.

NEIGHBORHOOD NEWS Cut the back off of a large box and then cut a hole in the front side to use as a television screen. Put a chair in the 'studio.' Get a microphone or use a paper towel roll.

Have the children take turns being on television, telling one or two incidents that have happened or are going to happen in the neighborhood.

ACTIVE GAMES

CLEAN-UP DAY Have a 'clean-up day' at school. Get extra pails, brushes, brooms, rakes, waste cans, etc. The day before remind the children to wear very old clothes.

On 'clean-up day' pick up the discarded paper, sweep the playground and sidewalks, wash the trikes and outdoor equipment, rake the sand areas, etc.

PARK CHARADES Have the children think of all of the activities that they like to do in the park. Have a child come up to the front and pretend to do a park-type activity. Let the other children guess what he is doing. Then encourage everyone to do the activity with the 'leader child.'

BOOKS

JOAN KAHN – *HI, JOCK, RUN AROUND THE BLOCK*
LORE SEGAL – *ALL THE WAY HOME*
NANCY CARLSON – *LOUDMOUTH GEORGE AND THE NEW NEIGHBORS*

221

COMMUNITY HELPERS

FOR OPENERS

BEFORE CIRCLE TIME MAKE A SERIES OF COMMUNITY HELPER FINGER PUPPETS. BACK EACH PUPPET WITH A PIECE OF FELT SO THAT IT CAN ALSO BE USED AS A FELT BOARD CHARACTER.

DISPLAY ALL OF THE COMMUNITY HELPERS ON THE FELT BOARD. POINT TO EACH ONE AND INTRODUCE HIM/HER TO THE CHILDREN. AFTER ALL OF THE COMMUNITY HELPERS HAVE BEEN INTRODUCED, TAKE ONE, SAY THE LIFE GUARD, OFF OF THE FELT BOARD AND USE IT AS A PUPPET. SAY TO THE CHILDREN, *"I'M HOLDING THE LIFE GUARD. SHE WORKS AT THE SWIMMING POOL WHERE MANY OF YOU SWIM.* (Child's name) *TELL ME ONE THING YOU KNOW ABOUT A LIFE GUARD."* THAT CHILD TELLS ONE THING. HAVE ANOTHER CHILD TELL ONE MORE THING ABOUT A LIFE GUARD. CONTINUE LETTING AS MANY CHILDREN AS POSSIBLE ADD TO THE LIST OF THINGS THEY KNOW ABOUT LIFE GUARDS. CHOOSE ANOTHER COMMUNITY HELPER AND REPEAT THE GAME.

PLAY THIS GAME AGAIN ON OTHER DAYS USING DIFFERENT COMMUNITY HELPERS.

RECIPES

ENERGY SNACK

To do a good job and stay healthy, people need to have nutritious snacks. Try some of these during the day.

YOU'LL NEED

A variety of dried fruit:
  Apples
  Bananas
  Apricots
  Pineapple
  Raisins
  Dates

A variety of seeds and nuts:
  Pumpkin seeds
  Sunflower seeds
  Almonds
  Walnuts
  Pecans

LANGUAGE GAMES

WHO WILL WE SEE?

Take an imaginary trip with the children. Begin by saying, *"Let's take a walk around the town. On the way we might see some community helpers. I'll need your help to spot them.* (Have the children start walking by quietly tapping their hands on their knees.) *OK we're all together. We're going to walk along the sidewalk towards the gas station. Does anyone see a community helper yet?* (Stop walking. Let a child name whomever he sees. Let anyone who wants to, say something about that person. Continue walking.) *Let's keep on walking. Tell me when you spot someone else."* Continue with the story until you've come back to school.

ON THE WAY TO SCHOOL

Encourage the children to look for community helpers on their way to school each day. At the beginning of circle time ask the children to name the helpers they saw and tell what the people were doing.

IF I WERE A. . . . . .

Bring the community helper puppets, which you made for the *'For Openers'* activity, to circle time. Display them on the felt board.

Tell the children to look at all of the community helper puppets and decide which one each would like to be. Call on a child to come up to the felt board, choose his favorite helper, and put it on his hand. Have him hold it up for everyone to see and then say, *"If I were a (name) I'd (tell what he would do all day.)"* Then he should put the puppet back on the board. Ask the children, *"Who else wants to be a community helper?"* Continue until all of the children have had an opportunity to choose a helper.

WHO NEEDS THIS?

Collect a variety of tools and items which different community helpers would use, need or wear. Put them in a bag and bring them to circle time.

Tell the children that you have brought items with you that relate to different community helpers. Have a child come up and take one of the objects out of the bag and hold it up for the others to see. Have the children call out what it is. Then have a child tell which community helper/s would use that item and how s/he would use it. Continue until all of the items are out of the bag.

MY HELPER

Have the children name a community helper who assisted them at some time and what s/he did.

ACTIVE GAMES

WORK TO MUSIC

Bring different instrumental recordings to circle time. Tell the children that you are going to name one of the community helpers and then begin the music. They should do something that the helper would do as they move to the rhythm of the music. For example, if you said, *"Lifeguard,"* they could swim to the beat of the music, call out another helper (custodian, sweep the floor; waiter, carry trays of food) and continue the music. Play several recordings for a variety of rhythms.

HELPER CHARADE

Say a series of three words only one of which is a community helper. When the children hear the name of the community helper, they should begin doing things that the helper would do. After a short time say, *"Statue."* The children should freeze in their position. Call on several children to tell what they were doing. Continue the game by saying another series of three words.

BOOKS

ANITA HARPER – ***HOW WE WORK***
DOUGLAS FLORIAN – ***PEOPLE WORKING***
JEAN JOHNSON – ***FIREFIGHTERS A TO Z***
　　　　　　　　POLICE OFFICERS A TO Z
MARGARET MILLER – ***WHOSE HAT?***
ANNE ROCKWELL – ***WHEN WE GROW UP***
GENE ZION – ***DEAR GARBAGE MAN***

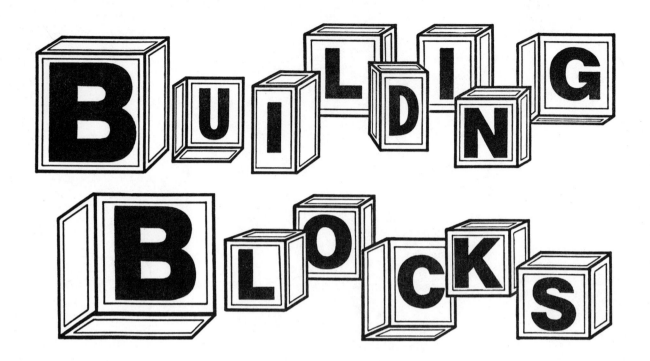

Building Blocks Library

The Circle Time Series

by Liz and Dick Wilmes. Hundreds of activities for large and small groups of children. Each book is filled with Language and Active games, Fingerplays, Songs, Stories, Snacks, and more. A great resource for every library shelf.

Circle Time Book
Captures the spirit of 39 holidays and seasons.
ISBN 0-943452-00-7   **$ 9.95**

Everyday Circle Times
Over 900 ideas. Choose from 48 topics divided into 7 sections: self-concept, basic concepts, animals, foods, science, occupations, and recreation.
ISBN 0-943452-01-5   **$14.95**

More Everyday Circle Times
Divided into the same 7 sections as EVERYDAY. Features new topics such as Birds and Pizza, plus all new ideas for some familiar topics contained in EVERYDAY.
ISBN 0-943452-14-7   **$14.95**

Yearful of Circle Times
52 different topics to use weekly, by seasons, or mixed throughout the year. New Friends, Signs of Fall, Snowfolk Fun, and much more.
ISBN 0-943452-10-4   **$14.95**

Paint Without Brushes

by Liz and Dick Wilmes. Use common materials which you already have to discover the painting possibilities in your classroom! PAINT WITHOUT BRUSHES gives your children open-ended art activities to explore paint in lots of creative ways. A valuable art resource. One you'll want to use daily.
ISBN 0-943452-15-5   **$12.95**

Gifts, Cards, and Wraps

by Wilmes and Zavodsky. Help the children sparkle with the excitement of gift giving. Filled with thoughtful gifts, unique wraps, and special cards which the children can make and give. They're sure to bring smiles.
ISBN 0-943452-06-6   **$ 7.95**

Everyday Bulletin Boards

by Wilmes and Moehling. Features borders, murals, backgrounds, and other open-ended art to display on your bulletin boards. Plus board ideas with patterns, which teachers can make and use to enhance their curriculum.
ISBN 0-943452-09-0   **$ 8.95**

Exploring Art

by Liz and Dick Wilmes. EXPLORING ART is divided by months. Over 250 art ideas for paint, chalk, doughs, scissors, and more. Easy to set-up in your classroom.
ISBN 0-943452-05-8   **$16.95**

CIRCLE TIME

ART

Parachute Play

by Liz and Dick Wilmes. A year 'round approach to one of the most versatile pieces of large muscle equipment. Starting with basic techniques, PARACHUTE PLAY provides over 100 activities to use with your parachute.
ISBN 0-943452-03-1   **$ 7.95**

Classroom Parties

by Susan Spaete. Each party plan suggests decorations, trimmings, and snacks which the children can easily make to set a festive mood. Choose from games, songs, art activities, stories, and related experiences which will add to the spirit and fun.
ISBN 0-943452-07-4   **$ 8.95**

Imagination Stretchers

by Liz and Dick Wilmes. Perfect for whole language. Over 400 conversation starters for creative discussions, simple lists, and beginning dictation and writing.
ISBN 0-943452-04-X   **$ 6.95**

Parent Programs and Open Houses

by Susan Spaete. Filled with a wide variety of year 'round presentations, pre-registration ideas, open houses, and end-of-the-year gatherings. All involve the children from the planning stages through the programs.
ISBN 0-943452-08-2   **$ 9.95**

Learning Centers

by Liz and Dick Wilmes. Hundreds of open-ended activities to quickly involve and excite your children. You'll use it every time you plan and whenever you need a quick, additional activity. A must for every teacher's bookshelf.
ISBN 0-943452-13-9   **$16.95**

Felt Board Fun

by Liz and Dick Wilmes. Make your felt board come alive. Discover how versatile it is as the children become involved with a wide range of activities. This unique book has over 150 ideas with accompanying patterns.
ISBN 0-943452-02-3   **$14.95**

Table & Floor Games

by Liz and Dick Wilmes. 32 easy-to-make, fun-to-play table games with accompanying patterns. Teach beginning concepts such as matching, counting, colors, alphabet recognition, sorting, and so on. Over 100 pages of patterns (foods, animals, transportation, feelings, nature, etc.) ready to trace or photocopy. Within a short time you'll have a variety of games to play with your children. You can also use patterns for felt board stories, bulletin boards, quick note paper, charts, newsletters, and children's dictations.
ISBN 0-943452-16-3   **$16.95**

All books available from
teacher bookstores,
school supply catalogs
or directly from:

38W567 Brindlewood, Elgin, Illinois 60123
708-742-1013   800-233-2448   708-742-1054 (FAX)

Thank you for your order.